ch 9-12

EDUCATION 2.0

EDUCATION 2.0
THE LEARNINGWEB REVOLUTION AND THE TRANSFORMATION OF THE SCHOOL

LEONARD J. WAKS

LONDON AND NEW YORK

First published 2014 by Paradigm Publishers

Published 2016 by Routledge
2 Park Square, Milton Park, Abingdon, Oxon OX14 4RN
711 Third Avenue, New York, NY 10017, USA

Routledge is an imprint of the Taylor & Francis Group, an informa business

Copyright © 2014, Taylor & Francis.

All rights reserved. No part of this book may be reprinted or reproduced or utilised in any form or by any electronic, mechanical, or other means, now known or hereafter invented, including photocopying and recording, or in any information storage or retrieval system, without permission in writing from the publishers.

Notice:
Product or corporate names may be trademarks or registered trademarks, and are used only for identification and explanation without intent to infringe.

Library of Congress Cataloging-in-Publication Data

Waks, Leonard J. (Leonard Joseph)
  The learningweb revolution and the transformation of the school / Leonard J. Waks.
    pages cm.
  Includes bibliographical references and index.
  ISBN 978-1-61205-035-5 (hardcover : alk. paper)
  1. Internet in education. 2. Public schools. I. Title. II. Title: Learningweb.
  LB1044.87.W35 2013
  371.33'44678—dc23

                                                                    2012042273

Designed and Typeset by Straight Creek Bookmakers.

ISBN 13: 978-1-61205-035-5 (hbk)
ISBN 13: 978-1-61205-036-2 (pbk)

To Dr. Veronica

CONTENTS

Acknowledgments		ix
Introduction		xi

PART ONE: SCHOOLING—THE INDUSTRIAL PARADIGM

Chapter One	Young People	2
Chapter Two	Education and Change	11
Chapter Three	High Schools	33
Chapter Four	School Failure I—Academic Underperformance and Administrative Inefficiency	42
Chapter Five	School Failure II—Social Irrelevance and the Loss of Political Legitimacy	53

PART TWO: LEARNING NETWORKS

Chapter Six	The Internet and the World Wide Web	68
Chapter Seven	Web 2.0 and the Net Culture	78
Chapter Eight	The Learningweb	94
Chapter Nine	The Web in the School	112

Part Three: Education 2.0: A Network Paradigm for Education

Chapter Ten	New Educational Visions	130
Chapter Eleven	Complex Organizations	147
Chapter Twelve	Open Learning Centers	159
Chapter Thirteen	The Clash of Paradigms	182

Part Four: Educational Revolution

Chapter Fourteen	The Learningweb Revolution	196
Chapter Fifteen	What Needs to Be Done?	212
Appendix		224
Notes		237
Index		257
About the Author		270

ACKNOWLEDGMENTS

Readers familiar with education literature will immediately recognize my intellectual debts to John Dewey, Richard S. Peters, Ivan Illich, Robert Dreeben, and Thomas F. Green. Francis Schrag gave me the push to begin work on the book. Books by Johnny Ryan and Clay Shirky guided my investigation of the social effects of the Internet and Web 2.0. Steve Hargadon, the leader of the Classroom 2.0 movement, provided me with an early forum for presenting my ideas. Curtis Bonk and Judy Breck, the authors featured in Chapter Ten, were generous with their time and ideas. Breck was a cheerleader, supplying steady encouragement. Sadly, she passed away shortly before the book was completed.

My brother David, director of technology for the Prodigy service—the first Internet portal, shared his vast knowledge of the Internet and read every word of the book carefully, making many very useful suggestions about both content and structure. He could enjoy great success in a second career as a book doctor. My book-buddy Kathleen Knight Abowitz and I worked in parallel during the thirty-odd months it took to produce this book and hers (*Publics for Public School: Legitimacy, Democracy, and Leadership*)—reading successive drafts and offering constructive criticism and advice—and I thank her. Jason Barry, my editor at Paradigm, was a fount of wise advice and support from beginning to end. Finally, I want to thank my wife, Veronica, my mother-in-law Zoya Kovalenka, and my son Sjoma for their endless support. Veronica and Zoya kept my life going smoothly so that I could focus on writing. Sjoma, a graduate of PA Cyber Charter High School and currently a computer science student at Temple

University, was enthusiastic about the project from the start, and we endlessly discussed every idea in the book. He was always ready with useful suggestions and telling examples. Veronica is the love of my life and my muse; the book is dedicated to her with great respect and admiration.

Introduction

This book offers a new vision for education in the age of global networks. It is not aimed at fixing, reforming, or improving today's schools, but at laying out a blueprint for an educational transformation—a shift to a new paradigm for new kinds of educational organizations.

Schooling as it has come down to us from the industrial era is now accepted as given, inevitable, and natural. But there is nothing natural about it. It is a human invention that has outlived its utility. We are educating young people to expect that school and college diplomas will lead to decent jobs—proverbial pots of gold—somewhere over the rainbow. But the pots of gold are illusory; in large measure because of Internet-related efficiencies and the reduced costs of finding contract workers, few such permanent jobs with benefits are being created today. We will have to build new models of living in today's global network society, complete with new means of earning our livelihoods and new forms of learning aligned with them.

I will be proposing that the Internet and its new social tools have much to contribute to such new social models of learning and living. Until now the computer has been used in education, without marked success, as an add-on to improve or refine or reform the operational processes of conventional schooling: conveying curricular information and test preparation materials and facilitating assessments of school learning. Even the new social tools, the blogs, wikis, and social networks, have been retrofit—reshaped—by educators to forge a fit with the conventional processes of schooling.

This retrofitting of the new tools to the old school processes, I will argue, simply cannot work; there is a fundamental contradiction between the conventional aims of schooling on the one hand—conveying pre-selected material and assessing how much of it has been learned or memorized—and opening the floodgates of information and platforms for creative, collaborative work accessible through the Internet, on the other.

I will be proposing the transformation of today's factory-like hierarchical schools into complex organizations that I will be calling, for lack of a snazzier term, "open networked learning centers" offering a complex assemblage of programs—what I will call "Education 2.0." These organizations will continue to offer something like a high-tech version of a conventional high school education for those who desire it. But the learning centers will do much more: they will support independent learning; they will generate, or collaborate in creating, new courses and programs to meet the changing needs, interests, and passions of their students. And they will develop certificate programs organized as task training workshops and quasi-apprenticeships, placing their students in real-world situations with adult coworkers, challenges, and responsibilities. In these programs learners will steadily acquire the habits and capabilities characteristic of thriving adults in network society. These programs will thus breathe new life into the intellectual, social, and practical dimensions of secondary education.

THE SCHOOL AND SOCIETY

Any proposal to improve education by using new technologies runs the risk of being read as touting new means for "improving instruction." Seen as such, some parents, teachers, and school children will be attracted to them while others will long for the "good old days" before such newfangled technologies existed. Researchers will conduct assessment studies pitting high-tech and no-tech instructional methods against one another in a horserace—with inconclusive results.

These responses inevitably miss what is most important about the new technologies—that they are already facets of new ways of life with their own distinctive processes and ends. As John Dewey argued more than a century ago, new education can only lose its "isolated character" as a product of "over-ingenious" minds when seen as "part of the whole social evolution and in its more general features at least, as inevitable."[1] My goal in what follows is to induce just this kind of shift in perception or paradigm shift—from the factory school to Education 2.0.

THE BOOK IN OUTLINE

I start Chapter One with a glimpse at today's web-using teens, who like teens throughout history exhibit high levels of intelligence and creativity combined with inexperience and naiveté. Many teens undeniably act like reckless kids, but that may be in large measure because most adults view them as kids and confine them in custodial schools that keep them from acting as adults. The question arises: How can educational arrangements be transformed to liberate their youthful energies in our networked world?

To answer this question I offer fresh conceptions of both "education" and "change" in Chapter Two. If "education" were confined to schooling, then educational change would be merely school change. Three decades of failed school reform suggest that more fundamental changes in our educational arrangements are now called for: we need to think about education beyond the limits of schooling. I conceive of education more broadly as a kind of initiation—providing *academic learning* but also *channels* for developing high-level action capabilities and *links* to adult activities, social and economic. Fundamental educational change is change in the entire institutional pattern concerned with meeting these needs; it involves a shift to a new education *paradigm*.

In Chapter Three I explicate the entrenched hierarchical paradigm or, as it is now frequently called, the *factory school* paradigm, and in Chapters Four and Five I consider the major failures of the schools—the lack of academic achievement, high drop-out rates, waste and inefficiency, lack of real world relevance, and loss of social and political legitimacy. In these chapters I focus on the high school, choosing this level of the system because it is arguably the most important one in providing broad general education and connecting young people to the larger society and because it is the most troubled level today. My argument, however, has broad applications for middle and junior high schools and to the early years of college; it addresses education in all higher branches of learning and their practical uses.

Part II is concerned with the Internet as an educational resource. Chapter Six explains the growth of the Internet and the World Wide Web. The key point is that the complex of computing power, including both the Internet and the powerful workstation computers serving as its terminals, evolved to free end users from central control to access and manipulate knowledge and information and to collaborate in creating and exchanging and using new knowledge and information. As a result it is not possible to adapt the Internet as we know it to learning in top-down, tightly controlled environments like the factory school. Chapter Seven turns to the breakthrough development of Web 2.0 and the new web learning culture, to demonstrate how Web 2.0 contains the seeds of a revolution in learning by facilitating the creative self-expression, collaboration, and collective social action of young people freed from tight institutional control. Chapter Eight then examines three elements of the Internet platform for learning—the "learningweb": online knowledge, teaching, and informal learning—illuminated by informal education in new Library 2.0 and Museum 2.0 environments.

Chapter Nine then investigates current attempts to introduce the Internet into contemporary schools. These attempts, we discover, fail because they run up against the barriers inherent in a hierarchical, centrally controlled organization: especially the centrally predetermined objectives and the tight micromanagement of curriculum and instruction. This factory paradigm endures even in new Classroom 2.0 programs and cyber-schools and in new policy initiatives for using the Internet in schools; the conclusion we draw is that you can't put the new networked wine in the old hierarchical bottles.

Part III presents a concrete vision for educational revolution, organized around "complex open networked learning centers" and Education 2.0. While hierarchical forms of organization seek radically to reduce complexity, teachers and learners are complex in ways that conduce to significant unpredicted learning. They all have distinct interests, talents, and passions that get lost in hierarchical forms of instruction. Their interactions with one another stimulate these unique characteristics and combine them in powerful but unanticipated ways for significant learning. A century of tight behavioral control and "classroom management" has not succeeded in taming them. New theories of complex networked organization provide helpful ideas about how networked organizations can harness this complexity for learning instead of suppressing it for control. From these theories, new models for new learning organizations can be generated to serve as successors to today's hierarchical schools.

Chapter Ten reviews recent visions for education that fully embrace the Internet as the source of ubiquitous "any time, any place, any subject matter learning"—educational arrangements where anyone can learn anything from anyone at any time. While these visions are liberating, they fail to answer some basic questions about teaching and learning in concrete terms; they leave too much up in the air about aims, leadership, teaching, subject matters, and assessment, and as a result they fail to generate the kind of concrete aims and action steps that can inspire and direct broad-based change toward new educational institutions that families, communities, taxpayers, educators and policy leaders can embrace. The bare-bones visions of networked learning that the learningweb visionaries advance need to be fleshed out in ways that convincingly explain how young people will get initiated into adult society—how they will get guidance, form adult capabilities, and obtain links to adult work situations.

Chapter Eleven sets out in somewhat abstract terms the kinds of organizations that can make effective use of today's information networks. Such "complex organizations" give up top-down control and free individual participants to act and interact creatively but within well-understood contextual limits. They then harvest the unpredicted value they create, periodically reshaping the overall mission and structural design to remain effective in the organization's ever-changing environment. Chapter Twelve translates these general ideas about organizational complexity into a concrete vision of schools as complex open networked learning centers, the promised embodiments of the new Education 2.0 informational paradigm. Chapter Thirteen sets out the educational commonplaces of the new network paradigm and shows how the new paradigm can resolve the four failures of the factory school.

Questions will certainly arise about whether the shift from hierarchical schools to networked learning is a real possibility or merely a wild fantasy. These questions are addressed in Chapter Fourteen. Serious thinkers have argued for some thirty years that fundamental educational change is impossible; the most change we can expect or hope for is a kind of "tinkering" around the edges of the entrenched system. The public, they say, knows what "real" schools look like and the social benefits they have conferred on advantaged groups, and it just won't accept anything else. As a result each new "reform" leaves the basic system unchanged and thus reinforces the factory school mind-set.

In the three decades since this argument was first advanced, however, our economic, social, and political leaders have actually withdrawn their support from the one-size-fits-all factory high school. In its place they press diverse smaller schools operated by diverse providers, including for-profit school corporations. These schools have been freed from some regulations to pursue experimental ideas for teaching and learning, but they remain confined by preset curriculum standards and assessment by high-stakes standardized tests. Like the Japanese mini–steel mills, these diverse charter schools are educational mini-mills. They have indeed destroyed the image of what a "real school" has to look like, but without laying the ground for a new educational paradigm. No credible evidence, however, suggests that these mini-factories can effectively resolve the pressing problems of American secondary education. The factory model even in this up-to-date form has failed, and the public is ready to consider new ideas and practical arrangements.

Having presented a framework for open networked learning centers, and shown the paradigm shift to be both desirable and possible, Chapter Fifteen lays out the concrete action steps readers, in their capacities as learners, parents, citizens, school leaders, teachers, and policy makers, can take to move the learningweb revolution forward.

* * *

Many questions remain about both the Internet as a learning platform and about the impact of information technologies on contemporary adult social and economic lives. The Internet has enabled firms to outsource jobs and replace employees with contract workers. It has destroyed trusted information media—magazines and newspapers and music publishers—rendering it impossible for many who thrived in these industries to earn a living. Information technologies have made work processes more efficient and eliminated many jobs. Industrial robots have replaced routine workers throughout the world. The corporate elites have concentrated wealth and power and, by distorting the electoral process with money, have weakened democratic control over the direction of society.

These issues are profoundly troubling. They may cause us to look back with nostalgia to past modes of learning and living. But there is no road back to the past. It is more useful to look to the present and future, to think about building effective and just institutions for our times.

I will not be addressing these issues directly in what follows. I focus narrowly on educational change. Suffice it to say that I share these troubling concerns. Nevertheless, expanding the Internet as a learning platform can open the world of learning to everyone on a global scale. That seems to me to be an unmitigated good. Blocking this educational transformation, by contrast, is merely a reactive move that exacerbates rather than resolves the problems of today.

Part One
Schooling—
The Industrial Paradigm

Chapter One
Young People

In March 2008, eleven-year-old Tavi Gevinson of Oak Park, Illinois, a suburb of Chicago, connected to the cyber-community, "casting a net" by posting a first entry in her aptly named blog *Style Rookie*:

> Well, I'm new here. Lately I've been really interested in fashion, and I like to make binders and slideshows of "high-fashion" modeling and design.[1]

A year after this first online post Tavi was declared the "new darling of the fashion industry." Her blog was getting 1.5 million hits a month. While her classmates struggled with long division and parts of speech, Tavi dashed off to front-row seats at runway shows in New York, Paris, Tokyo, and the world's other major fashion centers. *USA Today* profiled her and soon she was seen on the cover of *Pop* and in feature articles in *Sassy*, *Love*, and the *New York Times Magazine*. Top fashion designers Kate and Laura Mulleavy, hooked on Tavi's cutting-edge fashion commentary, highlighted her in their 2009 Rodarte collection for Target. Soon other top designers came running with new projects. In October 2011 Tavi was selected as cover girl for the 90th anniversary issue of *L'Officiel*, the leading Paris fashion magazine.

Critics have been astounded by the range, elegance, and sheer professionalism of *Style Rookie*. Some question the blog's authenticity, declaring that no eleven-year-old could have produced anything like it. Child advocates worry that young girls like Tavi, in exposing herself so openly to the adult world, court danger. Lawyer Parry Aftab, of the online protection site WiredSafety.org, says, "Parents have no idea what their kids are doing online.... Most parents have no idea what a blog is." Aftab could have been speaking for Tavi's father, English teacher Steve Gevinson, who hardly knew about his daughter's blog until Tavi asked for permission to appear in the *New York Times Magazine* article. He says, "It was a kind of non-thing to know.... I didn't look at it. I wasn't terribly interested in it." Today Steve is a proud father, and a spirited defender of youth bloggers.

Of course, not everyone can be Tavi Gevinson.[2] Tavi is clearly an exceptional young person. But teen fashion blogging is an important industry trend and many other young fashionistas are making their mark. Jane Aldridge, the sixteen-year-old native of Trophy Club Texas and publisher of the blog *Sea of Shoes,* receives 25,000 hits a day. Julia Frakes, who started *PaperMag* as a high school student in Scranton, Pennsylvania, started a second blog, *Bunny Bisous,* to handle the more whimsical, offbeat stories that didn't fit in the first one. At eighteen, when Frakes moved to New York City to cover the fashion scene, she was receiving 800 emails a day from PR people pitching her stories. The industry friendships she made through her blog have helped her score many inside scoops; she tags along with the models and listens in when they talk about the clothes that turn them on. Her competitive advantage: few industry insiders enjoy the direct access to the models Frakes has gained through her blog or bring her youth perspective to the table.

And out in the Philippines, when blogger BryanBoy posted a home-brew video tribute to top designer Marc Jacobs on his self-titled blog, Jacobs emailed to say he was a fan. Jacobs then named a bag from his 2008 collection, the "BB," in Bryan's honor. "Marc sent me the original prototype via courier from New York, in a box bigger than a fridge, and I literally had tears running down my face when I opened it," Bryan reports.

* * *

Some may complain that the obsessive interest in fashion runs counter to our highest educational aims. Fashion, however, is not the only field affected by young bloggers. Teens and preteens are doing amazing things in many fields, casting nets far and wide.

Fifteen-year-old Jayralin Herrera, for example, might be considered an anti-fashion blogger. Jayralin lives in a 2,800-square-foot mini-mansion in suburban New York. Two years ago she rejected her family's consumerist lifestyle.

> I was sick of all the excess. So, I began to pare down to the essentials. There were over eight big bags of stuff I got rid of and threw away. I slowly began to realize the excess we really own.

Jayralin started reading blogs about alternative "minimalist" lifestyles and began her own minimalist blog. Eventually she attracted the attention of senior lifestyle bloggers like Leo Babauta of *Zen Habits* and Francine Jay of *Miss Minimalist*. Jay invited Jayralin to do a guest post, exposing her views to tens of thousands of readers. In that post she writes,

> The whole idea of a house, cars, a huge closet full of clothes ... it overwhelms me! Everything I own now fits in my single closet, with plenty of room to spare. I now own less than 55 things and keep trying to get rid of more. Seeing the way the environment is being torn apart and not cared after destroys me inside. Sustainability, along with "minsumerism," and proper knowledge on what goes on with the world helps for the right decisions.[3]

Unlike Tavi, Jayralin isn't rushing off to Milan, Tokyo, or Paris for the latest fashion shows:

> My plans for the future include backpacking from my single backpack, walking everywhere and having a garden.

Jayralin's own blog, reminiscent of Thomas Merton's journal, is filled with acute philosophical and religious insights. In June 2011, I interviewed her by e-mail and asked first about her experience in high school. She said that overall it provided a positive learning environment, but she added,

> I just wonder if we could someday change the schooling system to become something that focuses on the individual's needs a lot more than it does at this moment. We're all fed this stuff in one system, all the same way, so creativity is squashed.

She added that beyond excellent training in basic academic skills like spelling, grammar, and arithmetic, conventional school subjects are not really necessary for everyone. She would prefer her studies now to focus more directly on her writing. I also asked her about the role of the Internet at school and in her life. She said,

> The school doesn't force us to get familiar with the web, [but] we all do it out of habit. Since all our friends use Facebook, Twitter, and Tumblr on an everyday basis, we all get used to it. Not to mention the handiness of the mobile web.

Finally, I asked about whether she had opportunities to study or discuss her ideas about frugality and minimal lifestyles in school.

> Frugality, minimalism. Those things don't come up often in school, honestly. Consumerism does, actually. Everyone in school simply wants to buy, buy, buy, and show off what fancy goodies they brought. I express my opinions with my peers, not so much my teachers. They actually think I'm some kind of crazy dreamer. Everyone thinks what I want to do in the future is a bit crazy. [But] I usually get positive feedback: people ask me more and more questions and think I'm a genius when it comes to what I own and my ideas. These ideas are open and should be shared with the world; people need to be aware. The reason why people don't debate about things is because they aren't aware, and to make them aware opens their eyes to tons of new possibilities.

Let's take note of four features in these teen blogger stories that can help us frame a larger vision for the Internet and education:

- *Anyone, Anywhere:* The young people are not located at industry power centers. Tavi is out in the Illinois suburbs, Jane Aldridge in Trophy Club, Texas, Jane Frakes in Scranton, Pennsylvania, BrianBoy in the Philippines, Jayralin Herrera in the New York suburbs, Priyasha (whom we will meet in a moment) in Indonesia.
- *Building on Basic Skills:* All four possess some basic communication skills—writing, editing, organization and selection of images, videography—which they put to creative use.
- *Channeling Personal Interests to Build Powerful Capabilities:* All channel a personal interest or passion and express a unique point of view in communications addressed to particular public cultural communities.

- *Connecting to Adult Communities:* Their activities connect them to other participants, influencers, and leaders in those communities, opening doors for further development, visibility, and professional opportunity.

Teens Are Awesome

Priyasha, a fifteen-year-old blogger from Indonesia, writes in a guest post titled "Simply Said: Teens Are Awesome," on the multiauthor youth activist blog *Itstartswith.us,* that "teenagers are awesome, because (some of us at least) still have little bits of innocence from our childhood combined with maturity as we turn into adults."[4]

Priyasha is certainly on to something. Teens really *are* awesome, with or without the Internet. Psychologist Robert Epstein, a former editor of *Psychology Today,* in his recent book *Teen 2.0: Saving Our Children and Families from the Torment of Adolescence,* argues convincingly that teens are true adults whose development is artificially inhibited by constraining institutions, especially schools. Freed from these constraints, teens are highly capable—in some ways more so than adults.[5]

Epstein points to studies demonstrating that by age fourteen the brain is at its state of highest development. Studies based on Piaget's test of formal operations show that all formal operations—those involved in adult thinking—are acquired by age fourteen, and if not demonstrated by fifteen will probably never be acquired (165). Intelligence matures at age fifteen; the nonverbal and culture-free progressive matrices scores peak at age fourteen (172). Scores of memory improve until age thirteen or fourteen and then level out or decline (177). Even on tests of judgment, the scores of fourteen-year-olds did not differ significantly from those of either eighteen- or twenty-one-year-olds, and they are significantly better than those of nine-year-olds. Markers of creativity are high in childhood, peak again during the teen years—with a dramatic leap between fifteen and eighteen—and then decline throughout adulthood (255).

As a result, teens have surprising and sometimes even shocking mental and emotional capabilities. Blaise Pascal invented the mechanical adding machine when he was nineteen; Anton van Leeuwenhoek made his famous perfections of the microscope at sixteen; Louis Braille developed his system of reading for the blind at fifteen; Philo Farnsworth provided the critical breakthrough for electronic television at fourteen.[6] Tennessee Williams was only sixteen when he wrote his first book, Edith Wharton fifteen, Jane Austen fourteen. Jorge Luis

Borges was only nine when he prepared his Spanish translation of Oscar Wilde's "The Happy Prince."[7] Mozart, who composed his first piano pieces at age five, wrote his first successful opera at fourteen and all of his violin concertos during his nineteenth year; Chopin wrote his first two polonaises at age seven and many of his most important works before age twenty; Mendelssohn composed his first symphony at fifteen and his beloved overture to *A Midsummer Night's Dream* at sixteen.

Recent examples from the news of astonishing teens (alert readers will regularly find similar news stories) include these:

May 27, 2012: Shouryya Ray, a sixteen-year-old Indian immigrant living in Germany, was the first to solve a problem posed by Sir Isaac Newton more than 300 years ago—how to calculate precisely the path of a projectile under gravity and subject to air resistance. His father, an engineering technology professor at a technical college, says that Shouryya never discussed the problem with him until it was solved and that it relied on mathematics "way beyond my reach." Labeled a genius by the German media, Shouryya explained his discovery as a result merely of "curiosity and schoolboy naivety." He said, "when it was explained to us that the problem had no solutions, I thought to myself 'well, there's no harm in trying.'"[8]

June 4, 2012: Sho Yano, who graduated summa cum laude from Loyola University of Chicago at age twelve, has graduated from the combined PhD/MD program of the medical school of the University of Chicago at age twenty-one, making him the youngest MD graduate in the school's history. He picked up his PhD in neurobiology along the way. He hopes his graduation will silence those who questioned his readiness when he entered medical school. The University of Chicago took a chance on Yano after other medical schools refused to admit him, concerned that the challenges of medical school would hinder his chance of having a "normal adolescence." He said, "I never understood that. Why would being allowed to challenge yourself be considered more damaging than being totally bored?"[9]

While these stories of individual achievement are amazing, idealistic teens also can work together to improve society. Lots of teens, Priyasha says, "have ideas on how to change the world around us." She adds,

> This teenage generation has the power of the Internet, and we are stronger than ever, if our "powers" are used correctly. Since a mass percentage of the teenage generation is connected on the Internet and frequently uses it, if we

put our "powers" together, we could start something really big, or change the world in a really big way.

Aristotle would have agreed. He said that "young people long to do noble deeds ... because they have not been humbled by life or learned its necessary limitations; moreover, their hopeful disposition makes them think themselves equal to great things."[10] Perhaps we adults can help them do great things and even join with them, instead of raining on their parades.

Jayralin Herrera's parents and teachers, for example, do not share her minimalist views, and she, in turn, does not discuss her ideas much with them. Like many young netcasters, she is flying solo. But few young people can discover passions and shape life projects without some adult support. Priyasha thinks "it would be incredible if teenagers and adults could work together more often to combine our thoughts and hopes to create something of greater good."

This is an educational vision worth pondering: teens combining peak mental capabilities with childlike naiveté, learning at high adult levels; becoming valued members of society; making creative discoveries in science, the arts, scholarship, and invention; and putting their powers together, working with adults for the greater good. In what follows we'll see where Priyasha's vision takes us.

What's So Awesome about Ordinary Teens?

A nagging thought, however, is that the teens mentioned above are *so* awesome, *so* exceptional, that their experiences shed no light on learning prospects and potential achievements of "ordinary" teens. In response it is worth considering that such teens share the same humanity with their amazing counterparts. They have the same vast number of brain cells—up to 500 billion by some estimates. It is a commonplace that most people use less than a tenth of their brainpower. All "normal" humans have astonishing capabilities—their brains are millions of times more powerful than the most advanced computers.

Aristotle famously said that "all men by nature desire to know." We delight in our senses and especially our sense of sight, he said, "because it makes us know and brings to light many differences between things."[11] Today he would say "all people." Harvard philosopher John Rawls developed this insight as what he called the "Aristotelian principle." Stated simply, "other things equal, human beings enjoy the exercise of their realized capacities (their innate or trained abilities), and this enjoyment increases the more the capacity is realized, or the greater its complexity."

Rawls regarded the motivation to richly develop our capabilities and to enjoy their exercise as a "deep psychological fact" about human beings[12]—not a rare trait of "exceptional" people. Rawls regarded the values of personal affection and friendship, meaningful social cooperation, the pursuit of knowledge, and the fashioning and contemplation of beautiful objects as very widespread. These familiar values, moreover, tend to be interdependent and complementary: each person's pursuit of them both depends upon the cooperation of others and is likely to enhance the good of others. This is a major reason why good societies single them out as especially important values. Indeed, for Rawls the very essence of a just society is that it is one where all human beings can obtain basic goods—including civil liberties and education—so that they can pursue these values and develop richly, in accord with their own aims and plans. It is no part of a just society, however, to impose compulsory treatments on young people or anyone else having nothing to do with their freely chosen aims and plans. If that is what "equal educational opportunity" is about, we can well do without it.

Why then do we tend to think so many kids are "ordinary" and incapable of rich, complex growth? Epstein suggests a distinction between teen competence and performance. The tests of formal operations, IQ, memory, and creativity all show that teen *competence* is equal or even superior to that of adults. Competence remains latent, however, under conditions preventing or forbidding its expression in *performance*. Adults, Epstein shows, infantilize teens and block their access to adult roles—especially by confining them in schools. Epstein provides many examples of otherwise unexceptional teens who, in suitable settings, perform at high adult levels. There is no telling what ordinary teens might do if freed from constraints and placed in nourishing, unconstraining environments with appropriate support and guidance. Why write teens off and kill Priyasha's dream before giving them a chance to show what they have in them?

* * *

Despite the pleas of child safety advocates like Parry Aftab, parents of young bloggers appear less concerned with the privacy and security of their teens than with distraction from school work. Parents know that education is more important than fashion or lifestyle trends. And they don't recognize youth blogging as "education." Maybe they are wrong. Maybe writing with passion each day for discerning audiences, honing a personal style, and connecting to the adult world of action and opportunity is just as much a part of education as mastering long division, sentence diagrams, or parts of speech.[13] In the next chapter we will explore the concept of education to see if we can discover a place for such activities.

CHAPTER TWO
EDUCATION AND CHANGE

WHAT IS EDUCATION?

Blogging about fashion and lifestyles has no place in conventional secondary education. This book, however, sets forth a revolutionary proposal for educational change, a paradigm shift from a hierarchical, school-centric industrial model of education to a networked, learner-centric model—Education 2.0. In this paradigm the passionate activities of young people—often mediated by the Internet—play a central role. The Internet, not the school, is the centerpiece of this network model. Schools retain a place in the new model, just as the Internet has obtained a role in today's school-centered education. But in the network model conventional curriculum-based schooling will play a different and a smaller role, though one itself deeply affected by the Internet; for example, most classrooms will have "Google jockeys" appointed by teachers to amplify curriculum content. Meanwhile, the Internet—beyond the confines of schooling—will play a different and greatly expanded one. If diagramming sentences and learning parts of speech, balancing chemical reactions, and finding roots for quadratic equations are typical educational activities in the entrenched, school-centric educational model, the efforts of Tavi, Jayralin, Priyasha, and their fellow youth bloggers will be equally typical examples of education on our network model.

Broad and Narrow Senses of "Education"

The term "education" has a broad general sense and a more specific or narrow one. According to the Shorter Oxford Dictionary, to "educate" is "to bring up (children) so as to form their habits, manners, intellect, aptitude, etc.," and also, more specifically, "to instruct, to provide schooling for." "Education" itself is defined as "the process of nourishing and rearing" and also as "the systematic instruction, schooling, or training of young people, or by extension, instruction obtained in adult life."

In the broad sense, "education," like "health" or "welfare," is an open-ended value term. We can agree that education, like health or welfare, is good while still debating about what it contains and how it proceeds. But these disputes have their limits.

Some recent definitions help us understand these limits. My late friend and colleague James McClellan said that the concept of education is concerned with a "particular way of becoming a person-in-society." The great educational historian Bernard Bailyn also brings out this social dimension, defining education as "the entire process by which a culture transmits itself across the generations." Lawrence Cremin agrees that this broad definition is needed and adds that to qualify as education the process must be "deliberate, systematic, and sustained."[1]

Education as Initiation

Richard Peters offers a particularly illuminating definition of education as "initiation into worthwhile activities."[2] For Peters "initiation" involves processes of gaining knowledge, understanding, and an active cognitive perspective involving ways of thinking and judging specific to social practices. To be an initiate in an activity is to know its traditions and rules, to understand its point, and to be able to participate as a social "insider."

The Internet adds a new dimension to education as initiation. The initiation concept fits Tavi Gevinson's case well; through her avid attention to fashion and style, mediated by the Internet, Tavi gained the knowledge, understanding, and perspective that informed her own thought and judgment and led to her acceptance, again mediated by the Internet, within the fashion community.

Education for Peters also involves conveying a sense of the point of the activities, grasping and sharing and caring about the values inherent within them that make them worthwhile. A chess player who learned how to move the pieces but had no sense of why anyone would ever play chess is not an *initiate* in the world of chess. Initiation implies building up active capability sufficient to perform with enjoyment in activities and share in their values. This eliminates rote learning unconnected to performance as *mis*-educative. Tavi, on the other hand, profoundly grasps the point of fashion in shaping personal style and young adult identity. As a recognized blogger she's an insider in the world of fashion—she talks today's talk and walks today's walk.

Peters adds that "education" implies a degree of voluntariness, a willingness to learn. While this would clearly eliminate a lot of what passes for education in today's high schools, it fits Tavi and other youth bloggers well; indeed, their participation is not merely voluntary or willing, but passionate and sometimes obsessive.

Reconsidering Education as Initiation

Peters's definition of education as initiation has not been universally accepted. Peters offered the initiation metaphor as an alternative to the molding or shaping metaphor of conservative educators and the growth metaphor of progressive educators. Initiation into ongoing worthwhile activities provided learners with vital fields of ongoing activity to enter; instead of being passive recipients of molding or shaping, they became active participants in an evolving culture. Meanwhile, these cultural activities set some constraints on growth; learners weren't growing helter-skelter, but along lines already acknowledged as worthwhile.

Not surprisingly, Peters's idea met with opposition from both conservatives and progressives.

Mary Warnock argued from the conservative side that education as initiation overemphasized "insider" understanding and voluntariness. She claimed that all learners had a moral right to acquire basic facts and skills. While accepting that the deeper and more nuanced understandings and capabilities deriving from education as initiation were worthwhile, they were trumped by the moral obligation to provide the basics. Insofar as time and effort devoted to education as initiation took time from the basics, she argued, it violated that moral obligation.[3]

An answer to Warnock's criticism is that becoming an initiate in academic forms of thought logically requires acquisition of many basic facts and skills. One can hardly hold one's own as an "insider" in history, for example, without knowing a lot of history. While learners may become adept at historical thinking while remaining ignorant of important areas of history, armed with the tools of historical thought and available reference sources, including today's Internet, such deficits can readily be eliminated.

From the progressive side, Gert Biesta countered that the initiation metaphor retained the cultural transmission model of education. He offered an "agency" model stressing each individual's growth in uniqueness or difference.[4]

Initiation versus agency is, however, what John Dewey would have called an "untenable dualism." The worthwhile activities intended by Peters include transformational as well as normal ones and thus allow for the differences and new identities regularly exhibited in intellectual and artistic fields. In art education, for example, it is a given that mature artists develop unique perspectives and practices. They do this by working through traditions and conventions, as filtered through their unique life experiences and those of their generation, discarding outmoded forms while extending their fields in new ways. They do not study the old masters to become different from them; this would be immature and shallow. Rather they study to learn from them and to qualify themselves as insiders or initiates—as creative members of the artistic community.

The failure of Biesta's critique hardly implies that Peters's analysis of "education as initiation" is completely adequate. Peters's own formulations are one-sided, highlighting formal learning and neglecting the role of informal education in the process of initiation.

The term "initiation" frequently calls to mind the initiatory rituals of simpler societies, where norms of kinship, religion, economy, politics, and culture are tightly intertwined. In these the young can demonstrate knowledge and competence in adult life in one unified process or ritual and gain adult status at once. Modern societies by contrast are institutionally differentiated.

Peters's notion of education as initiation is focused squarely on education in the narrow sense, on the intellectual dimensions of academic disciplines. His account highlights school teachers and lessons; education aims at initiations into science, history, literature, and the like. Education is thus a package of particular academic initiations.

For Mircea Eliade, initiation refers to a "body of rites and oral teachings whose purpose is to produce a radical modification of the . . . status of the person to be initiated"; the novice emerges from the initiation ordeal "a totally different being." Eliade distinguishes between two types of initiations: (1) obligatory collective initiation rituals whose function is to effect the transition from childhood to adult status by introducing novices to the spiritual and cultural values and practices of the community and assigning them adult responsibilities, and (2) voluntary particular initiations into, for example, secret societies and occupational guilds, which distinguish initiates from other members of society.[5]

At first glance, education, taken as a whole, appears to fit the notion of *general* initiation: obligatory initiation into society. The child emerges from education as an adult—a "totally different being." The various disciplines, however, do have their own occult languages, so education in history, literature, and the sciences can be conceived as *particular* initiations. But what is the relation between education as general initiation and education as a package of particular initiations? And why did Peters not think of education in terms of general initiation?

Significantly, Peters was well aware of this distinction and actually did consider this question carefully. In "Ritual in Education," an article Peters coauthored with Basil Bernstein and Lionel Elvin, the authors mark out this very distinction.[6] The function of general rituals is, they say, to unify the social whole through shared repetition of symbolic behaviors. Many vivid examples of such general rituals can be found in the history of education, including athletic contests in English public schools and weekly sermons at Bryn Mawr and Morehouse Colleges. Wellington reputedly stated that "the battle of Waterloo was won on the playing fields of Eton," suggesting that general school rituals—not academic lessons—generated the patriotism and leadership in the elite class that sustained the British empire. In her sermons Martha Carey Thomas directed Bryn Mawr women not merely to excel academically but to devote themselves to leadership in all walks of life. At Morehouse, President Benjamin Mays told young black male students that "Morehouse holds a crown over your heads, and expects you to grow into it." These colleges, through such general rituals, sent forth astounding cadres of female and black leaders.

But in highly differentiated modern societies, Peters and his coauthors assert, the number and significance of general rituals declines: such rituals can only be effective when a high degree of social consensus and uniformity among students prevails in a school. In today's comprehensive schools, they say, these conditions simply do not exist. As a result, general school rituals wane and students develop their own youth-culture rituals outside of school to form their transitional identities. In short, for Peters and his coauthors, educational agencies have lost the power to perform general social rituals and initiate young people into responsible adult roles.

"Ritual in Education" appeared in 1966, amid a vital and widespread revival of youth culture and an economy boosted by social and military spending. The authors felt that schools could concentrate on intellectual development, while young people formed identities through the youth culture, found work in the growing economy, and affected their transitions to adult status in recognizable ways despite the absence of general rituals in schools. Today, however, youth culture has broken into thousands of little pieces while opportunities for work disappear. Pathways to adult status are obscure for both former working- and middle-class young people. More and more high school and college graduates, regardless of their academic attainments, languish in their parents' basements. General rituals of initiation—genuine rites of passage to adult status—are needed more than ever. And once initiation is freed from Peters's narrow definition, it can be reshaped to guide the development of such rituals.

NESTING PARTICULAR ACADEMIC INITIATIONS IN GENERAL SOCIAL INITIATION

My reconstruction of education as initiation *conjoins* particular initiations and general social initiation, and nests the former in the latter. The overriding aim of education on this account becomes transition to adulthood, and education becomes a rite of passage. Schools guided by this notion assess themselves primarily by how well they move their charges forward to independent adult status. Academic initiations serve as *both* introductions to activities with their own inherent values *and* steps in the passage to adulthood. Academic lessons and courses are nested in, and qualified by, the larger purpose of *general social* initiation. Such schools mark successful transitions to adulthood in public ceremonies: their honor rolls, halls of fame, and graduation rituals give primary place not to those with the highest academic marks but to those demonstrating well-documented adult knowledge-in-use, in jobs, internships and apprenticeships, independent research projects, and business ventures.

But what of Peters's doubts about the possibility of general initiation rituals in comprehensive schools? My earlier examples—Eton, Bryn Mawr, and Morehouse—were selected to illustrate how such rituals work in the opposite kinds of schools—those serving distinct groups defined by class, race, and gender. Such rituals conduced to solidarity, and Peters doubted that they could be effective where student groups shared little in common.

But today's school students are not as diverse as they may appear. Children from elite families do not attend comprehensive schools, while those who do, the children of so-called working and middle classes—black or white, male or female—all face similar life challenges and thus can respond to common rituals.

Steady jobs of all kinds are disappearing. Young people need high-level knowledge and skills for decent work of all kinds. They need further education that does not drive them into unmanageable debt. They need attitudes of flexibility and adaptability to turn knowledge and skill to account in responding to unpredicted occupational opportunities throughout life. They need networking skills to connect with others and make themselves and their capabilities visible. Without schools conducting general rituals responding to these needs, just who will be "holding a crown" over the heads of *their* students?

Putting these definitional strands together, we may speak of education as initiation, in a broad sense, as involving the deliberate processes by which social groups initiate young people into their ways of living and valued activities by developing knowledge, understanding, perspectives, capabilities, and values—and thus bringing them into their social worlds.

The processes of education, so understood, are exceedingly diverse, including conventional procedures of early child rearing; provision of libraries and museums and playgrounds and arenas for public speech; internships, apprenticeships, and on-the-job training programs; publication of books, magazines, and newspapers; broadcasts of radio and television programs; publication of websites and blogs; support of social and athletic clubs like the Boy and Girl Scouts and little league baseball; Internet-mediated meetups; and many other things.[7] Education as initiation also requires access to adult communities of practice and informal learning incidental to practice. Today many communities of practice combine physical and virtual worlds. Initiation also requires aid in composing a life that is self-sustaining. This last requirement highlights the central importance of mentors and role models on the one hand and access to remunerative work on the other.

Education and Schooling

In a narrow sense, as noted above, education means "formal instruction and schooling." In this sense we speak of people as "educated people" if they have been instructed in the higher branches of knowledge over many years in secondary schools and colleges, and we think of improving education as reforming these schools and colleges.

Until the twentieth century, however, schools and colleges did not play a major role in the education of most citizens. Thomas Jefferson, who among the American founding fathers placed the highest value on public schooling, considered the press more important as an educative force. Even John Dewey, the patron saint of the American public school, considered schools to be minor players in the public education of citizens compared with radio, magazines and newspapers, libraries, and even saloons where working people gathered for conversation.

Mark Twain said, "I have never let my schooling interfere with my education." He learned elementary lessons about writing in school, but as a writer he could not be confined by them; he had to push and test and even break them, adopt and adjust them to his expressive purposes. Or as contemporary novelist Elmore Leonard puts this point, "I can't allow what I learned in English Composition to disrupt the sound and rhythm of the narrative."[8] As mature participants in life activities we are all, to some extent, in the same boat. Even if we need schooling, we can't let it interfere with our educations.

Actually, schooling is not a necessary component of education at all. In colonial New England most children of literate parents learned the Three R's at home. According to census figures for 1840, only 1 percent of white New England adults lacked basic literacy, long before the common schools had a significant impact.[9] The unschooled colonial craftsman, long considered a "jack of all trades but master of none," was in reality a "master of all," a maker of fine houses, furniture, and farm tools.[10] Early American lawyers learned their trade by "reading at the bar." Nineteenth-century engineers learned how to build railroads and bridges by apprenticing themselves to senior engineers. Professional schools played a very minor role until late-nineteenth-century economic growth demanded recognizable "professionals" with standard knowledge.

The Higher Branches of Learning

This book focuses on the high school. Even ancient civilizations marked a distinction between elementary and higher branches of education. In ancient Athens, young male citizens attended private elementary schools, typically from ages seven to fourteen, to learn reading and writing, "music" (including poetry and drama), and gymnastics. Drawing was also a common school subject by 350 BC. The age-fourteen cutoff is not arbitrary: as we saw above, by that age humans reach peak levels of brain development and intelligence and in preindustrial societies get initiated into adult status. Past that age they are no longer children, unless their childhood has been arbitrarily extended into "adolescence" to keep them from productive work.

What, then, was higher education for young adults? After leaving the lower schools, Athenian young men went to gymnasiums (from *gymnos* = naked) where they exercised and trained for athletic competitions, considered useful for moral development and military preparation. Teachers established higher schools alongside these gymnasiums: for example, Plato's famous Academy at the gymnasium in the olive groves of Academe. Studies included logic, rhetoric, mathematics, geography, natural history, and politics, subjects that evolved into the "liberal arts." This education prepared those young men free from remunerative employment for the demands of public life: speaking in the forum, arguing a case of law, serving on municipal committees, and so on. In the Athenian direct democracy public life was a full-time job requiring its own (liberal) arts just as mechanics required mechanical arts. The studies comprising the liberal arts remained roughly the same throughout the classical and medieval eras, long after the link to the public life of democratic citizens was broken.

Higher Learning and the Two Cultures

During the Renaissance, humanists working outside the universities restored the classical liberal arts as instruments of public life; by the sixteenth century the humanist spirit entered the universities and "the humanities" became a dominant force. That century also saw the rise of discovery; scholars responded to the demands of navigators, merchants, overseas traders, engineers, inventors, and scientists for scientific knowledge. The English crown wanted the universities to embrace the new practical impulse in scientific spirit, but the self-governing university colleges resisted. Other venues were needed to foster scientific and technical discovery and creativity.

In London, organized meetings of scientists and practical men began in 1597 at Gresham College. This non-degree-granting institution also offered free public lectures in liberal subjects, for example, logic, rhetoric, astronomy, and geometry; but it expanded and reinterpreted them to include the new scientific and technical knowledge, creating a new "liberal-modern" paradigm for higher learning. The liberal arts thus forked into two cultures: a humanities branch in the universities and a liberal-modern scientific and technical branch outside them. The leading seventeenth-century scientists—Robert Boyle, Robert Hooke, Christopher Wren—all Gresham professors—formed the Royal Society in 1660, and the Society continued to meet at Gresham's mansion until it acquired its own headquarters during the presidency of Sir Isaac Newton early in the eighteenth century.

The two cultures came back together under one roof only in the late nineteenth century, when science, technology, and professional studies came to dominate English and American universities and the humanities were reformed as quasi-scientific academic disciplines alongside them. As C. P. Snow demonstrated, they have not lived comfortably together.[11]

Many of the Puritan leaders who established Harvard in 1636 were Cambridge men; Harvard was a copy of an English university college, and its professors were humanist scholars. Admission to Harvard required proficiency in Latin and Greek. A year before the college opened, a Latin grammar school was established in Boston to prepare young men for Harvard. Boston Latin was the first public school for higher learning in America. This pattern for higher education—grammar schools plus liberal arts colleges—remained fixed throughout the next century.

By the middle of the eighteenth century, however, leaders in American business and industry, overseas trade, and navigation, like their forebears in London, felt the need for scientific and technical knowledge and scientifically educated personnel. At first, ad hoc academies responded to this market with courses in bookkeeping and accounting, navigation and geography, surveying and mechanical drawing. The academies grew topsy-turvy, without any fixed structure, appalling New England elites who valued fixed and coherent order.

Ben Franklin organized a coherent plan for a model liberal-modern academy in his 1750 plan for an English academy in Philadelphia.[12] His vision was similar to the program at Gresham College. But much to his disappointment, William Smith, when assigned to implement his plan, retreated to the classical liberal arts model. But in 1821 Boston's industrial and civic leaders finally established an English High School, offering an orderly course of study in "all branches required for advancement in life, in all useful occupations." The English High School fulfilled Franklin's vision for his academy. Its founding principal, George B. Emerson, was a natural historian who later founded the Boston Society of Natural History and was its second president, as well as the designer of the Geological Survey of the State of Massachusetts. The English course had finally found its responsible sponsors and leader.

A battle then ensued between the private academies and the public high school. With public funding the high schools offered job stability for teachers and low-cost education for students. Eventually the high schools drove the ad hoc academies out of existence.

High Schools and Colleges

Starting in 1821, then, high schools and colleges offered two distinct forms of higher education in the liberal arts: the high schools emphasized science, technology, commerce, and modern languages and literatures, while the colleges offered the humanities, mathematics, and ancient languages and literatures. Teachers at the English High School were designated as "professors." High schools were frequently referred to as "people's colleges." Students went to college for a classical liberal education or to high school for a liberal-modern education. Central High School in Philadelphia even conferred a bachelor's degree.

In America, and throughout the world today, however, high schools and colleges are two levels in a sequentially organized system; young people seeking to advance through education have to go to both. There is nothing natural or inevitable about this arrangement. It is no more than a negotiated arrangement between the high school and college leaders at the end of the nineteenth century assuring that both could capture the education market. The arbitrary line between the two levels even today is demonstrated by the existence of vast duplication of the high school curriculum in colleges, by AP high school courses that carry college credit, by early admission and dual admission programs, and by high school–level and even remedial courses in colleges. Mass secondary education is an accident that turned into an institution. As we reimagine education in the Internet age, remember that today's system is an unshapely human invention that today's humans can replace by another invention better suited to our times.

High Schools for All

Thinking of a person without a high school diploma as woefully uneducated is an error of recent origin. Before the twentieth century very few Americans went to high school, as will be seen shortly. Even in the twentieth century many leaders acquired their education through life experience. To cite two examples, Sidney Weinberg, CEO of Goldman Sachs from 1930 to 1969, dropped out of a Brooklyn junior high school at age thirteen and started at the firm as a janitor's assistant. Dave Thomas, founder of Wendy's restaurant chain, dropped out of high school at age fifteen to work full time in a restaurant (he had been working part time in restaurants since age twelve). We can draw up a long list of performing artists who lack high school diplomas: Drew Barrymore, Tom Cruise, Russell Crowe,

Jim Carrey, Robert DeNiro, Whoopi Goldberg, and Ellen Burstyn acquired their high levels of general culture and occupational skill on the job.[13]

Even long after high schools became an established component of the educational system, few students attended and *very* few graduated. In 1890, there were only 3.5 high school graduates among every 100 seventeen-year-olds, and into the second decade of the twentieth century that ratio remained under 1 in 10. No one thought of leaving school as "dropping out." But in the twentieth century education became uncritically equated with schooling. In 1920 about 17 of every 100 seventeen-year-olds held a high school diploma, and except for the World War II years that ratio grew steadily until, by 1950, 59 percent held diplomas; by 1960, 65 percent; and by 1970, 76 percent.[14] With no need for child labor, elites tried to keep all youngsters in school; those who left were stigmatized as "dropouts" and blocked from employment. Just about every "educable" person received a diploma, and the diploma became a requirement for a decent job. Only then did getting an education came to *mean* going to school.

Keeping young people in classrooms was important throughout the industrial period regardless of the relevance of the curriculum to adult knowledge needs, because prior provisions for child care and youth learning were disappearing. The high schools also prepared young people for the expectations of industrial society, a point expanded in the next chapter.

The Internet has changed all that. Anyone with access to the web can today interact with limitless information and people anywhere in the world. The free access to and use of information is now central to human activities in every sphere; the Internet is the global communication hub and work platform: increasingly, people learn, work, communicate, and even play online. Initiation into the adult life of global network society quite simply is preparation for networked action. Confining learning to constricted, information-poor environments, and subjecting it to the tight hierarchical control of school teachers and a curriculum, is now simply perverse. We need new educational conceptions and practices for the information age.

But when we think of education as schooling, we can't even conceive of less school-centric alternatives; improving education simply *means* fixing the schools. It is especially important, therefore, to reclaim a broad sense of education as initiation when we explore opportunities for fundamental educational change. What is needed today is not just change *within* schools and colleges, but a change in the place such organizations play within our broader pattern of education.

INITIATION, PARTICIPATION, AND PERFORMANCE: FORMAL AND INFORMAL LEARNING

We can get a fresh start by returning to the idea of education as initiation into the world of worthwhile adult activities. Education as initiation implies preparatory learning for mature performance, obtaining the knowledge, understandings, perspectives, action capabilities, and values associated with worthwhile adult life activities and demands. Initiation consists in preliminary learning, access to adult communities of practice, and early stages of learning incidental to practice: getting ready, showing up, showing your stuff, and participating until you are accepted and recognized as a full member.[15]

Formal Learning and Didactic, Discursive, and Heuristic Teaching

An important subset of initiating activities consists of three kinds of overlapping episodes that usually (but not necessarily) involve teaching.[16] These episodes work together in an interdependent whole that I will call the "formal education complex."

Didactic teaching-learning eventuates in "I know." This kind of teaching imparts information and routine skills and processes to be mastered. Imagine the history teacher lecturing about names and dates, or the arithmetic teacher going over the process of long division, followed by drills and quizzes, or the English teacher diagramming sentences and explaining parts of speech. Didactic teaching aims at stocking the mind and memory. A well-stocked grid of ready-at-hand knowledge available in operational memory, however obtained, is a necessary condition for performance in any sphere. Note that the youthful bloggers were all able to read and write and had rudiments of cultural literacy. Thinking involves the selection and organization of knowledge to some purpose, and without an underlying framework of available knowledge learners have nothing to think with or about. Just how well-stocked in advance of significant activity in adult spheres this grid of knowledge must be, however, is subject to debate. We have to be careful to avoid overloading initiation with didactic teaching; the didactic curriculum can be infinitely, and pointlessly, inflated. Especially in our information era, when every learner has the entirety of the world's knowledge at hand on a PC, laptop, smartphone, or iPad, this stock of knowledge-in-memory needs to be held within reasonable limits.

Discursive teaching eventuates in "I understand." It involves setting up opportunities for speaking and listening. A discursion is a trip, a journey, with an unpredictable route and destination. Discursive episodes—for example, classroom discussions, panels, and debates—presuppose that students already have some didactic knowledge and hence something to talk about and fill in with new knowledge acquired for the immediate task at hand. Given expectations about background knowledge, a teacher may read a passage from a text, ask an interpretive question, and then facilitate a discussion or set an inquiry problem.

Discursive teaching helps students discern *why*. Students are asked, for example, to *explain why* one event gave rise to another, or *why* an author used a particular phrase in a literary passage and what it means, and what effect an alternative choice of phrase might have. Such intellectual acts—of explaining causal sequences or interpreting literary texts, or drawing implications from given facts—are at the heart of *understanding*. Students who have acquired didactic knowledge in a rote fashion but are unable to explain what they have memorized, consider its logical implications, or expand upon it by making connections in an organized way have not really understood it. Understanding is the ability to *use* facts and concepts, to go on, taking matters further in relevant and interesting ways. By speaking and listening students make knowledge their own, bring it to life, and move it along. This is why Aristotle says that the best way to learn anything is to teach it, to explain it to different people with different background knowledge and perspectives.

The discursive phases of lessons are opportunities for engaging in the liberal arts of logic and rhetoric. Mortimer Adler, who wrote a classic book on speaking and listening,[17] says that intellectual values central to education—for example, judgment, prudence, and discernment—can *only* be learned in discursive episodes. The young bloggers probably had few opportunities to discuss fashion in their history and social studies classes. But they did learn early lessons in critical discourse in discussing stories and plays and historical episodes. And they probably discussed clothing choices and personal styles with friends in the schoolyard before they shared their observations online.

Heuristic teaching is teaching *how-to* and eventuates in "I can do." Athletic coaches or journeyman workers *explain how* or *show how* by demonstrating, guiding, and correcting learners who follow their examples. This practice of a learner following in the train of an exemplary model is the root of our concept of training as teaching *how*. Such teaching is of course central to sports and games and vocational subjects such as auto mechanics. The coach explains the surprise play, then demonstrates its parts, and then supervises the players as they repeat it and master it. The mechanic explains the procedure for repairing the auto body, demonstrates the procedure on a dented fender, then supervises the students or apprentices as they work on other cars.

Heuristic teaching, however, has an essential role in all academic subjects. A course in history, for example, does not merely fill a student's head with names and dates or facilitate discussions but also imparts something about techniques and methods of history as a field of knowledge. Teachers may, for example, introduce students to history databases, demonstrate computer searches using them, and then guide students in making parallel searches for topics related to class projects. Or they may provide model explanations of particular historical events, abstract from these to indicate the components of a good historical explanation, and then guide students in offering explanations of the events taken up in their own projects. A course on literature does not merely populate student minds with names and dates of, and passages from, important books; it trains them to interpret the texts as well as to emulate them and build on them in their own writing of stories and interpretative essays. Or to take an example familiar to all, geometry teachers prove a number of theorems. But then they abstract from their proofs the general features involved in any proof and guide students in proving other theorems until they grasp how to go about constructing such proofs on their own. In the course of this instruction, they introduce such heuristics as "work backward from the conclusion to be proved" or "assume the opposite of the conclusion and work toward a result that contradicts what has already been established."

Even elementary schools provide many training opportunities, with units on creative writing and increasingly even on the use of multimedia tools like digital cameras. Today they may even provide lessons in blogging—how to use a blogging platform, name a blog, and use the blog editor program. Many eleven-year-olds today can "do" blogging, even if they can't yet, like Tavi, create active, popular blogs.

While these three elements—didactic, discursive, and heuristic—can be distinguished as separate methods of teaching and learning, what is indispensable, as Mortimer Adler insists, is the "dynamic flow from one to the other." I *know*, I *understand*, I *can do* form a complex whole. Whether school lessons and courses are offered in live classrooms, online, or through some blend of the two, we expect to find all three types of teaching and all three kinds of associated outcomes: knowledge, understanding, and action capabilities. School knowledge is of no value if it is poorly understood and cannot be constructively used. Assessment routines that do not measure all three of these dimensions of learning, in a balanced and integrative way, are invalid: they don't measure what we need to know about student learning. I'll return to this major point frequently in what follows.

Informal Learning and Performance in Worthwhile Activities

Preliminary knowledge, understanding, and ability engendered through formal learning do not in themselves grow into adult capability. In a frequently cited study, Sally Ann Moore of Digital Equipment Corporation estimates that in learning for adult-level performance about 5 percent of time must be devoted to the didactic dimension to develop the "I know," 20 percent to the discursive and heuristic dimensions for "I understand" and "I can do," and an additional 75 percent to the informal education dimension of "I adopt and adapt." Her figures may not be precise, or the same for all fields, but they give us a ballpark sense of how adult capabilities develop.

The first three components can be organized in formal courses: teachers can present, explain, and discuss the basics and then guide the first steps of practice. The last stage, however, requires many hours of informal learning through applying and augmenting formal lessons. Teachers can help us learn to read and can guide our early reading, but only years of self-directed reading can make us readers. Coaches can introduce us to the rules and guidelines of a sport like tennis and provide lessons to teach us basic strokes, but only years of self-directed practice and play can make us tennis players. Foreign language courses can teach us vocabulary and basic grammar and guide us in informal dialogues, but only immersion in the language through travel or overseas living can make us capable speakers.

Malcolm Gladwell, in his bestseller *Outliers,* popularized the notion that it takes 10,000 hours of concentrated practice to become proficient at any activity. According to Gladwell the statistical outliers with unusual skill do not generally have extraordinary talent but rather possess the drive and opportunity to master the skill.[18] This "adoption and adaption" stage usually consists of three types of informal learning: individual or group study, learning incidental to practice and subjected to explicit criticism, and tacit learning that remains deep in our hearts, muscles, and bones.

Schools and colleges specialize in the initial 25 percent. Much of the additional 75 percent takes place out of school and often after formal education has ended. But there are limits to this frontloading of the formal aspects of learning. We cannot simply excuse schools and colleges from developing meaningful adult capabilities. If they cannot foster 10,000 hours of informal learning, they can at least actively promote it, taking responsibility for it as an essential component of their overall task. If these capabilities are not fostered during the school years, most young people will graduate without them. Their future employers and college teachers will have every reason to complain that the students can't effectively *do* anything.

Some schools provide times and spaces for informal learning through the extracurriculum. But they rarely focus on it and, all too often, prevent it completely by filling all available time with an unnecessarily bloated and didactic curriculum.[19] Classroom lessons and homework fill all hours of the day. The young bloggers, however, owe their successes to that 75 percent devoted to informal learning. The parents and teachers who worry about online distractions ignore the crucial role of informal learning for performance. They risk emptying their children's education of its purpose and robbing them of its benefits.

The Bill Gates story is as instructive as that of Tavi Gevinson. Gates essentially dropped out of his high school's curricular program in the eleventh grade. His private high school was one of the few in the country to have access to a time sharing computer, and during his junior year Gates spent his days and evenings on it. His school then arranged for him to devote his entire senior year to an independent study project working full time as a computer programmer. Instead of punishing him for his passion, his school facilitated its development. He says of that time, "it was hard to tear myself away from a machine at which I could so unambiguously demonstrate success." At age seventeen he had already formed a computer business with Paul Allen. The basic conceptual question that follows is this: did his school, in easing his access to computers, *foster* his education or collude with him in *avoiding* it?

Hundreds of thousands of young people are computer literate; they have taken a course about computers, learned some important facts, and performed some programming exercises. In this minimal sense they can do programming. Gates, on the other hand, was by seventeen a capable professional programmer. When the MITS-Altair computer was released in 1975 and needed an operating system and other programs, Gates already had his 10,000 hours of learning for performance. He was more prepared for the MITS-Altair job than any person in the world. At age nineteen he dropped out of Harvard (he had never engaged with the university curriculum, spending almost all of his time at the computer center) and formed Microsoft with Allen. The rest, as they say, is history!

Of course we can no more all be Bill Gates than we can all be Tavi Gevinson. That hardly implies that we can't learn anything from his experiences and achievements. Many young people, from all social and economic groups, have interests and passions that can be developed and productively channeled during their school years. Their schools should help where they can, through guidance and access to informal learning opportunities. Where they cannot help, they can at least get out of the way. Young Tavi and Bill didn't need more lectures or coaching sessions to do amazing things; they just needed plenty of time for learning. If we as educators did what we could to facilitate young peoples' growth, or at least cleared up the time and space for their own self-directed efforts, we might just be amazed at the results. As Priyasha says, teens are amazing, and "it would be incredible if teenagers and adults could work together more often to combine our thoughts and hopes to create something of greater good."

Fundamental Change

Priyasha's dream is revolutionary. Moving from today's schools with their fixed, bloated, and outdated curricula to new arrangements where young people have the time and encouragement to follow their passions and cast their nets in the web, assisted by adults when help is needed, represents a fundamental educational change, a transformation of our entrenched institutional arrangements from the factory school to Education 2.0.

A revolutionary change means a transformation in an institutional paradigm. Institutions introduce order and predictability; they consist of rules governing the practices that build up around all of the significant aspects of life in society. Institutions govern giving birth and dying, buying and selling, making war and peace, selecting leaders and worshipping gods. Social, political, religious, and economic institutions work together in an interdependent institutional order. When one institution changes in fundamental ways, all the others must adjust. Changes in the occupational order, for example, fuel changes in the family, which in turn compel changes in education. And changes in the industrial occupational order are now taking place all around us. Something will have to give.

Educational practices and behaviors are surrounded at all points by institutional rules. These rules determine which schools are legitimate; they establish curriculum formats including the division of educational levels and requirements for the completion of each level; and they regulate uses of space and time, the credentials for teachers, the legitimate authority of administrators, and the taxing powers of school districts.

These institutional rules assure a consensus about basic institutional assumptions and practices. These rules come together in any era to form a well-understood institutional pattern, a template that can be copied endlessly (even as it is modified in minor details to conform to local conditions). The expectations and behaviors of everyone interacting within the institution—taxpayers, teachers, parents, students, and community interest groups—all come to accord with that pattern. Habits form. Legislation builds up around them. Teacher training is adjusted to them. Textbooks are designed around their assumptions. The institutional rules guide our actions but also constrain them, keeping our actions within the guidelines. They form an exoskeleton around us, locking us in place.

More or less the same institutions surrounding the learning of so-called adolescents in secondary schools now extend throughout the world. These patterns of teaching and learning have been replicated from state to state and nation to nation, incorporated in state and national laws and the popular mind. They have been formalized in international comparisons based on standardized international tests that have in turn shaped the curricula of the schools of separate nations into a global standard. Because various features of the institution—curriculum, teaching, administration, assessment—work together to form a unified pattern, a template repeatedly copied, it is difficult to disentangle and rearrange the separate features. The pattern itself has a unified existence; it is "greater than the sum of its parts."

Educational Paradigms and Commonplaces

Following recent usage, we can call this unity a "paradigm," meaning (1) a conceptual *model* that (2) first becomes instantiated in one or several places as a real world *example*, and then (3) becomes normative—that is, the example becomes an *exemplar* that serves as the obligatory institutional model.

The terms "paradigm" and "paradigm change" gained popularity after they were used by Thomas Kuhn to account for scientific revolutions, such as the shifts from Aristotelian to classical mechanics and Ptolemaic to Copernican astronomy. The new texts of Copernicus, Galileo, and Newton replaced the Aristotelian corpus as scientific paradigms. They served as examples of the new scientific work that became normative in the scientific revolution of the seventeenth century. Since Kuhn introduced these terms, they have been adopted to explain changes in the social sciences and humanities and in practical fields like medicine, law, and education, and now their use, too, is normative—we cannot but think of fundamental changes as paradigm shifts.

Paradigms are not mere theories, ideas, or models, but all-encompassing worldviews built up in our minds through social conditioning that shape how we see and interpret objects and events. As Kuhn put it, "the proponents of competing paradigms practice their trades in different worlds."[20] Seeing young people as, for example, "ninth-graders" or "high school juniors," is a reflection of our entrenched age-graded educational paradigm. No one would have seen fourteen- or fifteen-year-olds as "school-aged" in 1800; those living at that time occupied a different world. And quite possibly those living in a near-future world will see teens not as school-aged kids but as genius-aged adults.

All of us are familiar with paradigm shifts in our own lives and those of our friends and neighbors. Imagine these: a young person, raised in a conventional religious family, questions her beliefs and leaves her church; or an adult living a secular lifestyle confronts feelings of meaninglessness and embraces a religion. Or these: a psychiatrist trained in psychoanalysis, frustrated by inconsistent results, shifts to cognitive-behavioral and drug therapies (or vice versa); or a full-time employee loses a job and becomes an entrepreneur.

Thinking and acting within a given paradigm simplifies our tasks. As Kuhn puts it, our problems get reduced to "puzzles" that can be approached using standard methods. The entrenched education paradigm reduces education to schooling, learning to attainment of specified learning objectives, and assessment to measurement of results against objectives. Educational problems in turn are narrowed and simplified into puzzles: How can we fix the schools, attain objectives more efficiently, and measure them more accurately? A paradigm shift is like the famous gestalt shift picture—it's one and the same picture, but look at it one way and it's a duck, look at it another way and it's a rabbit. If we reject the entrenched paradigm, the duck becomes a rabbit—the ground shifts under our feet; new problems open up, old problems are reframed, and new kinds of solutions, appealing to new clienteles, become both possible and necessary. We will no longer judge schools in terms of their production of widget-like specific learning objectives or perceive young people as "adolescents" or captive "school-aged children." Instead of fixing the schools, we may think about entirely different arrangements for education outside of schooling altogether. Instead of efficiency in meeting prespecified learning objectives, we may reconsider our aims in terms of powerful but unanticipated emergent results of learning beyond schooling.

In "preparadigm" situations, workers in a field or discipline share no guiding assumptions or authoritative models. In a "multiparadigm" situation, the allegiances of workers are divided between several paradigms; they are guided by different models. Humanities and social science disciplines are frequently multiparadigmatic. Recognized professional philosophers, for example, may be divided into analytic, continental, and pragmatist camps, each accepting different exemplars of practice and employing different philosophical methods. Psychological therapy is notoriously multiparadigmatic: some therapists rely on the Freudian paradigm, others on behavioral, cognitive, or gestalt paradigms. They view their clients in different ways, conceive their symptoms in different terms, and even judge the effectiveness of their treatments against different criteria of success. They "live in different worlds."

Because of the powerful standardizing role of the modern state, many practical fields exhibit a hegemonic paradigm: a central paradigm or set of institutionalized assumptions, models, and approaches bolstered by legislation and state funding and surrounded by a number of weak alternatives. A hierarchical paradigm, one that many have called the "factory school" paradigm, was established for education in the period from 1820 through 1870 and was further refined in the 1890s through the 1920s. The popular comprehensive American high school is the result of that process. There is nothing natural or inevitable about the hierarchical organization of education when conceived of as initiation. But it is hard to break from the hierarchical view because schooling is the paradigm: we have all imbibed the schooling "Kool-Aid."

This dominant factory school paradigm is now surrounded by an array of weak alternatives, ranging from Waldorf schools and Summerhill-style free schools to home schools and home-based "un-schools." Today the factory paradigm is strained. Sensing its problems, educators have created charter schools of many kinds, including cyber-schools. Until now the impulse for change, however, has been contained by the dominant paradigm. Policy makers have tolerated considerable variation in the surface elements of schools so long as the deep structural elements of the hierarchical school—the predetermined curriculum sequences, distinct subject matters, and standardized tests—remain in place. It is as though school officials have followed Henry Ford, who declared that customers could buy a Model T Ford in any color, so long as it's black.

To date no comprehensive model deviating from this structure and capable of capturing the imagination of the educational public has even been formulated, much less implemented and tested. Any new educational paradigm must attend to all key features or commonplaces of organized learning—learning and learners; teaching and teachers; subject matters; methods; authority and leadership; aims and assessment—the who, what, why, when, where, and how of education. The commonplaces function at a level of abstraction higher than those of specific institutional practices. The notion of a "learner" is more abstract than that of a "school student"; the notion of "subject matters" is more abstract than of a "school curriculum." Commonplaces can thus survive through changes that wipe out their historically specific forms; there will still be learners and things to learn even if we eliminate schools and curricula. A *fundamental* educational change is a change of paradigms, a transition from one paradigm, from one way of grasping and filling out educational commonplaces, to another. New paradigms provide new meanings for the commonplaces and a new pattern for relating them to form a new whole.

This book considers a fundamental change in the learning arrangements for young people from roughly age fourteen, when they mature biologically, until they enter the workforce or college. I will propose a fundamental shift to a new network educational paradigm suitable for the information era. This shift entails rethinking each commonplace. I start in the next chapter by explicating the currently entrenched factory school paradigm and its commonplaces.

Chapter Three
High Schools

The first American high school was established in Boston in 1821, just as the first American mechanized factory was established in the same place. The high school was a direct response to the emerging industrial situation; the growth of industry after 1800 called for machine operators but also workers and managers with commercial and mechanical capabilities. Factory production and high school education have run on parallel tracks since that time; hierarchical organization has prevailed in both. Today, however, industry is being re-engineered; flatter network organizations are replacing hierarchies. High school organization lags far behind.

Francis Cabot Lowell opened his first mechanized factory in 1814. In 1823 Nathan Appleton and Patrick Tracy Jackson of Lowell's Boston Manufacturing Company established an industrial town along the rapids of the Merrimack River, and they named the town Lowell in honor of the visionary founder, who died in 1817.

Lowell graduated from Harvard in 1793, entered the overseas trade, and sought to improve rum distilling on an industrial scale. After 1807, conflicts in Europe began to disrupt American overseas trade. He switched to cotton and with assistance from Jackson and Appleton formed the Boston Manufacturing Company on the Charles River in Waltham, Massachusetts, in 1814. He introduced technical improvements, mechanizing the entire process from raw cotton to finished cloth. When the firm exhausted the available power from the Charles, they expanded to the site along the Merrimack named after Lowell.

The mechanized industrial process introduced by Lowell became the paradigm of industrial production, a template copied throughout New England, the Midwest, and the South and eventually around the world.[1]

Mechanical Production and the Industrial Mindset

Lowell initially approached his workers as a paternal leader of an extended family. He introduced schools and cultural activities for his "mill girls" and provided housing in attractive dormitories. Economic recessions and increased competition in the 1830s forced the firm to eliminate benefits, cut wages, and raise dormitory rents. When his Yankee workers rebelled, the firm fired them and hired immigrant workers willing to work for low wages and do as they were told. Harsh industrial management replaced Lowell's paternalistic model of employee relations. These methods of industrial management were improved after the Civil War and further refined in the early twentieth century under the banner of "scientific management."

Frederick Taylor, in his classic *Principles of Scientific Management* (1911), focused on the active role of management in analyzing, planning, and controlling the production process in minute detail, compelling workers to do exactly as they were told. Each shop required a "functional foreman" who would teach workers the precise methods and then check all the work. Scientific management required analyzing manufacturing processes into (a) predetermined finished end products and then, working backwards from those ends, to (b) sets of explicit steps—small, measurable, and reproducible behaviors—for producing them. Management's job was to impose these methods of production upon the workers. In the process, the actions of high-skilled craft workers, based on long training and craft knowledge, were "engineered" as steps in the mechanical process. This method put productive knowledge and full control of production into the hands of management while reducing worker knowledge to a minimum, thus increasing worker productivity and reducing wages.

Hierarchical Organization

In short, production shifted to hierarchical organizations. In hierarchies *directive* links flow downward from the top level through subordinate levels of control and eventually to those at the bottom. *Report* links flow from the bottom back up to the top. There are few direct cross-level links. Workers do not go over their foremen's heads or behind their backs to contact division heads; managers may have an open-door policy for colleagues but not for line workers. Significant links, those that influence behavior, among same-level nodes are discouraged because exhaustive authoritative directives have already been handed down from above. Line workers do their jobs without help from coworkers. Top management establishes a comprehensive plan and sends directives down to functional division heads. These leaders then establish the subdirectives for their functions and send them down to middle managers until specific operational directives reach the bottom rung of operatives, whose performance outputs are then reported back up the chain. The workers at the bottom represent interchangeable sources of "labor power," mere "hands" to be managed. No account need be taken of their unique potentialities or capabilities.

In an automobile firm, for example, top management establishes the overall shape of the model line and sends directives to design, marketing, engineering, and manufacturing. When their various teams have completed their functional tasks they report back to top management, which pulls the model year together. In a hierarchical high school the district board and superintendent establish overall direction; the principal interprets it for his school and sends directives to department heads who convey them down to teachers operating directly on students. The department heads rarely confer because their faculties have distinct functional tasks; literature, social studies, and math courses proceed on separate tracks. In the classroom students do their own work and are assessed on their individual performances. Following the line of hierarchical authority, data are gathered on student achievement, reported back up the line to the superintendent, and then compiled and sent on to state and federal officials. The school is organized as a factory for the production of predetermined learning objectives, while students learn to submit to industrial order.[2]

The Industrial Paradigm

The spread of industrial methods in manufacturing gave rise to an industrial culture fostering a new paradigm, mindset, or mental model of rational action. This paradigm dictated gathering the productive forces in a single place, mechanizing the productive processes, and tightly controlling labor processes. The guiding value in this paradigm was efficiency in production—the increase of yield per unit of input. The primary input is dollar cost, as all factors of production—resources, machines, and labor processes—can all be purchased on the market.

From the early nineteenth century through the twentieth century, this mindset was extended from manufacturing to all spheres of life including domestic housework, medical and psychological therapy, and even sexual intercourse, conceived as the efficient production of orgiastic pleasure.[3] Acting rationally came to *mean* adjusting means to ends so as to improve efficiency measured in terms of the ratio of predetermined ends per unit of input.

Schools as Factories

As schooling expanded in the industrial culture, school leaders embraced the industrial paradigm; the school that emerged has justly been called the "factory school."[4] William Bagley was among the first theorists to conceive of schools and classrooms as factory-like systems. In his textbook *Classroom Management* (1907) he spoke of the teacher as a kind of functional foreman demanding "unquestioned obedience" from students.[5]

Following the publication of Taylor's *Principles,* The National Education Association rapidly established a Committee on Tests and Standards of Efficiency.[6] Educational efficiency came to be seen as maximizing the units of learning per input cost, with learning understood in terms of acquisition of specified learning objectives as measured by tests. Taylor's associates were recruited to consult with school "managers" about how to introduce scientific management, as the efficient production of learning objectives, in their schools. Educational leaders openly and proudly referred to themselves as "managers" or "chief executives" and to their schools as "factories of learning."

Development of the Factory School

Most early high schools consisted merely of a single room in a common (elementary) school, with a single college-educated teacher offering all subjects. This arrangement appears less strange when we remember that before the Civil War college students underwent the conventional liberal arts curriculum including standard literary and mathematical subjects. There were no college majors as we now conceive them; college graduates were prepared to handle all standard high school subjects. By the 1870s, in the wake of the new research universities, colleges became organized into disciplinary departments. High school faculties were then reorganized into parallel departments of math, science, English, and history–social science.

From the beginning, teaching and curriculum were shaped by textbooks with standard subject matter content.[7] Didactic lectures based on the textbooks, solo study of problem sets by students, and recitations rapidly became the norm. The recitation, where students were called on daily to stand and conjugate verbs or solve algebra problems, was taken over from classical language teaching in the Latin grammar schools, when former grammar school teachers were hired by the high schools. The recitation, first adopted for English grammar and foreign languages, spread rapidly to other high school subjects. The group oral recitation served as a convenient way for teachers to assess student learning, because it was less time-consuming than grading written work.

Critics complained from the start that this "system of cram" made it impossible for teachers to develop a creative art of teaching.[8] Normal school leaders and popular books on the theory and practice of teaching dismissed didactic teaching, rote memorization, and recitations as fit only for imbeciles. But even those who condemned these practices fell back upon them when forced to cope with the day-to-day demands of school teaching. The factory paradigm became entrenched because it fit the circumstances of the crowded classroom, with each teacher managing thirty-plus students. It continues to do so.

Students persistently complained that teachers deviated from the textbook-based curriculum when lecturing and that they made subjective, biased judgments of recitation performances. Faced with complaints from parents, school principals and superintendents introduced standardized tests to solve the problem of teacher bias; tests were designed to keep teachers on track by selecting test items exclusively from the official curriculum represented in the textbook and by introducing an objective measure of performance that undercut complaints about subjective bias.[9]

The main structural features of the factory high school paradigm were thus already in place prior to the age of scientific management, but that movement consolidated them and locked them firmly in place.

Factory Schools: Seven Features

The industrial, hierarchical, or factory high school paradigm has been well described over the past quarter century by leading scholars.[10] It can be defined in terms of seven key features:

(i) It is an age-graded school organized into departments and disciplines. The high school course is a secondary level of the system of formal education between the primary and tertiary levels; it consists of four age-graded steps from freshman to senior years.

(ii) Instruction is organized in roughly identical "egg-crate" classrooms (that radiate out from central corridors). The term "egg-crate" points to the essential identity of each classroom—like the cells for eggs in a Styrofoam egg package. Some of these rooms, such as the chemistry labs and art studios, have special features, but these are mere variations on a single pattern, and these special rooms are readily used as, or converted to, general purpose classrooms.

(iii) A single certified professional teacher in each classroom provides instruction in accord with directives imposed by officials higher in the chain of command, assesses learning, and reports results back up to superiors. The teachers, in turn, have received a structured teacher training course that accords with directives set by state officials and professional accreditation bodies.

(iv) The high school subject matters are predetermined and presequenced in a curriculum (generally) supported by a textbook, with specific learning objectives. The high school course of study, with minor variations, has been constant throughout the history of the institution. The subject matter contents are adjusted over time to reflect new developments in the academic disciplines.

(v) Didactic instructional methods, with lectures, recitations, and work on prepared worksheets, dominate teaching. Teachers are "functional foremen" who teach facts and precise methods and then carefully check results. Discursive and heuristic methods play only minor roles, and time and opportunity for informal learning are sharply limited. With only minor variations, the teaching and organizational routines of the high school have remained constant, and they habituate learners to the conditions of bureaucratic organization. This habituation is often referred to as the "hidden curriculum" of the school, and it comprises the most lasting and consequential learning of school students.

(vi) Assessment is based on tests of specific learning objectives, typically reflecting memory of prescribed content and application of standard routines emphasized in the curriculum.

(vii) The manifest aim of the educational process is scholastic: to facilitate learning of basic academic skills and disciplines translated into "school knowledge." Other aims, such as the full development of personality, effectiveness as a worker, and the development of good citizens frequently appear in mission statements but rarely figure as guides for teaching or benchmarks for assessment.

The Grammar of Factory Schooling: The Seven Features in a Pattern

David Tyack and Larry Cuban, among others, have described this paradigm of age-graded and departmentalized schools, egg-crate classrooms, didactic instruction, and assessment by examination as determining the "grammar" of schooling. They explain that the structure of relations between these commonplaces of teaching, learning, setting, assessment, and others gained political support in the nineteenth century and has proved so efficient that it has crystallized, preventing consideration of alternatives.

The late Ted Sizer echoed this point, noting that the basic architecture and grammar of contemporary schooling haven't fundamentally changed since the nineteenth century. He added, "we understand that the culture and economy have changed, but we are so stuck in what has become the conventional way of schooling that we don't think twice about it."[11]

Indeed, this factory pattern is now institutionalized throughout the world. As K. Anderson-Levitt noted, schools everywhere share this age-graded, egg-carton format where "teachers rely mainly on lecture-recitation and seat work."[12] The subject matter content, especially in literature and history, may be somewhat diversified to serve different national cultures and political regimes, but the structural grammar remains the same; it is uniquely well adapted to industrial and industrializing nation-states.[13]

The seven features of the factory paradigm are connected by this grammar; they work together as a pattern, just as words are connected by grammatical rules to form sentences. If learners are assessed by standard subject matter tests (feature vi), these subject matters *must* be organized in a predetermined sequence (iv) that can fit into a definite time frame, which *must* be one school year or one half school year (a semester) if the school is age-graded (i). Because teachers *must cover* prescribed subject matters within that period to prepare students for tests, they *must* control learning tightly through didactic methods, as discursive and heuristic episodes are less predictable and controllable (v); so whatever the *stated* aims (development of human personality, democratic citizens, etc.), the operational aim *must* be acquisition of the subject matters for memory and routine application (vii).

The Factory School and Industrial Society

Each feature of the hierarchical high school has thus been fine-tuned to fit with its other features, and the institution as a whole has remained in a rough harmony with other institutions in the industrial social system throughout the nineteenth and twentieth centuries.

Robert Dreeben of the University of Chicago, a leading sociologist of education, documented in his 1968 classic *On What Is Learned in Schools* that the primary upshot of mass schooling has been habituation to norms of industrial life rather than academic learning. Long after young people forget most of the academic content of the curriculum they ever learned, they continue to adjust their lives to norms regulating their everyday behaviors in social settings—norms they learned in school.

School students learn to adjust behavior in schools to norms imposed by school rules and regulations. If they fail to accommodate to these institutional norms they get into trouble, get suspended, and eventually get pushed out or drop out. By providing a steady diet of the same norms over twelve or more years of schooling, schools also shape young peoples' expectations about how the world outside of the family works and what it demands from them. Schools thus can be said to prepare young people for life in society by habituation in an impersonal normative order that replaces the close personal order of families and neighborhood ethnic communities.

Dreeben provides a short list of the most important norms learned in school: he calls these independence, achievement, universalism, and specificity.

The norm of *independence* means being self-sufficient, accepting personal responsibility, and handling tasks by oneself that in other circumstances might be best handled in a group. Students learn the norm of independence by being physically separated from one another and having their interpersonal communications blocked. Tests are monitored so each test booklet reflects the work of a single, isolated student.

The norm of *achievement* means mastery, measured against an external standard of excellence. Students learn the norm of achievement by being subjected continually to tasks that do not reflect their personal aims and being evaluated by superiors by reference to impersonal criteria that they have no hand in shaping. They learn to work hard to succeed at what others rather than they themselves regard as important and to face the consequences of failure.

The norm of *universalism* means responding to others as bearers of categories rather than as unique, holistic individuals, while the norm of *specificity* means confining our attention to those characteristics of others relevant to the institutionally structured activities where we interact. Students learn to regard themselves and others as, for example, tenth-graders, as students of geometry;

they learn to see others as teachers or principals, sixth-graders or seniors. And they learn to confine their interest in teachers or sixth-graders to characteristics deemed relevant to their institutionally defined interactions; for example, they are not supposed to take an interest in a teacher's inner feelings or out-of-school personal life.

The norm of independence is essential in a social order where most individuals function as employees accountable to employers. The norm of achievement is likewise essential in a market society where an individual's value is based on mastery of impersonal tasks. Universalism and specificity are crucial in a mass society where it is not possible to relate to the people we interact with holistically because we can't be expected to know much about them beyond their institutional positions and roles. Thus Ms. Jones is reduced to "the algebra teacher" and Billy Smith is reduced in Ms. Jones's viewpoint to "a freshman algebra student."

In the late twentieth century, however, in the wake of global information networks, hierarchical forms of organization began to give way to flatter network paradigms in many "postindustrial" industries. People work together in teams. The teams are often composed of freelance contract knowledge workers. The workers have to work together collectively to figure out project goals and methods, drawing on any knowledge and insight they possess, including deep knowledge of their own and their coworkers' capabilities. Any new paradigm for education will have to reflect these new normative demands, or it will fail to prepare learners for their emerging adult roles. It will thus have to alter each commonplace feature of the industrial paradigm and, what is much more important, arrange them in an entirely different pattern—a new "grammar" of education—accustoming learners to new norms in synch with the needs and expectations of information, or global network, society.

Today educational leaders of many persuasions agree that the factory high school is failing. In the next two chapters we evaluate this charge. We consider the high school's performance in achieving what we demand from the education of young adults: basic academic skills and disciplines, channels for interests and passions of students, and connections linking students to the real world of adult activities and opportunities.

Chapter Four
School Failure I
Academic Underperformance and Administrative Inefficiency

Today's pundits berate our schools as failing—failing to perform as expected, to deliver on their promises, even to maintain past levels of achievement. The schools, these detractors say, fail to teach: students fail to learn and drop out in unacceptable numbers. School critics complain that teachers are inefficient and often incompetent; recently they have even charged that teachers are overpaid and coddled because of their powerful unions and have proposed eliminating tenure and collective bargaining rights. Meanwhile even those students who persist with high school studies through graduation fail to adjust to adulthood; schools and even colleges are now "roads to nowhere." The critics, moreover, insist that the public is losing patience with the schools and withdrawing its support from public education.

In this chapter and the next we examine these four purported failures of the schools. We start in this chapter with the issues of academic underperformance and inefficiency. In the next we turn to concerns about the social and economic irrelevance of the schools, and their declining social legitimacy. The school critics continue to view education through the prism of the industrial paradigm; their complaints are, for the most part, about the failure of the schools to adjust curricular treatments to achieve desired learning effects. I will be stepping outside of this paradigm, and, not surprisingly, my perspective on the failures of the schools will be quite different.

Failure One: The Academic Disaster

Most observers today agree that American high schools are failing academically; academic achievement is low and dropout rates, particularly among poor minority groups, are high. The academic crisis was noted thirty years ago, when the "excellence in education" movement began in earnest. What lies behind this alleged crisis?

In the past Americans were proud of their schools and were confident that they contributed to our prosperity and democratic way of life. Fears of declining economic competitiveness in the 1970s, however, led policy leaders to question the adequacy of our schools.[1]

A Nation at Risk and Excellence in Education

In 1979 President Jimmy Carter established a cabinet-level Department of Education, charged *to promote student achievement and preparation for global competitiveness by fostering educational excellence and ensuring equal access.* The focus on excellence for all was a political compromise between conservatives seeking a no-nonsense approach (labeled "excellence" because of its emphasis on high academic standards), and liberals seeking to ensure equal opportunity for disadvantaged groups.

The department was opposed by conservatives, who complained that federal intrusion into education was unconstitutional. When Ronald Reagan defeated Carter in 1980, one of his first priorities was to close the nascent department. His first secretary of education, Terrence H. Bell, however, saw political benefits in seizing leadership on education from the Democrats. Bell pushed for a no-nonsense, hard-core approach to education that would appeal to business leaders, who wanted an abundance of well-trained workers. Announcing his concern that something was "seriously remiss" in the schools, Bell established a blue-ribbon commission to recommend reforms.

Their report, "A Nation at Risk" (ANAR), declared the nation to be teetering on the brink of failure. "Our once unchallenged preeminence in commerce, industry, science, and technological innovation is being overtaken by competitors throughout the world ... the educational foundations of our society are being eroded by a rising tide of mediocrity that threatens our very future as a Nation and a people."

Bell's commission pointed to poor showing on international comparisons of educational achievement, declining scores on standardized tests, low attainment of higher-order thinking skills, and rising need for remedial courses in colleges as indicators of failure. It then announced twin goals of equity and high-quality schooling. Constrained by the status of education as a reserved power of the states, the federal department pursued these twin goals by selective funding of state and local efforts to impose challenging curricula, increase the number of challenging courses mandated for graduation, and expand opportunities for disadvantaged groups.

Before examining the success of these reforms, we must first stop and ask: How correct and useful was the commission's diagnosis of the problem? This is especially important because this diagnosis remains more or less unchallenged even today.

First, contrary to the scare tactics of ANAR there was no "rising tide of mediocrity." The commission claimed that SAT scores had declined by "over fifty points" on the verbal section and "nearly 40 points" in math. An independent, federally funded re-investigation by Sandia Labs revealed, however, that the *average* decrease in SAT scores was due entirely to the changing cohort of test takers; more students from lower scoring groups were taking the SAT because they were planning to attend college. Despite lower *average* scores, the scores of *each subgroup*, paradoxically, had actually increased.[2]

Second, the alarm about declining performance on international comparisons was also misplaced. Despite our conviction of national exceptionalism, the United States has *never* done well on international comparisons of student achievement. In the First International Mathematics Study in 1964, two decades *prior* to ANAR, for example, the United States placed eleventh of twelve industrial nations. It is difficult to imagine a significant decline from that level.

Now, how about the results of ANAR? Federal and state officials made the curriculum more challenging and focused more attention on academic achievement, but few indicators of achievement improved. The results on the International Trends in Mathematics and Science Study (TIMSS) are indicative: through the 1990s US students performed poorly despite these reforms.[3]

Goals 2000 and No Child Left Behind

In 1994 Congress passed Goals 2000: The Educate America Act, setting as aspirational goals that by 2000 our high school graduation rate would rise to

90 percent and US students would be "first in the world in mathematics and science achievement."[4] But faced with evidence from TIMSS that school reforms were failing to lift test performance, in 2000 President George W. Bush upped the ante with his signature No Child Left Behind (NCLB) law requiring states to establish statewide assessments. Officials would be forced to close any school unable to demonstrate annual yearly progress on tests mandated for grades 3 to 8 and high school. By 2010, forty-nine states had created standards tied to high-stakes tests, and twenty-two required students to pass high school exit exams.

Many states, however, then gamed the system by setting a low bar in order to prevent their schools from being tagged as "failing"—and thus losing federal funds. In 2010, 95.5 percent of eleventh-graders taking the Georgia High School Writing Test, for example, met or exceeded state standards. In 2009, a comparable 91 percent of Tennessee seniors tested at the proficient or advanced levels. But when, under pressure, Tennessee introduced new tests based on revised standards in 2010, the report of results was delayed amid claims that districts were cooking the books. Eventually more than half of the seniors failed the new exit exams. Only 21 percent of that cohort, moreover, scored at the "proficient" level or higher on the National Assessment of Educational Progress (NAEP) exam, the so-called nation's report card. Speaking of the schools graded as failing, Governor Bredeson said they would be taken over by the state and "they are all going to get body slammed."[5]

In New York, a report showed that only 23 percent of the 2009 high school graduating class was prepared for college or well-paying jobs. The study found that scores of 75 percent on the Regents English exam and 80 percent on the math exam were required to get a grade of C or better on entry-level college courses in those subjects. Those with lower test scores would require remedial work in college. But New York standards for graduation only required scores of 65 percent on *any* four Regents exams. Less than 17 percent of graduates in some city districts, including Buffalo, Rochester, and Syracuse, could meet the higher standard deemed "college ready." In Rochester only 5 percent achieved that level! David Steiner, New York's state education commissioner, remarked "It's a national crisis!" and declared that he would personally hold all principals accountable for higher state standards in 2012.[6]

All the news was not as bad. By 2003 US students had finally started to improve their standing on TIMSS.[7] However, neither US fourth- nor eighth-graders showed any measurable change in the percentage testing at or above the *advanced* level; the sharp focus on teaching for tests raised the so-called proficiency of our students but did not raise the percentage of those scoring at a high level.

Even the positive TIMSS results were unfortunately overshadowed by those of the Program for International Student Assessment (PISA). PISA tests fifteen-year-olds and follows TIMSS methodology. However, like the original NAEP, PISA adds items from varied real-world contexts alongside those from the school curriculum, so it is a better measure of broad educational achievement; the real-world items make it more difficult to teach for the test. PISA data were first gathered in 2000 and have since been gathered every three years. Each three-year cycle tests for a different subject: reading literacy in 2000, math literacy in 2003, and science literacy in 2006. In 2009 PISA administered tests in all three subjects. On this broad test American students returned to their mediocre performance.[8]

Conservative educational critic Chester Finn immediately called PISA a "Sputnik moment," and a "wake up call to those who think American schools are globally competitive."[9] The "Sputnik moment" and "wake up call" phrases were soon echoed by President Obama and his education secretary Arne Duncan.[10]

The Real Meaning of PISA and High-Stakes Tests

Just how bad was US performance on PISA? Our fifteen-year-olds scored right at the PISA average in science and reading and an insignificant tad below average in math. But Secretary Duncan asked, "Have we ever been satisfied as Americans being average in anything? Our goal should be absolutely to lead the world." The PISA scores became exhibit #1 in the movie *Waiting for Superman,* which pushed for the privatization of the public schools as the strategy to raise our international standing.

But one has to ask *why* anyone should expect America to be first in the world in educational test performance? Our scores in international comparisons have been mediocre ever since these tests were first introduced. Asian American students, however, score just about the same as their Asian counterparts, European-Americans the same as their European counterparts, Hispanic students similarly to their Latin American peers. Cultural factors thus explain almost all the variance in school performance. Why should we expect our students to outperform those from Asian nations? Do we have a more school-centric culture? And should we want one? Do we value teachers more and recruit our brightest young people into the education profession? Singapore—where a young person can be lashed for chewing gum—consistently scores at or near the top of every international comparison. China—with its one-child policy, low university enrollment, and gross income inequality—also does well; failure to test at a high level condemns not just students but their parents and children to a life of poverty.

Are these the cultures we wish to emulate? Vicki Abeles, director of the documentary film *Race to Nowhere,* does not think so. Her film documents the stress of being a child in a school and a society obsessed with standardized testing. She shows kids tired yet deprived of sleep; the pressure for grades and test scores drives kids to plagiarize schoolwork, cheat on tests, and turn to addictive drugs to stay awake and concentrate.

Taiwan has scored near the top on all international comparisons, but until recently the mainland Chinese have not participated. But the city of Shanghai participated in the 2009 PISA and finished first. Perhaps the Chinese should feel proud, but the reaction has been decidedly mixed. Yong Zhao of Michigan State University noted that from a young age, children in China are relieved of any other burden and deprived of opportunities to do anything other than school work so they can focus on getting high grades and test scores. "The result is that Chinese college graduates often have high scores but low ability."[11] Jiang Xuchien, deputy principal of the Peking University High School, agreed. "Chinese schools are very good at preparing their students for standardized tests," he said. "For that reason they fail to prepare them for higher education and the knowledge economy." He added,

> China's most promising students still must go abroad to develop their managerial drive and creativity, and there they have to unlearn the test-centric approach to knowledge that was drilled into them. The dictates of the examination have left students with little time and room for learning on their own. Shanghai's stellar results on PISA are a symptom of the problem. One way we'll know if we are succeeding in changing China's schools is when these PISA scores come down.[12]

Low Test Scores Do Not Place the Nation at Risk

Secretary Bell's blue-ribbon committee tied the nation's economic performance to educational achievement. It aimed to use the schools to build a globally competitive workforce.[13] Since then American students have performed at a reasonably steady, unimpressive level on tests of educational achievement. Meanwhile, its economy has had dramatic ups and downs. A little logic thus reveals that very little, if any, economic variance is explained by educational achievement as measured by standardized tests. Further evidence for the independence of educational and economic achievement is provided by the consistent stellar performance of nations with basket-case economies, like Japan, on international comparisons.

The real drivers of the US economy during the years since ANAR have been high-tech entrepreneurs like Steve Jobs, Bill Gates, Michael Dell, and Mark Zuckerberg, college dropouts all, not by straight-A students and good test-takers.[14] Venture capitalists in Silicon Valley now look for young entrepreneurs fitting a specific profile to fund; being a dropout is one of the cardinal features. Peter Thiel, PayPal founder and Silicon Valley venture capitalist, upset a lot of people last year when he proclaimed that a higher education bubble had replaced the housing bubble and would be the next to burst:

> A true bubble is when something is overvalued and intensely believed.... Education may be the only thing people still believe in in the United States. To question education is really dangerous. It is the absolute taboo. It's like telling the world there's no Santa Claus.[15]

Thiel has established a fund to pay scientists and technologists under age twenty to drop out of school and stay out; so far it has awarded $100,000 grants to each of twenty-four Thiel Fellows to pursue entrepreneurial ventures, research, and self-education.[16] Thiel's conception of higher education as a bubble has been listed as one of the top ten educational technology ideas of 2011.[17]

David Karp, the founder of the Tumblr blog platform used by Jayralin Herrera, dropped out of the Bronx High School of Science at fifteen. Perhaps we will know we are succeeding in changing our schools when more students like David Karp drop out. If fueling our economic engine is an important educational goal we will have to do more to liberate our most talented, creative, ambitious young people. Freeing them for net-based learning and networked action may be a big part of the solution; the time-consuming, bloated, mandatory curriculum is certainly a large part of the problem.

School Reform and School Failure

The school reform movement since A Nation at Risk in 1983 has not challenged the factory paradigm. Instead, it has strengthened it. By mandating more years of mathematics, English, social studies, and science, the reforms further locked in the fixed course of age-graded study. High-stakes tests have further narrowed the curriculum to what is covered on the tests. Narrowing the subjects tested has marginalized or eliminated other subjects including the social studies and arts. The NAEP, when first introduced as a broad measure of national educational performance, covered twenty-one subjects. As it became reduced to a tool for assessing school reform it was narrowed to six subjects with a special emphasis on English and math. Not surprisingly, a 2010 report showed that our students scored worse in history and social studies than in all other academic subjects.[18]

School reform, in short, has tightened the grip of top-down hierarchical control, which is itself the source of familiar school problems. Here are the most obvious ones:

The emphasis on didactic methods of teaching fills classroom time with a steady diet of monotonous and largely unnecessary memorization of inert, useless knowledge and drill. Students have to sit still and listen to didactic lessons and practice limitless routines to learn something they have no interest in learning. Most hate it. This places a large burden on teachers to manage classrooms full of alienated students, many of whom drop out. Teachers might wish instead to devote much classroom time to interpretive discussions and heuristic learning. They know that "I understand" and "I can do" are necessary elements that make "I know" educationally meaningful. They know that students greatly prefer teaching that blends discursive and heuristic learning with didactics. But these kinds of learning are difficult to assess objectively, so they are not measured on standardized tests. Studies have consistently demonstrated that the introduction of high-stakes tests is quickly followed by increased time devoted to didactic instruction. As a result, discursive and heuristic teaching is reduced or abandoned, and students' depth of understanding and capabilities for knowledge use (e.g., in projects and problem-solving activities) are consequently weakened.

The "efficient" teaching of bits and pieces of knowledge and standard routines requires keeping distinct subjects isolated. Math facts and routines are taught in math, science facts and procedures in science, history facts in history. Teachers in different disciplines don't have to know the topics outside their fields or cooperate to forge a multidisciplinary curriculum synergy. But the world is not divided into neat categories. Arranging subject matters under grand hierarchical organizing concepts like math, science, and history deprive them of context. Make a Google search of any science topic, for example, and you will find many links to related historical and mathematical topics. Real-world problem solving depends upon contextual thinking: drawing relevant facts and concepts together from across the map of knowledge and applying them in creative ways to the messy problems of practical life.

Few would deny that deep understanding, capability building, contextual thinking, and creative problem solving are as important as rote memorizations. As Sir Ken Robinson notes, however, we squander the opportunity to develop these by a steady diet of didactic teaching and a bloated mandatory curriculum. Creative problem solving requires conjectures, trying out different approaches, getting things wrong, "creative fast failure": try many things—learn quickly from your mistakes, adapt, and adjust. Students unwilling to get things wrong will never come up with anything original. Didactic teaching and standardized testing teaches the exact opposite: there is only one right answer—never make mistakes.

It is time to recognize that our hierarchical response in educational reform efforts to the worrisome academic problems of our schools is itself a catastrophic failure.

Failure Two: Educational Inefficiency

The hierarchical organization of education has from its inception been touted as increasing efficiency. Citizens are presented by media accounts of waste in school budgets: unions are said to protect grossly incompetent teachers; school buildings that open late and close early are decried for inefficient use of space; teachers abuse their collective bargaining and strike privileges to force districts to pay high salaries; teachers get tenure and eight-week summer vacations while "working Americans" struggle.

The complaints are endless. And proposed solutions impose stronger industrial discipline, by compelling longer school days and school years and evaluating—and paying—teachers for their students' test performances.

The touted efficiency of factory production of learning objectives, however, is an illusion. Industrial discipline of teachers is in fact a monumental waste of human resources. The most important educational inputs are not dollars, but the time, energies, motivations, and capabilities of teachers and students. The most important educational outcomes are not measurable fragments of rote knowledge and standard routines, but authentic capabilities useful in the worthwhile activities of adult life. The fixed nature of the factory school curriculum and its test regime builds inefficiency in—it mandates that only a tiny proportion of teacher or learner motivations or capabilities can be put to use. Remember the norms of universalism and specificity identified by Robert Dreeben as necessary for industrial society—reduce people to categories and then attend only to characteristics relevant to these categories in their institutional roles and interactions. These bureaucratic organizational norms are toxic in settings requiring rapid and flexible response to changing circumstances—those typical of the information age.

Let's start with the learners. Fifteen-year-old men and women are more than high school students. They may be film buffs, bloggers, computer technicians, Irish dancers, or aspiring videographers. They may be fashionistas like Tavi or seers like Jayralin. They may be aspiring scholars of Asian culture or jazz innovators, as we will discover later in Chapter Twelve. They may be environmentalists, marine biologists, or inventors. Two recent examples will illustrate the point: (1) Aiden Dwyer, a thirteen-year-old New York inventor created a tree-like design for solar panels after observing tree leaves catch sun light in the forest at age eleven. (2) The research on "The Effects of Physical Environment and Predators on Phenotypic Plasticity in Geukensia demissa" conducted by Samantha Garvey, a homeless seventeen-year-old student from Long Island, New York, under the care of her science research teacher Rebecca Grella, qualified her as a semi-finalist in the prestigious Intel science talent search after she spent two and a half years immersed in New York's Long Island salt marshes. "I have a lot of plans for the future," Garvey said. "I'd like to continue what I'm doing now—continue with science research and just get a doctorate and keep on trucking."[19]

In school the energies of these amazing young people are frequently wasted; they are bored and frustrated because their capabilities and youthful energies have to be suppressed.

The schools block their opportunities for mastery of skills that would make them distinctly valuable in subsequent years. Today schools forbid smartphones and block websites. Young netcasters like Tavi Gevinson and Julia Frakes have to work around school rules and expectations to follow their passions, to learn and to grow. Jayralin keeps her passions hidden from her teachers. Remember Malcolm Gladwell's estimate that it takes 10,000 hours of practice to attain mastery in a musical instrument, photography, computer programming, or a sport. It takes that many hours—or more—simply to master spelling, as is demonstrated by the stories of finalists at the national spelling bee. It is natural for young people to seek mastery, to distinguish themselves in valued activities. Most students, however, are compelled to spend most of that hypothetical 10,000 hours sitting in classrooms, undergoing a bloated curriculum while doing nothing to build mastery in anything. It is no accident that many in the national spelling bee and other national competitions are homeschooled.

Teachers' energies and capabilities are also wasted; their endless repetition of didactic lessons to disengaged students leads to boredom and burnout. People who teach in high schools are also more than school teachers, and many of them are amazing: they coach sports teams, write books, run small businesses, participate as activist citizens.[20] They cannot be reduced to institutional categories or restricted to behaviors defined by institutional roles. History and French teachers may know how to read and write Mandarin, and art teachers may know calligraphy, as we will also see later in Chapter Twelve. As they grow in their adult knowledge and intellectual powers, in curiosity and awareness, teachers have more to offer than can be channeled into narrow institutional roles and the delivery of standard lessons. They feel this constraint acutely. They know that leading discussions and coaching learner-directed projects can make more significant educational impact than didactic teaching.[21] But they don't have the time for discussions or coaching; they have to teach for the tests. So as they are confined to didactic teaching their work becomes alienated labor—they are working against themselves as educators. As a result they burn out, leave the profession, or go through the motions while devoting their energies and capabilities to outside-of-school activities. A recent survey demonstrated that teacher satisfaction is now, after thirty years of high-stakes testing, at an all-time low.[22] The most experienced teachers are leaving the profession in droves. This is not efficient use of human resources; it is gross waste.

Introducing more and better industrial-era processes into the factory school will not remove their academic failures. These stem in large measure from overreliance on these very processes. In the next chapter we turn to the social failures of today's education.

Chapter Five
School Failure II
Social Irrelevance and the Loss of Political Legitimacy

In the last chapter we considered the schools' internal failures—failing to generate learning and to use their resources efficiently. The upshot was that these worries are overstated and misleading. The real problems lie elsewhere. In this chapter I turn to the external problems with public education. The first is that graduates of high school and even college are finding it increasingly difficult to adjust to the social and economic demands of adult life. The second is that the political support for, and even the very legitimacy of, public education as an institution is in question. These problems, we will see, are more pressing and cannot be resolved by increased production of learning objectives or scores on standardized tests. The solutions require a fundamental rethinking of our educational arrangements.

Failure Three: Broken Connections between Youth and Adult Worlds

The next failure to consider is the broken link between schooling and adult opportunities. Schools and colleges are failing at the central educational task—initiating young people into adult life. Schools, and increasingly colleges and professional schools, are "roads to nowhere." The system of allocating job slots and as a result, positions in the social structure, on the basis of diplomas—what I will call the academic allocation of socioeconomic positions—has expanded beyond its limits.

Limits to Growth

The economic and social benefits of formal education suffer from a limits-to-growth paradox. When only a small percentage of any age cohort earns a diploma, the diploma naturally distinguishes its holders from a large proportion of the cohort. If only 20 percent of an age cohort graduate from high school, for example, diplomas differentiate their holders from 80 percent of their peers. But as more and more young people earn high school and college diplomas, these diplomas differentiate them less and less from their nongraduate peers. Today a high school, and even a college or professional school, diploma does not sufficiently distinguish its holder from peers to assure access to a decent job. There are simply too many graduates—and too few jobs—to create a meaningful advantage for diploma holders.

Students and parents seek diplomas as necessary credentials for decent jobs. As more learners have gone to high school and on to college, the educational institution has acquired the power to determine their life chances by assigning them to their future roles in the economy and thus in society—where and how they live and with whom they interact. But as the percentage of high school and college graduates in the cohort has grown, this system of social allocation has broken down.

In the industrial period, schools and colleges grabbed hold of job training roles that previously had been assigned to apprenticeships and on-the-job training. Until after the Civil War there simply weren't enough graduates to make it worthwhile for employers to use diplomas as a filter for any employment decisions. After around 1880, however, the diploma became a useful signal of standard levels of knowledge, capability, and diligence. After the Smith Hughes Act of 1917 established vocational tracks in high schools, more employers demanded diplomas for decent jobs. The diploma thus became a highly valued job qualification by differentiating its relatively few holders from the many less schooled.

But as a simple matter of logic, as the percentage of young people receiving diplomas increases, the differentiating value of the high school diploma decreases; and as that diploma becomes more nearly universal, its differentiating value approaches zero. This result is Thomas F. Green's law of last entry: those groups entering any level of the educational system later get less value than those entering earlier, and those entering last get the least. Green's data suggested that once the percentage of high school graduates exceeds 60 percent, the differentiating value drops precipitously. The diploma at that point becomes expected but no longer rewarded. We have been well past that percentage for fifty years. In the three decades ending in 2008, the average salary of male college graduates rose slowly, but the average salary of high school grads without college sharply declined in real terms. Students stayed in high school—or college—not to earn a reward but only to avoid the catastrophic punishment of a dropout status.

Now, as even students least prepared and most resistant to formal education remain in school through graduation, and tales of illiterate graduates spread, the diploma has also lost all credibility as a proxy for academic effort or achievement. Those with a high school diploma but no further education are sliding further down the occupational ladder while the wage gap between high school graduates and dropouts actually declines.

Everyone Will Be Above Average

The simple fact is that the goals of high achievement and high graduation contradict each other. In 1961 John Gardner, in his book *Excellence*, asked, "Can we be equal and excellent too?"[1] If the question means "can we all get equal test scores and yet all score as 'excellent'?" the obvious answer is "no." "To excel" quite simply means to perform *better*—better than average, better than others. Only in Lake Wobegon are all children above average.

Fortunately, Gardner didn't intend this silly question. Instead he pointed out the many different ways in which people can excel, and he proposed multiple pathways from school to careers to accommodate all learners. Our society has failed to heed this wise counsel. Recently, however, *New York Times* columnist Thomas Friedman has propounded a new solution: in a world where our young people face relentless competition from educated third-world counterparts, they all now need to be "above average."[2] This kind of punditry gets us nowhere; the only way in which all young people can be above average is by being themselves. Even the ones who are not yet very good at that are better than anyone else in the world. Helping all of them realize their unique potentials makes a lot more sense than pushing them all into a competitive race and expecting them all to perform better than the average.

The only way we can retain 90 percent of high school students through graduation is to have very low graduation standards. Conversely, we can maintain a standard of excellence as a condition for graduation only by failing or otherwise pushing many students out. It should come as no surprise that districts claiming very high achievement and graduation rates have covertly pushed students out prior to the state tests. Rod Paige, the Texas chief state school officer who served as George W. Bush's secretary of education, was famous for his "Texas miracle"—raising test scores for all groups. It would indeed have been a miracle, had it not been a fraud: the gains resulted from pushing low scorers out of school. A bit of honesty compels us to recognize that there will be inevitable trade-offs between the graduation rate and the required standard of achievement for high school graduation.

How Many Graduates?

Green argued that the only way of restoring any significant meaning to the high school diploma would be to move back below a 60 percent graduation level for seventeen- to eighteen-year-olds. If this proposal sounds morally odious, perhaps that is because we have no pathways to dignified adult life that don't move through the high school. We will always need home-care workers, hospital orderlies, security guards, and product assemblers; these are socially *valuable* jobs that don't require much formal education. We can, moreover, make them more socially *valued* than they are, following the examples of such nations as Germany. Only neoliberal capitalism requires that we push the wage level of these jobs below the subsistence level and rob these workers of their dignity.

There is nothing inevitable about the lack of alternative paths to careers; Germany has an apprenticeship program, linking directly to dignified professions whose value is recognized by society, for those leaving school at age sixteen. Perhaps a corporatist German-type program would not work in the liberal United States,[3] but we should be able to find some variant that can motivate many high school students to study hard and graduate, while providing attractive links to the adult world even for the minority that don't. I'll have more to say about this later.

High School to College: Diploma Inflation

The same process that has destroyed the signaling value of the high school diploma in the job market is now being repeated at the college level.[4] The percentage of twenty-five-year-old Americans with a bachelor's degree has been steadily rising for many decades. In 1950, it was barely above 5 percent. It crossed 10 percent in 1970. By 1990 it reached 20 percent, and today is pushing 25 percent.

The meaning of these numbers is clear; college degrees are exactly one-fifth as differentiating for their holders as they were in the middle of the twentieth century. As more young people graduate from college, the meaning of the college diploma erodes: graduates become an increasingly less elite group, and as more young people from less educated families enroll they need more remedial work and thus graduate with fewer academic accomplishments, so their diplomas no longer signal high-level capabilities. As Louis Menand recently put this, "if you are a theory-person, you worry that with so many people going to college the bachelor's degree is losing its meaning and soon it will no longer operate as a reliable marker of productive potential."[5]

Many of the new and untraditional students have been convinced they need a diploma to get a decent middle-class job. They are not motivated by the adventure of learning—a somewhat elevated goal for anxious kids from postindustrial working class or disadvantaged families. A recent study casts some light on these students. Richard Arum and Joseph Roksa, in *Academically Adrift*, asked whether today's young people were learning what their teachers claimed to be teaching: critical thinking, analytical reasoning, creative problem solving. Using the Collegiate Learning Association measure of these skills (CLA), the researchers found that the scores of a large percentage of today's college students did not improve after two and in many cases even four years. It should hardly surprise us, given the skills tested by the CLA, that liberal arts majors improved most while those in business and occupational majors, where the nontraditional college students are concentrated, improved least.

One "Professor X" commented in *Atlantic* that many of these students are "unteachable." They are caught in the system—they go to college because they're told a degree is a job requirement and because they see no alternatives. Professor X thinks that today's race for diplomas is like the recent real estate bubble and will soon burst, leaving these vulnerable students holding the bag.[6] While Menand does not accept the Arum-Roksa findings uncritically, he says that *if* there is a decline in the motivation of today's students, it may mark the end of "an exceptional phase" in the history of American higher education. For the students entering college in the expanding period after 1950, he notes, college was "central to the experience of making it" and was "supposed to be hard." But many students no longer expect, and will not even tolerate, tough intellectual challenges. For more and more of them, college is now just an empty ritual. It has become what high school became when its diploma no longer differentiated its graduates from their peers, no longer stood for (or was taken for) an extra level of competence and stick-to-itiveness, and no longer assured access to advantageous jobs.

In an op-ed in the *New York Times,* Arum and Roksa say that today's students tend to think of themselves as consumers or customers and seek to attain their credentials effortlessly and comfortably; their attitude is that "the customer is always right."[7] Maybe a more generous assessment would be "they don't put a lot of themselves into something from which they don't expect to get a lot." This is just good sense.

And it would be folly to expect very much. A 2012 study by economists at Northeastern, Drexel, and the Economic Policy Institute, based on US government data, demonstrates that at least half of recent college graduates are either jobless or underemployed in jobs requiring no more than a high school education—waiters and waitresses, bartenders, retail clerks, or receptionists. As the report notes, median wages for college grads have dropped since 2000 because of technological changes eliminating mid-level jobs. Meanwhile, future job projections show growth in lower-skilled positions such as home health-care aides; only three of the thirty occupations with the largest projected number of job openings by 2020 will require a bachelor's degree or higher. "Most job openings are in professions such as retail sales, fast food and truck driving, jobs which aren't easily replaced by computers."

An Associated Press story on the report worries that longer-term government projections are not factoring in degree inflation. The growing ubiquity of bachelor's degrees will make them commonplace in lower-wage jobs but inadequate for higher-wage jobs. Employers will be able to demand applicants hold graduate degrees for desirable jobs, regardless of the actual knowledge and skill demands of these jobs. Kelman Edwards Jr., who recently graduated with a bachelor's degree in biology, for example, has found no work opportunities six months after earning his diploma. "Everyone is always telling you, 'Go to college,'" Edwards said. "But when you graduate, it's kind of an empty cliff." And what advice do job counselors give Mr. Edwards and his peers? "Pursue further education."[8] That is a very poor, ill-informed suggestion.

From College to Grad School: Law School Replaces Baseball as the National Pastime

The erosion in the college diploma pushes the problem of differentiation for advantageous jobs on to graduate and professional schools. These represent the top rung of our educational ladder. When diplomas from these top-level schools fail to differentiate adequately to assure graduates great jobs, the academic allocation of favorable social positions reaches its terminus, its limit to growth.

Law school provides an excellent example, because law school enrollments have been rising dramatically. Unlike graduate students in the humanities and social sciences, who have faced a grim job market for decades but love their studies and no longer expect immediate payoffs from their doctorates, law graduates still seek and expect high-paying, prestigious jobs.

In 2009, forty-three thousand students earned law degrees in the United States. That was up 11 percent in just a decade. But jobs for law grads are rapidly disappearing; since 2008 fifteen thousand attorney and legal staff positions evaporated. Legal work has been outsourced from employees to temporary contract workers, here and overseas. According to the National Association of Legal Career Professionals, fewer than 40 percent of those 2009 grads were employed as full-time attorneys nine months after graduation.[9] Many of the others, according to David Segal, were waiting tables or babysitting or were altogether unemployed; the Association put the total unemployment rate of the 2009 law school class nine months after graduation at over 20 percent. Segal reports cases of students wallowing in debts exceeding $200,000 with no job prospects in sight. Meanwhile the law schools fudge or lie outright about the prospects for their graduates, claiming that the average entry level pay for attorneys is upwards of $160,000 a year. Professor William Henderson of Indiana University calls these "Enron-type numbers" and says, "Every time I look at them I feel dirty."

Law schools continue to be big cash cows for universities, with tuitions over $43,000 per year and rising even in the mediocre schools. Despite the desperate situation of law graduates, nine new law schools have opened in the last decade and five more are waiting for approval. Segal concludes, "Today American law schools are like factories that no force has the power to slow down."[10]

Alternative Methods for Allocating Social Positions

The allocation of economic and social positions by school and university diplomas is a fairly recent human invention, and it is already becoming obsolete.

Before the spread of the industrial mode of production, social and economic positions were rarely allocated through diplomas. Small farmers and merchants handed over their farms and skills to their sons; craftsmen taught their sons their trades. Families possessed the land, skills, and tools to reproduce themselves—we can call this the method of social allocation through physical and human capital, or simply allocation through capital.

As all fertile land in the eastern United States became distributed in the eighteenth century, many farm families went west and continued to live off their land and wits. In the nineteenth century they were joined by waves of immigrants. In the east, the factory system, and especially the regime of scientific management, drastically reduced the skill requirements of most productive jobs. While industry expanded, potential workers could show up with little beyond their labor power as capital—as a source of a stream of income. Children of farm families pushed off the land by the industrialization of agriculture migrated to industrial cities and took up work in factories.

But starting in the 1870s, and continuing to this day, the academic system of allocation—the culture of professionalism—began to spread until it eventually became the backbone of modern society.[11] This culture defined job credentials and positions of almost all citizens—for school and college grads seeking advantageous jobs and even dropouts, who didn't bother to seek them because they knew they were excluded. With vast reserves of workers, employers were able to use diplomas as filters to eliminate dropouts even from jobs requiring little formal learning. Diplomas—or their lack—determined where and how one worked, where one lived, and with whom one associated.

Today industrial jobs have shifted to low-wage nations and industrial robots. Professional tasks are also being outsourced or assigned to network-savvy workers who can make themselves known and can demonstrate their capabilities online. Decent jobs simply no longer exist for all the high school grads—or even many college and professional school grads—who seek them. The academic allocation of social positions is breaking down.

The Internet and Network Allocation:
The Decline of the Professional Worker

The Internet in particular is undercutting the culture of professionalism and its mystique. Those with professional credentials are increasingly competing with those who lack them—mere "amateurs"—for work opportunities in a new "network allocation" system.

The academic allocation system of the industrial period responded to a particular historical situation; "professional" and "amateur" are historically specific notions, acquiring their current sense in the late nineteenth century, when the

American universities and national corporations came of age. As the scale of industrial organizations expanded, firms needed to locate and assess managers and engineers and other knowledge workers for their increasingly standardized tasks. The lack of any corresponding systems of training and certification made this task time consuming, costly, and inefficient—in economic lingo it had high "transaction costs."

The framework of professionalism emerged to address the need to lower transaction costs. Before the late nineteenth century standardized university-based professional education hardly existed. But by the twentieth century being a professional came to mean having a university-based credential signaling a standard level of competence for increasingly standardized job descriptions. Employers could for the first time cut transaction costs by using a diploma from a professional school as an effective filter in assessing job applicants.

The Internet is now weakening that link, undercutting professional status and the professional mystique. Employees with professional credentials are increasingly competing with contract workers—with and without diplomas—for work opportunities. In *Here Comes Everyone*, Clay Shirky notes that people online have *dual visibility*: they can rapidly be *found* and *assessed*. Like Tavi Gevinson, all can use new web services—blogs, LinkedIn, Facebook, and YouTube—to make themselves known. Others can then inexpensively find and assess them using tools like Google search and LinkedIn. In addition, the Internet and inexpensive digital tools place many professional-level capabilities into the hands of nondegreed amateurs, challenging the elite status of professionals.[12]

The Internet, in short, has drastically reduced transaction costs for bringing even those without diplomas onto work teams. It has also sharply reduced management costs, as workers use it to self-organize for collaboration. Workers no longer need management and expensive infrastructure to do significant things. They can gain high-level skills, connect up to others for work experience, and leverage the web to collaborate and publicize themselves and their capabilities, without having "professional" status.

This drop in transaction costs is a boon to firms, which can now cheaply find, assess, and hire lower-cost temporary contract workers anywhere in the world. Firms no longer have to bear additional costs and long-term obligations associated with full-time workers, even professional "knowledge" workers. Many of the fifteen thousand legal jobs that vanished since 2008 are not coming back; as the work ramps up, much of it is going to temporary contract workers.

The rapid evolution of technologies also speeds up the obsolescence of knowledge and skill. As a result, firms do not wish to be encumbered by long-term contractual obligations, and workers don't want to get stuck in dead-end jobs that don't push them to keep their knowledge and skill at the cutting edge. The market system of allocation favors highly specific cutting-edge knowledge and skill over standard professional categories.

Lou Gellos of Microsoft explains why his firm makes such extensive use of contract workers: they do only the part of the project where their capabilities are needed. "They're experts at it. Boom boom, they're finished." Jeff Barrett of Eggrock, a manufacturer of prebuilt bathrooms, adds that contract workers are especially appealing in cyclical industries: "We have been able to get really good talent. Off the charts." Maynard Wells, a former COO at eBay who now runs the labor services firm Live Ops, stated the primary advantage of contract workers to firms: "You have access to the talent you need. And when the need is gone, the talent disappears."[13]

Further, titles associated with diplomas, like "engineer" and "manager," simply say too little about whether those bearing them have the right capabilities for specific tasks. Firms need and are looking to buy capabilities, not diplomas. This is a big challenge both to professionals clinging to elite status and to the top-heavy, expensive schools and colleges that credential them. Those lies about the $160,000 jobs waiting for law school graduates are wearing thin. As Professor X says, the academic bubble, like the real estate bubble of 2008, is about to burst.

The Return of the Entrepreneur

Those with the energy, ideas, and risk tolerance to start a business never needed diplomas. In the era of industrial expansion large corporate firms absorbed their smaller competitors and their markets, and hired professionals—workers with standard levels of knowledge and skill. Today, as large firms hollow out and outsource many tasks to small partner firms, entrepreneurialism is again on the rise. In her article "No Jobs? Young Grads Make Their Own," Hannah Seligson reports on a group of young people in New York making individual entrepreneurship a viable career pathway and "not just a renegade choice." Their experience is important "especially since the promise of 'go to college, get good grades, and then get a job' is no longer working out the way it once did." The new occupational reality, Seligson says, has "forced a whole generation to redefine what a stable job is."[14]

Moroccan Aziz Senni, responding to the high unemployment among young North Africans from immigrant families in France, with and without diplomas, details how he and other young North Africans successfully overcame prejudice and economic exclusion by sidestepping the "broken" social escalator of higher education and "took the staircase" to their own small businesses. Senni, who received a bachelor's degree in economics in 1994 and a graduate degree in transport logistics in 1997, was unable to find a suitable job. Hustling up 60,000 Euros in public and private funding, he started a private taxi service in 2000. In 2002 he created what has become the National Association of Young Entrepreneurs, and in 2005 he authored an important book documenting the entrepreneurial successes of many young people. Since that time he has won numerous awards, including the prestigious Social Entrepreneur of the Year Award from INSEA. In 2007, he launched Business Angels des Cités, the first investment fund dedicated solely to economic development through entrepreneurship in the *banlieues* where Muslim youth are concentrated. His point: university reforms have done little to ease the job problems of young French Muslims and probably cannot; "the escalator is broken." But "taking the staircase" by building strong skill portfolios, connecting widely in the community, and creating businesses to meet commercial and community needs has provided a viable pathway to satisfying careers for many.[15]

School reform—"fixing the escalator"—has failed. The network paradigm presented in this book moves beyond that strategy, embracing the Internet to "broaden the staircase" and make it accessible for all. Only further experience will show what proportion of young people can create and sustain self-sufficient lives in the entrepreneurial and freelance economies.[16]

FAILURE FOUR: THE CRISIS OF LEGITIMACY

The final failure of the schools is the breakdown of perceived legitimacy and political support. "The schools are failing" is an old story, but the schools have been very resilient; for 150 years school leaders and politicians have been able to turn every complaint about schooling into a demand for more and better schooling. You say there are problems in the grade schools? Then reform them and open more access to high school. High school grads lack skills? Reform them by adding vocational programs, and send more grads to college. You say the teachers are no good? Well, require them to go to graduate school for master's degrees. Such has been the American faith in schooling that all failures of our schools have been taken as signs that more schooling is needed—and that leaders have been able to sell academic solutions to academic problems is a sign of the incredible *success* of the schooling institution, not a sign of failure.

Academic Allocation and Legitimacy

All of this is now changing. Previous failures never undermined the legitimacy of the system, so long as educational leaders adopted a posture of reform, acknowledging the problems and addressing them with additional programs and layers of schooling. Today this does not appear to be sufficient. Why is that so? A good place to look is the failure of diplomas to secure decent jobs for graduates.

Stanford sociologist John Meyer argued thirty-five years ago that we cannot understand the power of education by looking at its effects on individual learners. The direct knowledge and skill effects of schooling are quite weak; when the effects of diplomas are corrected for, Meyer found, different levels of knowledge or ability explain almost nothing about occupational success. Education's authority is based almost entirely on the academic system of allocation, its power to define individuals on the basis of the duration and type of education they receive.

Schools and colleges have retained legitimacy because, as Meyer put it, students and parents know that if you want to get ahead you need a diploma. Graduates know it even better, through their direct experiences in society; they are accepted or rejected for positions based on their diplomas. Dropouts know this power best—they are allocated to failure, anticipate it, and adapt to it. Education has thus come to define individuals for life: "its levels and content categories have the power to redefine [them] legitimately in the eyes of everyone around [them]." Though people may gripe about the failures of education, they must shape their lives around it if they hope to fare well, and therein lies its legitimacy.[17]

The power of schools and colleges to define individuals and determine their life chances, however, is not a given; its continuing power depends on the day-to-day successes and failures that diploma holders experience. How legitimate can the system remain when, as Mr. Kelman Edwards says, "Everyone is always telling you, 'go to college,' but when you graduate, it's kind of an empty cliff"? Or when Professor William Henderson of Indiana University can look at the promises law schools make to students and say, "Every time I look at them I feel dirty"?

The crisis in legitimacy, then, has less to do with low test scores or operational inefficiencies than with broken links to adult life. The crisis is fundamental; the breakdown in allocation of advantageous jobs to diploma holders threatens not only the educational system but the structure of the entire modern social system. Today we are reluctantly coming to grips with this breakdown and working our way toward new paradigms of living, working, and learning suitable for global network society. That explains a lot about new concerns about austerity, frugality, and minimalist styles of living advanced by bloggers like Miss Minimalist and Jayralin Herrera and many others. As the academic system of allocation breaks down, the legitimacy crisis will deepen and entrenched educational arrangements will lose their legitimacy.

Conclusion

Current educational arrangements sap students of natural motivations for learning, while offering them little in return that can be converted into economic opportunity. A new education must release the passions and aspirations of learners while linking their studies in direct and transparent ways to adult opportunities. The open networked learning paradigm to be presented in Part Three does just that. But first, we must learn more about the Internet and the learningweb themselves in Part Two.

Part Two
Learning Networks

Chapter Six
The Internet and the World Wide Web

Individuals like Tavi Gevinson are finding their ways into society by casting their nets: developing their unique capabilities through online learning, making themselves visible and assessable through blogs and social networks, and connecting up with resources and individuals who want to associate with and support their projects. The Internet underlies a new network system of economic and social allocation competing with and, in some cases, triumphing over the system of allocation through school and college diplomas.

If we are going to rest our hopes for educational transformation on the Internet, we need to understand what it is and how it stimulates and supports the kinds of learning and social behavior suitable for today's world. In this chapter we'll examine the origins of the Internet and the World Wide Web. The story itself is fascinating, but there is an essential lesson we must take to heart if we are to construct a new informational paradigm for education—that Internet architecture *by design* undermines hierarchy and liberates the end users at their powerful personal computers and mobile Internet devices.

The Internet and workstation computers were designed from the beginning to free end users from central control. New Web 2.0 technologies and the emerging Web 2.0 culture accelerate this shift of power to end users. Today all areas of adult life are being transformed by the Internet. It is not merely a new technology but the grid of a new, global network form of social life. For education to embrace the Internet and take advantage of its incredible power to foster learning, advance knowledge development and use, and link young learners to adult opportunities, it too will have to break free from top-down hierarchical control. It will have to be transformed into Education 2.0.

What Is the Internet?

The Internet is the global network of interconnected computer networks accessible to the general public, transmitting multimedia digital data by packet switching using standard Internet protocol (IP). It is a super-network of millions of interconnected smaller networks, including personal, academic, commercial, and governmental networks, support structures for email, and the linked hypertext documents of the World Wide Web (WWW). The Internet with its billions of end-point networked computers is the largest and most powerful machine the world has ever known.

The real power, however, lies not in the machinery and wires but in the end users who create, share, collaborate, and act collectively. The machine is really a giant centrifuge, forcing power outward from hierarchical systems to computer end users, individually and collectively forming a networked global society. Many "netizens" came of age in the Internet era. Tavi Gevinson and her fellow netizens engage almost instinctively in networked action or "netcasting"; they make their intentions and projects known online and solicit support people and collaborators. Through their actions they are building a distinct network culture with specific norms and values that is spreading outward throughout the world. The web culture is the antithesis of the industrial age hierarchical culture that still dominates our schools. It is crucial to grasp the extent to which the shift from hierarchical control to autonomous computer users has guided Internet architecture right from the start.

The Origins of the Internet

The Internet and the World Wide Web are children of two strange bedfellows: the Cold War and an antihierarchical philosophy—Dr. Strangelove meets the hacker ethic.

The Cold War began shortly after World War II, and intensified after Russia developed and tested its first nuclear weapon in 1949. The United States' response spawned key ideas regarding computer hardware and software that eventually became the Internet. A "person-centered" democratic ethic featuring the unique creative capabilities of individual people, acting alone or in collaboration, also played a starring role; in its manifestation as the "hacker ethic" it prescribes that powerful technologies should be distributed from central system administrators to individual users.

The Nuclear Threat and Packet Switching Networks

The first chapter of the Internet story begins with packet switching, a brain child of Paul Baran of the RAND Corporation, created by the US Air Force in 1946. RAND operated as a network of interconnected individuals and groups—its studies drew from many disciplines and placed problems in multiple contexts, a style that came to be known as "systems analysis." In 1958 Burton H. Klein, a former RAND researcher, argued in *Fortune* that conventional military research suffered from "too much direction and control" and was crippled by "the delusion that we can advance rapidly and economically by planning the future in detail."[1] By loosening planning and control, RAND fostered creative thinking and a context for collaboration to optimize its power and relevance to emerging problems. Another former RAND researcher spoke of the "anarchy of both policy and administration" that gave each worker a unique degree of individual freedom.[2] RAND leaders gave up the illusion of control to stimulate and harness the complexity within the network.

Senior analyst Alfred Wohlstetter joined RAND in 1951. Skeptical about deterrence through mutually assured destruction, Wohlstetter, the model for the fictional Dr. Strangelove, focused on the survivability of US military assets, especially communications lines to coordinate military responses to a first nuclear attack. In 1959 Paul Baran, impressed by the freedom at RAND, joined Wohlstetter's group, studying the vulnerabilities of a telephone grid organized around central hubs: destroy the hubs and you destroy the whole system. Guided by an analogy with neural networks, Baran imagined a communication network system that was robust in the face of attack because it would be capable of continually rerouting messages from destroyed lines to those still active. Baran demonstrated that a network with nodes averaging three or more links could function reliably even if 50 percent of the nodes were eliminated.[3]

On Baran's model, a message with a given target doesn't go to a central hub. Instead it is broken into small bits (packets) in a numerical sequence. Each bit is sent to a linked node, and then on to another node until it reaches its intended destination. Eventually all packets reach their destination and the original messages are reassembled. The important point to remember is that Baran's network design was shaped to eliminate the need for central control. Significantly, Baran saw that a packet switching communications network would also make government censorship and repression difficult, as a network of interconnected points prevents a central point from being critical, so no central actor can control networked communication. As John Gilmore, another Internet pioneer, put it, "The Net interprets censorship as damage and routes around it."[4]

When the air force asked ATT to test Baran's model, ATT's top executives not only refused to cooperate but ridiculed Baran's ideas and humiliated Baran. As a result Baran's work on networks was shelved, not resurfacing until 1966.

Vannevar Bush's Memex and the Origin of the Workstation

The Internet story now shifts from network architecture to the powerful workstations as the end nodes of the networks. In 1945 Vannevar Bush, director of the US Office of Scientific Research and Development, argued, in an *Atlantic Monthly* article "As We May Think," that scientists needed to organize the store of knowledge generated during wartime and make it accessible to, and useful for, individual researchers. He envisioned a new kind of "Memex" machine, with search, scanning, and reproduction capabilities, using documents marked up with what are now called hypertext links capable of imitating the associative processes of human thought. Our present ineptitude in getting relevant documents from the record to stimulate and sustain new thought, Bush said,

> is largely caused by the artificiality of systems of indexing. When data of any sort are placed in storage, they are filed alphabetically or numerically, and information is found (when it is) by tracing it down from subclass to subclass. It can be in only one place, unless duplicates are used.

Searching through hierarchical categories made the search for relevant ideas cumbersome and ineffective. Bush added, "The human mind does not work that way. It operates by association. With one item in its grasp, it snaps instantly to the next that is suggested by the association of thoughts, in accordance with some intricate web of trails carried by the cells of the brain."

Bush's imagined Memex would allow researchers to select and review any item of the scientific record and to make connections with other ideas and mark them in the device, leaving a permanent trace of the associations, a "hyperlink." "Thereafter, at any time, when one of these items is in view, the other can be instantly recalled merely by tapping a button," (or as we now might say, clicking a mouse). These trails do not fade and can even be reproduced and exchanged so that others can draw on the links each worker has already built up. This process, moreover, is cumulative, ultimately resulting in a body of searchable and linked documents offering thinkers rich associative trails through the world of ideas, unhindered by the artificial barriers of hierarchical indexing systems.[5] The takeaway is that Bush's Memex was conceived to support the natural processes of thought and knowledge use and to create traces upon which later thinkers could rely and build.

From the Memex to the Workstation

In 1950 a US Air Force study revealed that in a first strike, US air defenses could stop no more than 10 percent of incoming Soviet strike forces. In response a study group proposed setting a ring of radars around our borders. Lincoln Lab at MIT was formed to develop this plan. Its Semi-Automatic Ground Environment (SAGE) project was tasked with gathering data from the radar ring, combining and analyzing them in real time, and displaying them in an easily readable form on a computer screen.

At that time the only computers were large mainframes controlled by central systems administrators. Operators waited hours, or even days, for their punch cards to print and then had to decipher the results. These time delays made centrally administered computers unsuitable for SAGE; the radar station operators needed *instantaneous* actionable information about enemy air positions: they needed personal interactive computers. SAGE set out to design the first of these, the "Whirlwind." Those working on the SAGE project at the time included Ken Olsen, Lawrence Roberts, Wesley Clark, and Robert Taylor, as well as J. C. R. Licklider, widely credited as the guiding visionary of networked computing and the Internet empowering end users to collaborate without constraints of central control.

Clark and Olsen created the first interactive computers for SAGE in 1956. In 1957 Olsen left Lincoln Lab to form the Digital Equipment Corporation (DEC). Basing his work on the Whirlwind, Olsen and DEC released the first commercial interactive computer, the PDP-1, in 1960. Licklider, who left MIT in 1957 to join Bolt, Beranek, and Newman (BBN), bought the first PDP-1 sold by DEC and continued to explore human-machine interaction in computer networks. In

1962 he released a BBN memo envisioning an "Intergalactic Computer Network," the first vision of an Internet—a network of computer networks connecting all computer users. Licklider imagined a future where researchers anywhere could access useful resources over the network from anywhere else and where all could collaborate.[6]

Networked Computer Workstations: Licklider and ARPA

This vision shaped subsequent computer network development when Licklider moved to ARPA, the US military's Advanced Research Agency, in 1963. ARPA was established in 1958 in the wake of the Soviets' surprise launch of Sputnik in 1957. The Soviets had won the space race, and commentators blamed the byzantine organization of military research where each service had its own research arm and fought tooth and nail for available funds. The new secretary of defense, Neil McElroy, called for a civilian agency combining the best minds from all services to avoid duplication and interservice rivalry. ARPA was created over the howls of the members of the Joint Chiefs.[7]

Like RAND, ARPA operated as a network organization. Its leaders conceived grand projects and handed them over to university laboratories; central control from ARPA was tightly limited: when ARPA began its networking project, its Information Processing Techniques Office (IPTO) had only two staff members, the director and his secretary. Focused solely on long-term research, ARPA became a magnet for "far out" proposals, and Licklider's intergalactic network was hardly the strangest; indeed, its grand vision influenced IPTO director Ivan Sutherland as well as Robert Taylor, the Lincoln Lab colleague who replaced Sutherland at IPTO in 1966.

By 1968 Licklider was back at MIT and ARPA faced a more immediate problem than intergalactic computing: the researchers at the far-flung labs were unable to gain access to each other's documents, curbing collaboration. IPTO director Robert Taylor saw that this was a microcosm of the problem Licklider had set out to solve with his intergalactic network; he proposed a network of ARPA project networks based on Baran's packet switching model, and he brought Lincoln Lab colleague Lawrence Roberts on board to implement it. While most computer science corporations regarded the idea as outlandish, Licklider's former employer BBN was geared up to build the network, gained the contract in 1969, and, following Taylor's plan, constructed ARPANET, the backbone of the future Internet, in just nine months.[8]

The original ARPANET linked ARPA-funded research projects at five universities, but in 1973 added its first international node, the NORSAR seismic detection agency in Norway. ARPA also began work on a satellite network, SATNET, to link US and European labs. All of these agencies had different computers running different software, so translation protocols were needed to enable these machines to talk with one another. Bob Kahn and Vint Cerf at ARPA jointly developed TCP/IP, the Internet protocol, enabling researchers at far-flung labs to exchange documents.

That same year, however, the US Senate, irritated by the "far out" projects of ARPA, passed the Mansfield Amendment limiting further ARPA projects to those narrowly focused on immediate defense needs and renaming the agency DARPA, putting the defense mission up front. The DARPA budget was slashed and its computer networking projects closed. Funding for university-based ARPA projects dried up, and many university computer scientists moved to corporate settings including Hewlett-Packard, Apple Computer, and Sun Microsystems. In effect, the Mansfield Amendment gave birth to the contemporary computer technology industry.

An important beneficiary of this migration was XEROX PARC (Palo Alto Research Corporation), a California subsidiary of the Xerox Corporation. The 3,000-mile distance from Xerox headquarters, and the relative indifference of the Xerox leadership, afforded individual workers at PARC intellectual freedom comparable to those at the original RAND and ARPA organizations, enabling PARC to bring together the brightest and most innovative researchers. PARC was able to hire leading researchers from the ARPA sites, including Doug Engelbart, a specialist on human-machine interactions.

Doug Engelbart, the Mouse, and the Graphical User Interface

Engelbart enters the Internet story as early as 1945, when, serving in the Navy as a radar technician and living in a tiny hut on a small Pacific island, he received the recent issue of the *Atlantic Monthly* with Vannevar Bush's "As We May Think" article. Bush's challenge to make the entire body of knowledge available to all researchers for peacetime collaboration, and his imaginary Memex computer, planted a seed in Engelbart's mind. In 1951 Engelbart wrote out his lifetime mission statement: to make the world a better place by developing computers capable of stimulating creativity, enabling collaboration, and harnessing collective intelligence.

After completing his PhD, Engelbart went to work at SRI. By 1962, the same year that Licklider announced his intergalactic network vision, Engelbart expanded his mission statement as *Augmenting Human Intellect: A Conceptual Framework*. ARPA gave him a grant to found a human augmentation research center at SRI. In December 1968, Engelbart displayed his center's results, including the mouse, video conferencing, teleconferencing, hypertext, word processing, hypermedia, dynamic file linking, and a collaborative real-time editor, in a legendary performance that has been called "the mother of all demos."

When Engelbart's ARPA funding dried up in 1973, he and his SRI colleagues joined PARC. In rapid order they produced the first interactive workstation computer, the Xerox Alto. Two thousand of these machines were eventually produced for workers at Xerox, but the Alto was never commercially released because the chief executives at Xerox couldn't see the potential of workstations.

By 1973 the major pieces of the Internet—packet switching networks and workstation computers—were ready to be connected and made available for public use. In 1975 the greatly expanded ARPANET was fully operational, and by the early 1980s computer networking was available to the public through commercial videotext services like CompuServe in the United States, Prestel in the UK, and Minitel in France. In 1982 the TCP/IP protocol became the worldwide standard and the Internet as we now know it was born. The US National Science Foundation initiated a network for computer sciences that evolved into NSFNET in 1987. Three years later, in 1990, NSFNET absorbed the ARPANET, while the first commercial Internet service provider (ISP), The World, opened for business and Prodigy launched the first Internet portal. Five years later the NSFNET itself was decommissioned, and the Internet, no longer owned or controlled by the US government, was ready for unfettered commercial and creative development.

The World Wide Web

This brings us to the next major Internet development, the World Wide Web—a system of interlinked hypertext documents accessible from the Internet. Armed with a web browser, a computer user can select, view, and in some cases modify multimedia web pages and navigate between them via hyperlinks. Inspired by Bush's vision of hyperlinks leaving a "permanent associative trail," Tim Berners-Lee at CERN created the web between 1989 and 1990.

CERN, an international center for particle physics, was "home to a dizzying array of incompatible computers."[9] In 1980 CERN hired Berners-Lee to map the relations among all of them. The resulting database allowed Berners-Lee to represent connections between all the data at CERN on his own computer screen. Enabling all CERN researchers to access the documents on all CERN computers would require a program that could work with data on *any* computer platform, regardless of how formatted. So he created HTML, the hypertext markup language, plus a browser and editor that allowed users to find and edit HTML files and a server to host HTML web pages. Berners-Lee went public with his results on the alt.hypertext newsgroup on August 6, 1991. As *Time Magazine* stated in declaring Berners-Lee one of the 100 People of the Century, "He wove the World Wide Web and created a mass medium for the 21st century. The World Wide Web is Berners-Lee's alone. He designed it. He loosed it on the world."

In what is by now a familiar pattern, CERN leaders showed no interest in Berners-Lee's breakthrough. He proposed to build a web system for CERN but was rejected twice. He worked on the project without formal approval, knowing that at any time it could be shut down.[10] Lacking support from CERN, Berners-Lee tried to give the World Wide Web away for free, but found no takers—no one could see any value in it![11]

Marc Andreessen, a student at the National Center for Supercomputer Applications at the University of Illinois, was the first computer engineer to grasp the web's full potential. He released the first version of his browser, Mosaic, in February 1993 and in April 1994 left NCSA to found Netscape with Jim Clark. Sixteen months later Netscape went public in an historic IPO, and the world finally awoke to the web.

The original web was adequate for the early users: scientists, computer professionals, university-based scholars. But the web couldn't realize its full potential until the web pages morphed from reasonably static text and graphic files to rich, interactive multimedia experiences, that is, until it morphed into Web 2.0.

LOOKING AHEAD: NETWORKS AND EDUCATION

Let's consider a shift from classrooms to networked learning settings like RAND and ARPA. School leaders would have to give up the delusion that they can control learning and make it advance rapidly and economically by planning its processes and objectives in detail. They would have to welcome a degree of anarchy, giving each learner a degree of individual freedom. They would have to eliminate classroom management by teachers who worked as system administrators of central hubs and instead allow network design to facilitate the natural thought processes of learners as regulated by their own interests and stimulated by instantaneous access to the world's knowledge and information. The learners would not only be free to talk to their neighbors but to exchange information and ideas with them—and everyone else in the world—for collaboration and collective action to make the world a better place. In short, education would have to embrace Priyasha's dream.

In the next chapter we turn to the recent developments in the World Wide Web that place the full power of networked computers in everyone's hands.

Chapter Seven
Web 2.0 and the Net Culture

Web 2.0 is the most dominant force of our time, affording ordinary computer users some remarkable creative and collaborative powers for learning and netcasting action. In detailing the birth of Web 2.0, the year 2003 is as good a starting point as any. That year broadband Internet grew in presence from 15 percent to 25 percent of American households, permitting fast uploading of web pages by a critical mass of users; Google purchased Blogger, an early blog-publishing service instrumental in starting the blog craze; and Friendster, the first web-based social network, came online. As digital photography had by then gone mainstream, social network users could post photos to their social network profiles. A 2mp photo that would have taken two minutes to upload on a dial-up connection could with broadband be loaded in about five seconds. 2003 marks the popularization of Broadband + Blogging + Social Networks.

ABC News listed "Bloggers" among its People of the Year in 2004. That year MySpace and Facebook came online. Unlike Friendster, MySpace appealed directly to teens and young adults by allowing members to use pseudonyms and thus experiment with online identities. In a stroke of luck, MySpace inadvertently failed to block HTML mark-up on profile pages, making it possible for users creatively to decorate their pages with all sorts of images, graffiti, and music (most of which taken without permission from other websites). The teen culture had already been downloading music and photos from the web through file-sharing sites like Napster and mixing them up on blogs and custom CDs for friends. According to the oft-quoted Pew Center study, by 2004 20 percent of American teens had downloaded content from the web and mixed and mashed it up. By appealing especially to teen girls seeking tools to express themselves to, show off to, and connect with their friends, MySpace soon replaced Friendster as the leading social network site.

After recovering from the dot-com fiasco, the American economy was booming in 2004. Media revenue from advertising, however, which was expected to grow 7 to 8 percent, was flat, while online ad revenue grew by 33 percent. The trend was noticed by Rupert Murdoch, who promptly formed an Internet division for NewsCorp. In 2005 he bought MySpace for $580 million, stating at the time that integrating digital media into the broader media industry presented "a monumental, once in a lifetime opportunity … if successful, our industry has the potential to reshape itself and to be healthier than ever before."[1]

After the MySpace acquisition, Murdoch said that NewsCorp was "at a turning point in its history." Comparing previous NewsCorp turning points—going international and becoming a full media company by adding 20th Century Fox Studios—Murdoch said,

> This turning point will be the most fundamental … we must transform ourselves into a powerhouse of the digital age … the Internet is central to the revolution, it is a transforming technology that will have as great an impact on our civilization as the invention of the wheel, the printing press, steam power and the combustion engine.[2]

In 2006, *Time Magazine* named "You" as the Person of the Year. By "You," *Time*'s editors meant the masses of people, especially teens and young adults, participating in user-generated content on social networks, blogs, wikis, and media sharing sites. As *Time* editors put it, the new web was a

> story about community and collaboration on a scale never seen before … about the many wresting power from the few and helping one another for nothing and how that will not only change the world but also change the way the world changes.

Facebook explicitly eschewed the "wild west" climate of MySpace. Launched first as a service for Ivy League college students, it slowly expanded to high schools and then to the general public. Founder Mark Zuckerberg saw social networks not so much as platforms for self-expression as tools enabling the free and open flow of information and as representations of what he called "the social graph": the map of relationships among people.[3] Web users who would have felt out of place on MySpace—professionals, business executives, and corporations—soon found a social network home in Facebook. By July 2010 Facebook had recorded 500 million users, by February 2011 it had added another 100 million, and as I am writing this in May 2012 now has more than 800 million and is expected to reach 900 million to a billion by the end of the year. An astounding 41 percent of US residents had Facebook pages by the end of 2011. *Time Magazine* named Zuckerberg its Person of the Year in 2010, while *Vanity Fair* ranked him first among the "top 100 most influential people of the information age." In the White House photo of President Barack Obama's heralded meeting with high-tech leaders in February 2011, the president is sitting with Apple CEO Steve Jobs on his left and Zuckerberg on his right.

Let's pause a moment to contemplate this Web 2.0 phenomenon.

- "It is a monumental once in a lifetime opportunity."
- "It will change the world and change the way the world changes."
- It enables "community and collaboration on a scale never before seen."
- It enables "people to help one another for free."
- It is "central to the revolution."
- It is "a transforming technology that will have as great an impact on our civilization as the invention of the wheel and the printing press."

Understanding Web 2.0

Web 2.0 spreads the full power of the Internet and workstation to ordinary people armed with inexpensive networked devices. The first recorded use of the term "Web 2.0" was by Darcy DiNucci in her 1999 article "Fragmented Future." She there described the web as "the ether through which interactivity happens." Web 2.0 technologies, she said, made it possible creatively to break up web pages into their parts, to recombine and exchange their contents, and to distribute them as something new, hence her phrase "fragmented future."

The term "Web 2.0" didn't catch on, however, until reintroduced by John Battelle and Tim O'Reilly at the first Web 2.0 conference in 2005. O'Reilly's speech compared Netscape with Google: Netscape (Web 1.0) was a desktop application—users had to download it to their computers; Google search (Web 2.0) provided software power without a program download; the operating power was in the web browser. The web became a "platform," or as O'Reilly later put it, the computer's operating system. With software in "the cloud" and networks linking billions of people all over the planet, the personal computer became merely a terminal of the biggest machine in history.

O'Reilly's timing was perfect. The term "Web 2.0" perfectly captured breaking developments, and within months pundits were calling anything new "Web 2.0." Its applications in turn were soon labeled as so many more "2.0s": "library 2.0," "museum 2.0," "classroom 2.0," and many others.

Some voices were skeptical. Raju Vegesna of Zoho said, "Web 2.0 is just a buzzword."[4] Richard McManus of the *Read/WriteWeb* blog dismissed it as merely a "marketing term" that "means a lot of things" and is "very hard to technically define."[5] Gina Bianchini, cofounder (with Marc Andreessen) of Ning, said the term simply "doesn't matter.... The whole point of having a definition of something is to have something that people agree on, and people don't agree on what 'Web 2.0' means."[6] Web founder Tim Berners-Lee offered a more fundamental challenge, doubting that Web 2.0 was at all different from his original web. Asked whether the difference might be that Web 1.0 is about connecting computers, while Web 2.0 is about connecting people, he stated, "Totally not. Web 1.0 was all about connecting people. If Web 2.0 for you is blogs and wikis, then that is people to people. But that was what the Web was supposed to be all along. It was an interactive space, and I think Web 2.0 is of course a piece of jargon, nobody even knows what it means."[7]

Web 2.0 as a Developmental Phase

Despite these charges there is actually a surprising degree of underlying agreement about Web 2.0. Bradley Jones interviewed twenty leading technology and operations leaders from major web companies, and underneath their many differences a few central patterns emerged:

First, the term "Web 2.0" names a second period in web development, and it has generated a host of other "2.0" terms standing for changes in libraries, museums, and other institutions following adoption of Web 2.0 technologies and social practices. Developmental periods—the classical age, the renaissance, the enlightenment—are used to divide historical time; it's hard to get our arms around complex historical processes without them. The same is true about Web

2.0; it is a useful marker of an important period of change within the Internet era. Even when the technical community moves on to further stages, the Web 2.0 stage will leave a permanent and fundamental sediment.

Web 2.0 Is Not a Technological Development

The leaders agreed that social and commercial rather than technological factors marked the Web 2.0 divide. Technologies such as AJAX, Flash, Google Gears and Adobe AIR, and LAMP make Web 2.0 possible but don't define it.[8] They make the web experience more interactive and engaging, and they enable lots of smart people with creative ideas who are not computer engineers to do quick, inexpensive start-ups without multimillion dollar funding from venture capitalists.[9] It is this social and commercial milieu, not the underlying technologies, that is the essential mark of Web 2.0.

The new social and commercial climate is well captured in Mark Zuckerberg's infamous evening "hackathons" where developers get together over pizza and soft drinks and churn out web applications. "The idea is you can build something really good in a night," Zuckerberg explained to author Steven Levy.[10]

Consider the experience of eighteen-year-old Israeli Daniel Gross at Y Combinator, a three-month boot camp and business incubator for young entrepreneurs in Palo Alto, California. Daniel spent his days working on an Amazon application, but a few days before final presentations to the venture capitalists Amazon tweaked its terms of service and wiped out Daniel's project. In a nonstop forty-eight-hour session he hacked the first version of social networking search engine Greplin and was rewarded with $4 million in start-up funding from leading VC firm Sequoia Capital.[11]

Tutorials permitting ordinary users to create sophisticated websites with just a few keystrokes are now proliferating. If you like social bookmarking sites like Digg or Reddit, for example, and want to create a clone application, one tutorial claims, "Look no further. With PHP and MySQL, you can create your own Digg site in just five minutes."[12]

Web 2.0 Enables Networked Action or Netcasting

Web 2.0 is a platform for individual self-expression and social participation. It enables those without even a modicum of technical know-how to express themselves, share with others, create neat things individually using digital tools, collaborate, and act collectively. Anyone with web access can now almost effortlessly "cast a net." They can start a blog; embed links, images, videos, and music; and create a rich experience by publishing it. Using simple tools—digital cameras, flip video, MIDI-enabled musical instruments, and editing software—hobbyists can even produce their own art and music to embed on their blogs or publish to YouTube or other multimedia sites.

Other users in turn can find whatever is placed on the net, because blogs and media sites are searchable and easily syndicated with RSS ("really simple syndication") or ATOM. They can also comment and the bloggers or content uploaders can respond, providing an opportunity to further develop or refine their points of view or their creative expressions. The bloggers almost always link with one another and comment on one another's sites, building communities around common interests. Such communities form subgroups, while they also combine forces with other interest communities for social action. For education to embrace the Internet is for it to incorporate this culture and these practices. I'll have much more to say about this as we proceed.

Web 2.0 Is Widely Accessible and Increasingly Mobile

Today the web is a widely accessible and increasingly mobile platform that is very powerful, continually improved, cheap, easy, and intuitive to learn and use. Just as the power of telephones and fax machines increased as each new user joined the network, the Internet grows in power as it becomes more widely accessible.

In North America the number of Internet users has grown over the past decade from 108 million in 2001 to 273 million users in February 2011, representing, at 77.4 percent penetration, a growth of 146 percent. The number of users in Oceania and Australia has grown in that decade from 7.6 to 21 million users, representing a 61 percent penetration and a growth rate of 179 percent. Europe has gone from 105 million to 475 million, for a 55 percent penetration and a huge growth of 352 percent. In Asia the penetration lags at 22 percent but the number of users has grown 625 percent. In Latin America the number has grown from 18 million to 205 million, a growth of 1,033 percent. Africa has the lowest Internet penetration, at only 11 percent of the population, but has grown from 4.5 million users to 110 million, an astounding growth rate of 2,357 percent in a single decade.

A 2010 study by the Pew Center for Internet and Society found that wireless mobile Internet use is now growing rapidly: 60 percent of American Internet users used some form of wireless, with about half using Wi-Fi or mobile broadband with their laptops or netbooks and 40 percent using mobile smartphones. The center reported that the numbers had risen sharply in the past year; the 2009 survey had found only 50 percent using wireless connections. In February 2011 President Barack Obama announced plans to bring 4G wireless to 98 percent of Americans in just five years, saying, "Every American deserves access to the world's information; every American deserves access to the global economy."[13] The official White House statement reasoned that "the number of 'Smartphones' will soon pass both conventional mobile phones and computers around the world."[14]

Web 2.0 Is Increasingly Powerful, Easy to Learn, and Cheap

The web experience has continually improved due to new enabling technologies and the rapid spread of web applications on the browsers on laptops and smartphones.

Powerful: The web is constantly growing in power, and the growth shows no sign of slowing down. From 2003 through 2009 the top 500 web pages have grown in size 5.4 times, while the number of objects (links, photos, videos, audios, and assorted JavaScript files) has grown 2.5 times, from 25.7 to 64.7 objects per page. While growth in size and complexity places increasing load on servers, broadband speed has steadily increased so the download time has decreased.[15]

Easy to Learn: Thousands of excellent, free, online tutorials are available covering just about any topic, including the design and use of web applications and digital tools.[16] Anyone wishing to learn how to develop or use powerful web tools can easily locate attractive, simple, well-presented tutorials, making web tools easy to learn and easy to use without teachers.

Even poor illiterate children can rapidly learn how to use the web. A slum teeming with such children lies just outside the office building in New Delhi of computer researcher Dr. Sugata Mitra. Dr. Mitra installed a networked computer in a "hole in the wall" separating the slum from his building. He discovered that within minutes children figured out how to point and click. By the end of the first day they were browsing.[17] According to *Frontline*, "Dr. Mitra has replicated his unique experiment in other settings, each time with the same result. Within hours and without instruction, children began browsing the Web."

Free or Cheap: The vast majority of content and computing power on the web is free. Web-based free software-in-the-cloud is replacing commercial software-in-a-box for many applications. Google Docs and Open Office, for example, provide free alternatives to Microsoft Office Suite for word processing, database management, and presentation, while free open source Linux and Apache have successfully challenged commercial operating systems and server software. Google books offers free links to almost every book ever published, with generous clips from most under copyright and full text where copyright has expired. The world's museums, libraries, archives, and collections make their vast holdings available for inspection (and manipulation) online.

While broadband access remains expensive, sites such as dialupforfree.com offer free dial-up services for all.[18] Dial-up, however, cannot efficiently download web pages with large files, including video. So many municipalities, states, and even nations have plans to make minimal broadband access universal and free; the information highway, like the automobile highways, would then be a public utility.[19] The public has a profound interest in universal access, as it will grease the wheels of industry and commerce while improving access to and involvement in government services, health care, and education.[20] Free and convenient Wi-Fi access is available in libraries and cafes across North America and Europe and is expanding everywhere. It is only a matter of time until almost everyone on the planet will have some form of broadband access, whether at home, at school, in libraries, at cafes or public access kiosks, and Wi-Fi hotspots, and become a node in the web.

THE WEB CULTURE: CREATIVE EXPRESSION, EXCHANGE, COLLABORATION, AND COLLECTIVE ACTION

Generalizing from Web 2.0 experiences, David Gauntlett, professor of media studies at the University of Westminster, has proposed the reframing of new "media audiences" as a "making and connecting" culture harnessing creativity for self-expression and social problem solving.[21] In a recent interview Gauntlett sheds light on the role of Web 2.0 in this culture:

> When discussing Web 2.0 and social media I was talking a lot about making, and about connecting, "making and connecting"—as well as other words like sharing and collaboration and so on—but then it struck me that an "is" in the middle summed up pretty well what I wanted to say. And that I wanted to make this discussion not just about digital media but about creativity in general.

CHAPTER SEVEN

So "making is connecting" because it is through the process of making that we (1) make new connections between our materials, creating new expressive things; (2) make connections with each other, by sharing what we've made and contributing to our relationships by sharing the meanings which we've created, individually or in collaboration; and (3) through making things, and sharing them with others, we feel a greater connection with the world, and more engaged with being more active in the environment rather than sitting back and watching.²²

Creative Self-Expression

Gauntlett speaks first of making new connections among our materials, creating new expressive objects. Arthur Koestler, in *The Act of Creation,* offers an illuminating conception of creativity as the "bisociation" of ideas—connecting ideas from different idea frameworks to create interesting and often surprising novelty. Consider the idea of cubism. On Koestler's account this idea for visual expression results from taking the idea of abstract geometric forms and combining it ("bisociating" it) with the idea of the truthful or revealing portrait or still-life painting. In cubist paintings visual objects are taken apart, analyzed, and put back together so that they can be seen from multiple viewpoints at once, revealing new dimensions and opening up new avenues for creative exploration.

Building on Koestler's notion of bisociation, we can think of creative self-expression in terms of individuals and groups associating ideas, putting them into new combinations, seeing and exploring the new possibilities, selecting and refining and augmenting some for progressive self-discovery, identity formation, and creative production, and finally publishing them—making them available outside of themselves. In this way individuals can present themselves to a social world, sometimes in multiple and even contradictory ways, so that their discoveries and pleasures can be shared, reviewed and commented upon, and augmented by others in collateral acts of creative expression. Through sequences of public expression and review, a richer and more unified self can emerge in and contribute to an increasingly creative public world.

Web 2.0 tools such as blogs and social networks provide abundant opportunities for creative self-expression, social exchange, and collaboration. The freedom to use fake and multiple identities and to mark up pages in HTML appealed to teens and propelled MySpace ahead of Friendster in 2004. The idea behind blogging is scanning and linking to multiple sites, combining and rearranging images, words, music, and videos to make a public personal statement that can be stumbled upon or found in a web search and commented upon, altered, and republished so that communities of interest and mutual expression are formed.[23]

This idea is illustrated in existing Web 2.0 sites devoted explicitly to youthful creative self-expression. Two relatively simple examples illustrate the underlying concept. The first is PicLits, a creative writing site with attention-grabbing images and word banks. Users grab images and combine them with words selected from the word bank or added freestyle. The words can be freely arranged on the page to create a multimedia composite work. Other users then review and comment on the works and even rate them with a star system. The finished works can be placed on the users' own blogs or websites. PicLits suggests that teachers use the site as a source of prompts for creative writing or as visual and verbal support for ESL learners or reluctant writers.

A second is Glogster, a site for designing "interactive posters." Glogster claims to be "the perfect tool to express yourself." Users design their own posters, add words and images as well as audio and video clips, and post them online. They can also browse the Glogster site to get inspired by, and emulate, others' poster designs, and to comment on or rate other Glog posters, promote their own posters, attract fans, and build Glog communities. "No other site gives you a chance to be so creative," Glogster declares.

Sharing and Exchange

Gauntlett speaks next of making connections, sharing what we've made and contributing to our relationships by sharing the meanings which we've created. The web is hardly limited to creating and publishing individuals' own document files. Shared resources can be made available for common use by individual users, collaborative groups, or third parties. A user can develop a design template or a group can work together on it, or an impersonal firm can provide it, in each case making it available for general use on a website.

The sharing of computer files has a long and conflict-ridden history. IBM released the 8-inch floppy disc in 1971, introducing file sharing through removable media. This immediately raised issues of protection of intellectual property and led to media industry efforts to prevent "theft." The introduction of the World Wide Web by Tim Berners-Lee in 1990, and of the MP3 standard that made it practicable to share large audio files in 1991, raised the ante on illegal file transfers. The sharing of illegal files came to a head in 1999 with the introduction of Napster, a site indexing files on users' computers and facilitating peer-to-peer sharing. Napster use peaked in February 2001 with more than 26 million users. It was shut down by a legal injunction in July 2001, the same month that the BitTorrent protocol was released. After Netscape closed, many alternative P2P websites such as Pirate Bay appeared, and P2P file sharing has continued its rapid growth. Despite the lawsuits and media and school campaigns that discourage it, the sharing of files, regardless of copyright status, is considered acceptable behavior by most young people.

Organizations also now routinely share files. Governments seeking greater transparency and efficiency regularly provide information online about regulations and hearing schedules; they issue briefs and notifications and engage in two-way exchange with citizens who can post problems, comments, or requests and even dialogue with and transact their business with government agencies.[24] Documents that governments keep secret are also likely to show up online, as whistle-blowers, aided by Wikileaks and other websites, share them when they feel that secrecy harms the public interest.

The how-to knowledge base of workers in nongovernmental organizations is also available online. Zunia Knowledge Exchange, for example, is a site facilitating exchange among professionals working at poverty reduction in over 200 countries. Zunia users exchange knowledge, tools, and contacts, in dozens of specialized fields in environment, economic development, technology, human development, and education.[25] Cloud computing also facilitates shared use and exchange of software among nongovernmental agencies, reducing costs through the pooling of expertise.[26]

Collaboration

Once users exchange files they respond to them in creative ways. They can work collaboratively with others in their organizations or communities of practice, as several users contribute insights to improve products or think up new ones. As Phaedra Boinodiris, an IBM product manager, notes, "the closed business processes of the past have prevented enterprises from realizing their full potential for agility and flexibility." Web 2.0 enabled networks "now empower people to collaborate, co-create, and experience personalized business processes as never before." Web 2.0 is a platform that facilitates personal introductions across divisions and firm boundaries, transactions, and teamwork; it "creates knowledge environments that facilitate discovery and action."[27] Customers also contribute their insights and participate in the shaping of future products, at the same time making their unique needs known and helping the firm serve them better. Steve Lee and Lane Cooper add that users and workers now *expect* to be able to collaborate, and that as a result the greatest share of IT spending by 2013 will be devoted to collaborative tools. As more "digital natives" enter the workforce and shape its culture, this expectation can only grow.

These insights about collaboration can be transferred directly from enterprise to education. Closed learning processes have kept schools from being agile and flexible. Web 2.0 tools now enable educators across school, district, regional, and national boundaries to collaborate on materials, lesson demonstrations, and even the delivery of actual lessons; students can contribute their own insights and dialogue with peers, and in so doing they can assist educators in understanding them as people and thus better serving their needs. And in this new culture of making and connecting, learners increasingly *expect* to connect and will turn increasingly away from learning environments that constrain collaboration.

Collective Action

Gauntlett concludes that "through making things and sharing them with others, we feel a greater connection with the world, and more engaged with being more active in the environment rather than sitting back and watching." The connections made through online communities, social networks, blogs, and other Web 2.0 sites facilitate acting together for shared purposes. Action is essential to complete the cycle of learning; once something is learned it becomes inert and stagnant unless shared, discussed, incorporated into our action schema, and used to achieve our various ends. Many of these ends are essentially public, requiring discussion and collective action.

Harold Rheingold was an early commentator on the potential of the web, especially the mobile web, to facilitate social action. In his 2002 book *Smart Mobs: The Next Social Revolution,* Rheingold spoke of having an epiphany while viewing a crowd of teens in Tokyo organizing activities such as impromptu raves or stalking of celebrities through text messages on their cell phones. This led to his general idea of "smart mobs," groups behaving intelligently by using network links to connect to information and to others to generate social coordination.[28]

Even before Rheingold's conceptualization, smart mobs had become an important form of social action. After the disputed presidential election in the United States in 2000, activist Zack Exley created a website to coordinate demonstrations to demand a vote recount in Florida; more than one hundred protests took place without any traditional organizing effort. As Exley explained in December 2000,

> It was natural for people to be angry and want to protest after the election, but without the Internet there would have been no way for a single person to propose a day of protests and for word of it to spread to so many people. The Internet allowed me to post the proposal where tens of millions of others could see it.

Exley added,

> These protests demonstrated that a fundamental change is taking place in our national political life. It's not the Internet per se, but the emerging potential for any individual to communicate—for free and anonymously if necessary—with any other individual.[29]

The "fundamental change" was hardly restricted to the United States. In 2001, citizens in the Philippines used text messages to coordinate a demonstration to protest the corruption of President Joseph Estrada. The crowd grew quickly, driving Estrada from office. The 2005 civil unrest in France also employed smart mob coordination. According to Patrick Hamon, a national police spokesman, there was no central coordination of the riots; the youths, mainly of the Muslim faith, used text messages and blogs to arrange meetings and warn of police operations.[30]

2011 became the year of the Revolution 2.0, conclusively demonstrating the power of social media in collective action. Young people throughout the Middle East from Tunisia, Egypt, and Libya to Jordan and Bahrain have coordinated protests through Web 2.0, in some cases driving long-term dictators from power.

Let's focus on Egypt. On June 6, 2010, Egyptian Khalid Mohamed Saeed was, according to many witnesses, beaten to death by President Mubarak's police. Then in January 2011 citizens of Tunisia overthrew longtime Tunisian president Zine El Abidine Ben Ali by means of the web-coordinated "Jasmine revolution." The BBC proposed that the revolutionary movement could not spread to Egypt: "the simple fact is that most Egyptians do not see any way that they can change their country or their lives through political action, be it voting, activism, or going out on the streets to demonstrate."[31]

A Facebook page, "We are all Khaled Saeed," however, had already attracted hundreds of thousands of "friends" and brought worldwide attention to Mubarak's brutal regime. As the Egyptian protests began on January 25, Wael Ghonim, a Google executive, announced that he was behind the Facebook page. Female activist Asmaa Mahfouz posted a YouTube video challenging the people of Egypt to protest; this video went viral. The crowds, almost entirely nonviolent, withstood attacks by Mubarak's secret police and on February 11 drove Mubarak from power. Protestors praise digital media as the fundamental infrastructure for the revolution. According to one, "We use Facebook to schedule the protests, Twitter to coordinate, and YouTube to tell the world."[32]

The editors of *Time* declared "protesters" the people of the year in 2011, recognizing the young people from Tunisia and Egypt through Syria and Wall Street that are challenging outmoded dictatorships and unjust institutions. Educators should pay attention: if young people can drive brutal dictators from power and challenge age-old social injustices using Web 2.0 tools, it is likely that they can also coordinate study groups, workshops, and fieldtrips.

USER-GENERATED CONTENT

The Internet is a platform for exchange, collaboration, and collective action on a global scale. It is not entirely accurate to think of it as a "new medium" alongside newspapers and magazines, radio, and television. These earlier technologies were indeed *media,* things in the middle, large organizations with paid professionals selecting and editing information and passing it on to passive audiences. The Internet, by contrast, provides direct, unmediated links among people. Today, the web is breeding a participatory culture, and leading websites are built on user-generated content: user-made videos (YouTube), blogs (Blogger, Wordpress), information exchanges (Yahoo Answers), product offers (eBay), and massive information products (Wikipedia). Many commercial websites shaped by firm-made content, like Amazon.com, are particularly attractive because of the user-generated content they host (e.g., in the case of Amazon, book reviews, reading lists, author pages).

Where do computer users find the time to generate all this content, and why would they bother? Internet guru Clay Shirky notes that citizens of industrial democracies have had considerable free time since the forty-hour work week was established. Most of that time has been absorbed by passive entertainments, especially TV. Americans watch about 200 billion hours of television each year. By contrast, the creation of Wikipedia in its current state represents 100 million hours of invested human effort. 100 million hours is a lot of time, but Americans spend that much time each year just watching TV *commercials*. We have, as Shirky puts it, a huge "cognitive surplus": we have plenty of time to create content.

The more interesting question is why we would bother. Why would we reallocate time from passive entertainments to Internet content creation? Shirky answers that basic human motivations are reasonably constant throughout history: to work autonomously, to grow in competence, to belong, and to share. The Internet simply provides powerful new opportunities over passive media to channel these motivations, to do what we have always wanted to do, and on a grander scale. We can now treat the free time of educated citizens globally as a "general social asset that can be harnessed for large, communally created projects, rather than a set of individual minutes to be whiled away one person at a time."[33]

Television executives have not yet caught up with this trend. They still think the old media paradigm that sees viewers merely as their audience will prevail. They assume that what we hope to get from media is high production-value entertainment. But what if, Shirky asks, part of that job is not merely to entertain but to connect us, to help us to feel less lonely, to feel more competent and creative? Well, we got a tiny little bit of that from TV; we could talk with friends about ball scores or joke about sitcom developments at the tavern or beauty parlor. But the Internet does these jobs so much better. And if Shirky is correct that these are the jobs we want media to do, production values don't matter quite so much. When we make the content ourselves even if the production values are modest, we are channeling very basic needs: to work autonomously, to improve our skills, to attach to like-minded people and form communities of value, to share generously.

Shirky estimates that our global cognitive surplus of educated citizens exceeds one trillion hours a year. That is a cool million Wikipedias every year. We can channel that into activities serving individuals, communities, and broad publics. Wikipedia, for example, is an unparalleled public good, serving not only the Wikipedians who create it but the rest of us as well. And through collective action, Internet users like Egyptian Wael Ghonim can even transform society.

There are few motivations more inherent in humans than nurturing young people and bringing them into life in society by educating them. It is an accident of twentieth-century life that we have assigned this role exclusively to professional teachers in large bureaucratic organizations. It takes a village to raise a child, and it may take the entire global village to raise its young. That village now has adequate means, but it still lacks institutional channels for directing the cognitive surplus to the educational task. Creating these channels is one chief task of the learningweb revolution.

Conclusion

The Internet and workstation were designed to circumvent the limits of hierarchical control and empower end users. Equipped with mobile computers and Web 2.0 technologies and living within the web-based culture, today's teens have unprecedented powers to learn, create, share, collaborate, and act collectively. Sharing, questioning, collaborating, and critiquing, furthermore, enhance memory by building strong neural connections. Education can be reshaped for network society only by liberating these powers and harnessing the results for individual growth and the common good. In the next chapter we consider how the Internet introduces new, previously undreamed of possibilities for education.

CHAPTER EIGHT
THE LEARNINGWEB

The Internet is the structural core of Education 2.0. In this chapter I focus on three main components of the learningweb revolution: online knowledge, online teaching, and online informal learning. Taken together these constitute the new technical and social infrastructure for Education 2.0.

LEARNINGWEB ELEMENT I: THE KNOWLEDGEWEB

The Internet is a window on the world's knowledge. It provides limitless courses, tutorials, and structured learning opportunities in all fields. It is revolutionizing informal learning in libraries and museums and elsewhere, shifting learning power from schools and classrooms to learners. It is the hierarchy's worst nightmare.

Knowledge is at the heart of learning. As Plato conceived it, knowledge is an atemporal ideal, fixed and certain. As I will be using the term, knowledge is more temporal—consisting of the ideas that responsible people in various situations of life can attest to on the basis of experience and cognitive norms. "I know" means "take my word for it, I can give you my warrant based on relevant considerations." As such, knowledge is highly diverse. *Bodies* of knowledge are organized in textbooks and become subject matters for school and college learning. Knowledge *creation* is a process whereby researchers and scholars learn new things about abstract objects, nature, and society and then typically subject them to peer review and make available for use by other scholars, industry, and the public. Practitioners of every art and science have collective know-how or *practical* knowledge that they apply to the problems (often unpredicted, poorly structured, and "messy") arising in their domains of life. Students and scholars persistently *construct* and *reconstruct* their own *personal* knowledge in every act of learning.

Today a vast portion of the world's knowledge is freely available on the web. Learners can do a Google search, consult a Wikipedia article, or go to Yahoo answers or Answers.com and find instant answers to just about any question. If the question is of the how-to variety, they can go to YouTube and many other sites to find simple video tutorials for most practical tasks or problems. One website, Answers.com, provides one-stop-shopping by aggregating answers from Wikianswers, a site permitting anyone to ask, answer, edit, or collaborate on answers in thousands of categories, plus "who-is" and "what-is" answers from major reference sources plus "how-to" answers from video tutorials.[1]

Question-and-answer technology is constantly improving. Students at any level can already find clear, user-friendly lessons and tutorials and even entire courses on just about every school and college subject. Teachers, moreover, can find online knowledge for all teachable subjects, plus model lessons, units, and course curricula, many with video demonstrations.[2] Students and teachers can find open source textbooks for most school and college subjects, and they can add their own notes and comments and exchange them with fellow students and colleagues. They can even add their own home-brew units to augment or update the textbooks. Meanwhile, research is now rapidly migrating from commercially published journals to free, online journals. Harvard is encouraging its faculty to move to open access online publications, and other universities are certain to follow.[3]

Here we will merely skim the surface of the "knowledgeweb" to show how much it contains and to prepare the way for our discussion of the radical new possibilities for learning.

Search and Question Answering

Early web search engines such as AltaVista worked by searching for keywords. A search yielded millions of results, but users were unable to assess their quality or relevance and most results were not helpful. Google was a game changer. Founder Larry Page hypothesized, "If you can solve search, you can answer any question. Which means you can basically do anything."[4] Visionaries such as Richard Stallman saw the web, indexed through search engines, as "having the potential to develop into a universal encyclopedia covering all areas of knowledge, and a complete library of instructional courses."[5] And in a *New York Times* article on the closing of Microsoft's Encarta encyclopedia, Randall Stross, a professor of business at San Jose State University, stated,

> The Google search engine is an automated, continuously updated, always-expanding guide to information that is completely free. Authority now comes not from a small group of encyclopedia editors and famous contributors but from Google's algorithms, which analyze links that point to Web pages elsewhere and other clues to make an educated guess about trustworthiness.[6]

Page approached the problem of search by downloading the entire web. In 1995 he conceived that if he could download the entire web he could map it and rank each page in terms of the probability of reaching it by a random search through all web pages. His algorithm, called PageRank, assigns a numerical weight to each one of a hyperlinked set of documents in order to measure its relative value or importance. Using a "wisdom of the crowds" logic, Google PageRank assumes that pages attracting the most links are the most valuable.

Today search technologies also employ tagging methodologies to search images, videos, and other files. Current projects include devising algorithms for personal relevance based on the search habits and data streams individual users leave behind as they use the web. Brian J. Ford of Cambridge University calls contemporary search engines "truly revolutionary."[7]

E-Books

Digital libraries, searchable e-book repositories, and online booksellers are making more and more of the world's books available free or at low cost for the global public.

Project Gutenberg (PG) was among the first projects to upload books to the web. Founded in 1971 by Michael Hart, a University of Illinois freshman, its initial goal was to make the 10,000 most consulted books available free to the public by the end of the twentieth century. The Internet has eased its growth, and the project now offers more than 34,000 books, with 100,000 more on partner sites. PG is staffed entirely by volunteers.

In 2004 Google began scanning and uploading the world's most important books to its book repository, Google Books. It collaborated with the world's most prestigious libraries to scan their collections. Greeted as democratizing the world's corpus of knowledge, it has also been condemned as the wholesale theft of intellectual property because of its scanning of still-copyrighted material. Google has settled a suit brought by the publishers, but the settlement is now contested. However it plays out, Google's book project has without question opened the world's knowledge archives and made a large proportion of all books searchable.

E-Book Readers

Technology skeptics have long doubted that a computer screen could ever replace the printed page. As Clifford Stoll put it in his widely read *Silicon Snake Oil* in 1995, "No online database will replace your daily newspaper."[8] Few journalists today will find Stoll's analysis comforting. Practical e-book readers with e-paper and e-ink that emulate the look and feel of ink on paper have changed the game. Today book publishers and bookstores, newspaper publishers and journalists, are severely challenged by e-books and e-periodicals.

An e-book, for our purposes, is an electronic version of a printed book readable on a computer screen or a dedicated e-book reader such as an Amazon Kindle. Public libraries started offering e-books on their websites in 1998 and by 2003 were lending popular titles. By 2010 65 percent of public libraries in the United States were lending e-books out to members, and the numbers have been growing.

E-books have several obvious advantages over print books, and the equally obvious disadvantages are now being corrected. In the space occupied by a single small paperback an e-book reader can store more than 2,500 books, a number sure to rise rapidly. Books can be browsed, purchased, and downloaded immediately, eliminating the wait time between wanting a book and having it in hand. E-books can be stored in the cloud and thus can't be damaged by sunlight or water. More than 1.8 million titles are available for download to the popular e-book readers.[9]

High-quality e-book readers have been game changers. Amazon launched its first Kindle in 2007, and it sold out in five hours, demonstrating huge pent-up demand for such devices. In 2008 Sony introduced the PRS series, and the following year Amazon introduced the improved Kindle 2 and Barnes and Noble introduced the Nook, featuring an Android open source platform. The year 2010, however, was a major turning point. Amazon introduced the Kindle 3 and 3G, Barnes and Noble the Nook Color, Apple the iPad, and Google its e-books project. On Christmas day 2009 Amazon announced that for the first time in its history the sales of e-books outnumbered the sale of all print books including paperbacks. Though Amazon has not been forthcoming about its sales data, industry analysts in mid-2011 estimated that over 4 million Kindles had been sold. And after the release of the Kindle Fire in November 2011, Amazon announced that it had sold more than 3 million more in the three weeks leading up to Christmas. For three years the Kindle has been the most popular product sold on Amazon, outselling even the *Harry Potter* books, and the Nook has also been selling like hotcakes. Amazon offers 650,000 e-book titles for sale, in addition to the 1.8 million titles of out-of-copyright books that consumers can download for free. In just five years the e-book reader has evolved from a dream to a novelty to a common, everyday device.

Online Encyclopedias

Although compendia of knowledge on discrete subjects existed long before this, the modern general encyclopedia was born in the eighteenth century. The famous *Encyclopedie* of Diderot and D'Alembert established the standard format. Diderot, anticipating the age of search and hyperlink, saw the encyclopedia as an "index of connections" between areas of knowledge rather than as a compendium, believing that no single print work, no matter how large, could encompass all knowledge. The *Encyclopaedia Britannica* (1768–), which has set the standard for subsequent encyclopedias, became the first encyclopedia to adopt a policy of periodic revisions. Popular encyclopedias appeared early in the twentieth century, including *Funk and Wagnalls Encyclopedia* (1912–) and the *World Book Encyclopedia* (1917–), the first to make annual revisions.

Microsoft's Encarta (1993–2009) was the first encyclopedia designed exclusively for the computer. Microsoft incorporated *Funk and Wagnalls* and *Colliers Encyclopedia* into Encarta, dedicating a large staff to a costly effort to update and fact-check all articles and to augment them with multimedia files to create a new kind of reference experience utilizing the power of the computer. Microsoft, however, overestimated the hunger of its mass audience for this product. Faced with competition from free web-based encyclopedias, especially user-generated Wikipedia, sales of Encarta plummeted.

The encyclopedia has thus witnessed a clear evolution: from print to the computer hard drive, then to the web and finally to collaborative Web 2.0. As Randall Stross put it, "Microsoft learned that the public would no longer pay for information once it became available free." The public would also no longer pay for scholarly authority and authentication. As Microsoft stated in closing Encarta in 2009, "The category of traditional encyclopedias and reference material has changed.... People today seek and consume information in considerably different ways than in years past."[10]

Microsoft didn't have to mention Wikipedia by name. Its 365 million readers, who are all welcome to add or edit articles, make it the seventh most often used site on the Internet. But it wasn't the first web encyclopedia. Richard Stallman offered a framework for a free online collaborative encyclopedia, which he called GNUpedia, in 1999. GNUpedia was launched in 2001, but it generated very few articles. When Wikipedia was launched later that year, Stallman inactivated GNUpedia and threw his considerable clout behind Wikipedia.

Founder Jimmy Wales initially wished to create a free encyclopedia with authoritative articles penned by volunteer scholars and peer-reviewed by a distinguished board of editors. This project, named Nupedia, also generated very few completed articles. Hoping to prime the Nupedia pump, cofounder Larry Sanger proposed to generate additional content by using the Wiki software developed by Ward Cunningham in 1994. Wikis allow for the very rapid collaborative creation and editing of interlinked web pages. Cunningham coined the term "wiki" from the Hawaiian word for "very quick"; he described the Wiki as "the simplest online database that could possibly work."

From its 2000 launch until it was inactivated in 2003, Nupedia had generated only twenty-four complete articles. By contrast, from its 2001 launch until the end of that year, Wikipedia had generated more than 20,000 articles. A study in the prestigious journal *Nature* in 2005 found the accuracy of Wikipedia's scientific articles comparable to those in *Britannica*, with a similar rate of "serious errors,"[11] a claim rejected by *Britannica*.[12] Despite rearguard actions by teachers and professors, Wikipedia is now the go-to reference source for most web users.

Open Knowledge

The distinction between knowledge freely available to the public (public domain) and knowledge protected by copyright has long been established in law, but increasing claims over "intellectual property" in the information age have made this distinction more important.

In announcing the GNUpedia project in 1999, Stallman argued that corporations were increasingly mobilizing to "control and restrict access" to knowledge and learning, "so as to extract money from people who want to learn." He added that while we "cannot stop business from restricting the information it makes available, we can provide an alternative."[13] An "open knowledge" movement has taken shape in the past decade to promote and protect public knowledge in the age of the Internet.

The standard definition of "open knowledge" is provided by the Budapest Open Knowledge Initiative:

> By "open access" to this literature, we mean its free availability on the public Internet, permitting any users to read, download, copy, distribute, print, search, or link to the full texts of these articles, crawl them for indexing, pass them as data to software, or use them for any other lawful purpose, without financial, legal, or technical barriers other than those inseparable from gaining access to the Internet itself. The only constraint on reproduction and distribution, and the only role for copyright in this domain, should be to give authors control over the integrity of their work and the right to be properly acknowledged and cited.[14]

Academic knowledge—produced by professional scholars and vetted by a peer-review process prior to publication—becomes available through publication in scholarly journals. Today these journals are typically owned by commercial publishing houses and edited by major scholars aided by boards of prestigious volunteer reviewers. The authors are not compensated for their works; indeed they often have to pay a fee for publishing them. Moreover, they sign away their copyrights to the works to the publishers, who in turn sell the knowledge back to academic libraries and individual scholars including the authors.

As journals proliferated and became more costly, academic libraries were forced to drastically cut back on subscriptions. Universities and research institutions became more protective of their intellectual property, increasingly claiming ownership of the scholarly works of their faculties. Corporations gained greater influence in universities and research institutions, a trend that sociologists have closely monitored and labeled "academic capitalism," and they routinely influenced research and publication in many fields.[15] In short, academic knowledge was migrating from the public to the private domain, its reliability was being compromised, and its availability to the public increasingly restricted.

Commercial academic publishers became central to knowledge distribution because they had the necessary capital, marketing, and distribution networks. However, in the age of the interactive web, online knowledge networks can now take over the knowledge distribution process at low cost. Open access to scholarship can have two channels: open access journals and open knowledge archives. Open access journals publish articles like conventional journals, but are accessible in full without any fee or subscription charges; open archives are publicly accessible online repositories where authors or other right holders upload their pre-print or post-print articles.[16]

According to the Directory of Open Access Journals, headed by Lars Björnshauge, director of the Lund University Libraries, there are now 6,165 open access journals,[17] and a recent study shows that over 20 percent of peer-reviewed research is now freely available for open access online.[18] As noted, Harvard is now urging its faculty to publish solely in open access journals and to resign from journal boards keeping articles behind paywalls.

LEARNINGWEB ELEMENT 2: OPEN COURSES AND TEXTBOOKS

The use of digital tools and Web 2.0 makes it significantly cheaper and easier for people to learn anything, through free online courses and tutorials and free open source textbooks. The world of knowledge is open online. Free or low-cost online tutorials and courses, and free open source textbooks, provide instruction in just about all subjects for anyone interested in studying and learning them. I limit myself to three examples illustrating how today's school, college, and adult learners can study any topic with the guidance of excellent online teachers and textbooks, for free.

Khan Academy

The Khan Academy currently offers more than 2,000 ten- to twenty-minute video lessons on just about every topic in school and college math, science, and economics. Salman Khan, the founder and sole faculty member, earned his MBA from Harvard Business School, where he was the president of his class. He had previously received two bachelor's degrees, one in electrical engineering/computer science and the other in mathematics, and a master's degree in electrical engineering/computer science, all from MIT.

While working as a hedge fund analyst in Boston Khan was recruited by an aunt to tutor his cousin Nadia, who was having difficulty in eighth-grade mathematics because she kept stumbling over "unit conversion." When she caught up and pulled ahead of her classmates his aunt asked him to tutor Nadia's two brothers, Arman and Ali, as well. Khan started his tutoring sessions over the telephone, but found it easier and more effective to make short videos for them, which he posted on YouTube. When these videos went viral Kahn had a transformative insight: "With just a computer and a pen-tablet-mouse, one can educate the world!"

Khan's goal for the academy is ambitious: "we hope to empower everyone, everywhere with a free, world-class education." So far Khan has focused on math, science, and economics, but his goal is eventually to "cover everything." He says, "my goal is to keep on making videos till the day I die!" Considering that he expects to live another forty to fifty years, he says "that should give me time to make several tens of thousands of videos in pretty much every subject."

Khan teaches in a simple, accessible, conversational style, which he says is the "tonal antithesis" of what people associate with math and science teaching. He teaches in the way he wishes he had been taught. When he was in school, he says, fascinating and intuitive concepts were butchered into page after page of sleep-inducing text with lectures delivered in monotone. Even his most intelligent peers memorized mechanical formulas without any sense of the underlying intuitions or the big-picture contexts. Khan seeks instead to convey these concepts as they might be approached by a fascinated human being—not by a curriculum committee.[19] Khan's audacious project is to become the teacher to the world, replacing didactic teaching with his video mini-lessons and comprehensive video courses.

Khan makes an important point about video-based instruction: the teacher can repeat the lesson endlessly, and students who appear to be slow learners may in fact be bright students stuck on a particular concept. In traditional schools where they are forced to keep up with the pace of instruction, such learners may continue to appear slow because they don't grasp concepts that form the basis for subsequent lessons. But when allowed to learn at their own pace, such students may repeat lessons and eventually master those concepts and complete the sequence of lessons at a high level within the time assigned for the course. Video teachers don't get tired or frustrated; they are available 24/7 to repeat lessons.

OpenCourseWare (OCW)

One of the most highly touted online learning projects is OpenCourseWare (OCW). Initiated by MIT in 2000, OCW has spread to more than 150 additional universities and research centers, and it currently offers more than 4,500 courses in nine languages. Tufts, Duke, and UC Berkeley are among the major

US sources of courseware, while in Europe the Technical University of Delft has emerged as a leader, ranking second globally in technology courseware behind MIT. The famed Indian Institute of Technology (IIT) is among the leading sources in Asia. The source institutions have joined forces in the OpenCourseWare Consortium, a "worldwide community of hundreds of universities and associated organizations committed to advancing OpenCourseWare and its impact on global education."[20] A list of participating institutions and an interactive search tool to search for courses by subject matter and language are available on the consortium website.[21]

In 1999 Provost Robert Brown charged the MIT Council on Educational Technology with discovering the institution's role in distance learning. After exploring commercial opportunities the institution came to the conclusion that a free and open course platform was more in keeping with its mission: "to advance knowledge and educate students in science, technology, and other areas of scholarship that will best serve the nation and the world in the 21st century." The OpenCourseWare project was seen as a way of providing "a new model for the dissemination of knowledge and collaboration among scholars around the world, contributing to the 'shared intellectual commons' in academia, fostering collaboration across MIT and among other scholars." Because some faculty members expressed concerns about loss of their intellectual property embodied in course materials and lectures, MIT made the project voluntary. The visionary computer science professor Hal Abelson was put in charge of the project.

Users of OCW are offered course curricula and class schedules, assigned readings, lecture notes, and presentation slides. Many of the courses come complete with open source textbooks and streaming video lectures. OCW enables any learner, anywhere in the world, to acquire a free world-class university education. To matriculate in MIT and attend its courses, students would have to pass extremely competitive exams and then cough up more than $40,000 a year in tuition. To attend the same lectures online, the bill comes to $0.00. You don't earn credits or degrees, but you cannot beat the price!

MIT alone offers more than 2,000 courses in its OCW program. A 2010 list of the most frequently visited courses illustrates the university's strength in technology: computer science, introduction to algorithms, circuits and electronics, signals and systems, and computer language engineering are listed among the top twenty. But the sciences and liberal arts are also represented in that top group: physics, introduction to biology, principles of chemical science, calculus, linear algebra, and even principles of philosophy.[22]

The edX and Coursera Certificates of Mastery: A Game Changer

In December 2011 MIT announced *MITx,* a new initiative, starting in early 2012, to extend MIT's OCW program in significant ways. Led by MIT Provost L. Rafael Reif, the *MITx* project will include a campus-wide research effort focused on improving online education. *MITx* also aims to eliminate barriers to higher education by offering MIT courses online, in a form that allows learners across the globe the chance to earn "certificates of mastery." MIT is creating a not-for-profit organization within the Institute to offer these certificates. MIT will also make the *MITx* open source software infrastructure freely available to educational institutions everywhere. All *MITx* courses will be free, and the Institute aims to make the certificates of mastery available for a "modest fee."[23] In May 2012 Harvard announced that it will be partnering with *MITx* in this venture, and the combined program of their course offerings (and those of fellow participants Berkeley and the University of Texas) was called edX. With the most prestigious universities now committed to this project, the dream of universal, free or very low cost, top-quality higher education for all students throughout the world is at hand.Online offerings were expanded further when in April 2012, Daphne Koller and Andrew Ng, two computer science professors at Stanford, received funding to initiate Coursera, an organization making a comparable effort to provide free online higher education. The founders say,

> We hope to give everyone access to the world-class education that has so far been available only to a select few. We want to empower people with education that will improve their lives, the lives of their families, and the communities they live in.

So far, Stanford has partnered with Princeton, the University of Michigan, the University of Virginia, Georgia Tech, the University of Toronto, Duke, Rice, and a dozen other major universities to make the Coursera mission a reality. Certificates of mastery are listed among the components of Coursera offerings. In August 2012, Coursera announced that it had already enrolled over 1 million students from 196 countries.

Open Source Textbooks

Open (or open access, or open source) textbooks are textbooks published online either by the authors or through nonprofit or open license publishers. Users are permitted to read and download the books for free and sometimes to print them out for personal use. Some open source publishers also offer low-cost print or audio editions to raise revenues for royalties and other expenses. Many authors also grant users rights to add, remove, or alter the content, usually on condition that the original source is acknowledged and that the new creation is available for use under an open license.

Commercially published textbooks have suffered from three major problems: high cost to users, limited (or in some cases overabundant) content range, and frequent shortages or time delays: every college teacher has suffered the nightmare scenario of facing classes for weeks without textbooks due to such shortages or distribution delays. Publishers keep the costs high by frequently publishing unnecessary new editions. The high costs are a barrier to college access for poor and lower-middle-class students: a study by the College Board in 2008 found that the average college student invested between $805 and $1,229 in textbooks and associated supplies during the 2007–2008 academic year. Studies by Student PIRGs and by the Florida legislature found that the adoption of open source textbooks could save students approximately 80 percent of these costs. Let's examine a few open textbook projects.

The California Open Source Textbook Project (COSTP) has been a leader in the open textbook movement. Founded in 1991, COSTP has actively spread the word about open source textbooks and educational materials in both K–12 and higher education worldwide. It has advised Wikipedia and dozens of other organizations on educational licensing strategies and textbook marketing strategies, including the Gates, MacArthur, Hewlett, and Annenberg Foundations, Creative Commons, and the Soros Open Access Initiative.

COSTP founder Sanford Forte is also an officer of Flat World Knowledge, the first commercial firm providing free open source university textbooks. These are published under a Creative Commons Non-Commercial license. Founded in 2007, Flat World issued its first textbooks in beta in 2009. It aims to provide free textbooks for all 125 of the highest enrollment college courses by 2014. In addition to the free online editions, Flat World offers low-cost print and audio editions to generate revenues for author royalties and expenses of publication. In spring 2009, 1,000 students in 30 colleges used these textbooks; in fall 2009, 40,000 students in 400 colleges; in fall 2010, 150,000 students in 800 colleges. Flat World now has twenty-four titles in print, fifty more in the pipeline, and more than one hundred authors under contract. The aim of serving students in all popular courses by 2014 appears reachable. The Flat World business model shifts market power from publishers to learners, who can either use the textbooks for free or select low-cost print or audio alternatives. They claim they will save 150,000 college students $12 million in textbook costs in the 2010–2011 school year.[24] The American Library Association selected Flat World Knowledge's business and economics textbooks for their 2010 list of "outstanding business reference sources," and the firm has won a number of other awards for their "disruptive business model."

David A. Wiley, a professor of instructional psychology and technology at Brigham Young University, founder of the Open High School of Utah (which we will examine later), and a national leader in open education, serves as the chief openness officer at Flat World. *Fast Company Magazine* ranked Wiley among the top 100 creative people for 2009.[25]

Open source publishing is gaining attention as innovative, creative, and disruptive. Professors increasingly adopt open texts, and private foundations and federal and state governments are funding them. The business model is succeeding. The higher education division of the Association of American Publishers, however, is alarmed and has initiated legal action to block open source textbooks.

LEARNINGWEB ELEMENT 3: INFORMAL LEARNING

Informal learning, according to an oft-cited definition by David Livingston, includes "anything we do outside of organized courses to gain significant knowledge, skill or understanding ... either on our own or with other people." Web 2.0 is today transforming informal education and in the process suggesting new possibilities for formal education.

Most organized courses take place in institutions of *formal* education: schools and colleges. But such courses can also be found in workplace training programs and community centers. Yoga studios, art centers, and organizations such as Toastmasters all offer structured courses over weeks and months, led by instructors following curricula. The learning in these outside-of-school courses is sometimes referred to as "quasi-formal."

By contrast *informal* learning, whether in or outside of school, is independent of instructor-led programs, does not follow a preset curriculum, and is not necessarily consciously planned or aimed at the learning of designated subject matters. Informal learning activities are chosen and directed primarily by learners. While they often involve other people, these others are often not teachers but, for example, members of a book or drawing club, a golf caddy or tennis partner, or someone we stumble upon online. We can learn informally from books, videos and podcasts, library and museum visits.

As noted in Chapter One, Sally Anne Moore of Digital Equipment Corporation estimates that 75 percent of "learning for performance" involves the informal dimension of "I adopt and adapt." Teachers can in formal courses explain the basics and guide the first steps of practice. The later stages, however, require hours of informal learning through applying and augmenting formal lessons.

In what follows I consider recent changes in informal learning in libraries and museums. After the spread of Web 2.0 each of these settings for informal learning has undergone significant change from isolated, passive activities to those prompting creative expression and social connection. Analogous with Web 2.0, and through the use of Web 2.0 tools, they have been reconceptualized as moving to "2.0" stages of their own.

Library 2.0

Libraries are repositories of documents, principally books but also audio, pictures, and video. They store the documents, catalog them, and make them available to the public. Some of the materials circulate, while others may be used only in the library building or, in the case of, for example, rare books and drawings, under the supervision of trained staff members.

A recent study found that 93 percent of undergraduates find that using online information makes more sense than going to a physical library. Physical library use has been in sharp decline for decades. Between 1991 and 2001, for example, the libraries of the University of California experienced a 54 percent decline in physical circulation. Caught between the high cost of print materials, reductions in public and institutional funding, and declining use, today's libraries are at a crossroad.

The notion of Library 2.0 was first put into wide circulation in 2005 by the blogger Michael Casey.[26] It immediately generated a firestorm of debate. Interest in the concept spread throughout the library profession in 2006 after the influential *Library Journal* published the article "Library 2.0: Service for the Next-Generation Library."[27]

Casey had declared that today's potential library users work with information in new ways not supported by traditional libraries, for example, downloading information, then reusing, mixing, and mashing it up. Because these new uses are continually evolving, the library could best adapt to change by placing users at the heart of the change process. Library 2.0, for Casey, is a user-generated library, where users not only read books and articles but review them, comment on the reviews and comments of other users, and even submit books and articles of their own. The authors added that Library 2.0 would be a paradigm shift from a one-directional information flow from staff to users to a new model involving multidirectional networks supporting user-to-user, user-to-library, and library-to-library interactions.

Some librarians saw the point of innovation as getting more users into the library. A widely cited definition of Library 2.0 by Sarah Houghton stated that "library 2.0 simply means making your library's space (virtual and physical) more interactive, collaborative, and driven by community needs." She adds, "The basic drive is to get people back into the library by making the library relevant to what they want and need in their daily lives ... to make the library a destination and not an afterthought."

Paul Miller, however, in an important article in 2005 countered that the goal of Library 2.0 was *not* to get people into the building but "to reach potential audiences wherever they happened to be," including "far beyond the building," thus transforming the library, in terms popularized by Manuel Castells, from a "place" to a "space of flows." In 2006 John Blyberg, a *Library Journal* "Mover and Shaker" who took first prize in the 2006 "Mashing-Up the Library" competition, went even further, arguing that Library 2.0 involved not just a change in delivery system but in mission, especially in "drastically changing the role libraries play in the lives of our younger constituents." He added, "It's obvious that the Millennials have very little interest in the 'traditional' library."[28]

In Library 2.0, as in other Web 2.0 fields, the social, not the technical, dimensions are primary. Dave Lankes and his coauthors, in "Participatory Networks: The Library as Conversation," said that in adapting to the new web, "libraries should focus on the phenomena made possible by the technology" rather than the technology itself. Building on the notion that "knowledge is conversation," they say,

> Imagine a local organization coming to the library, and within a few minutes setting up a Web site with an RSS feed, a blog and bulletin boards. The library facilitates, but does not own, that individual's or organization's conversation.... It does form a strong partnership, however, that can be leveraged into resources and support. The true power of participatory networking in libraries is not to give every librarian a blog; it is in giving every community member a blog (and making the librarian a part of the community).[29]

In this new conception, the library is no longer a hierarchical information repository shaped by professionals, but a multidimensional institution shaped by users fulfilling a variety of their needs: for informal learning, creative self-expression, group formation, collaboration, and social action.

Library 2.0, as it has evolved, is not just a collection of online materials, though collections of e-materials are rapidly growing and becoming an ever-larger budget item for most libraries. In addition to the circulation of e-books and other digital documents, Library 2.0 involves catalogs with entries that are easy for users to understand and augment and that are readily translatable into multiple languages,[30] blogs by staff members with comments and guest posts by users, social networks among all members of the library community generating discussions and online or physical reading groups, user-generated book reviews, book lists, and subject guides linked to catalog items, user-based materials selection and acquisition, and chat lines with librarians available for real time, extended hours consultations.

An excellent example of Library 2.0 is Lib Guides, a website aggregating subject matter guides to reading and audiovisual materials prepared by librarians from hundreds of libraries, with real-time chat with librarians to assist users. Imagine Amazon's Listmania lists with subject experts available 24/7 to chat about the materials listed.

Museum 2.0

The Museum 2.0 concept, like Library 2.0, arose from the analogy with Web 2.0 and the creative and collaborative opportunities it opens for the museum institution.

A major theorist of Museum 2.0 is Nina Simon, a California-based consultant and the author of *The Participatory Museum* (2010). For Simon, Museum 2.0 is the transformation of the museum from a "static content authority" to "a dynamic platform for content generation and sharing." Web 2.0 opens up new opportunities for museums, but it also shines a spotlight on areas where museums are lacking.[31] Traditionally, museums have conceived of their users as individual content consumers served by professionals serving up authoritative exhibits. Museum professionals have frequently spoken about user engagement and participation—for example, about exhibits providing users the "experience of being an artist, scientist, historian, or inventor." But these aims rarely have received concentrated attention.

Museum 2.0 changes this situation. Simon offers a five-stage model for museums in moving from an individual consumer model to social participation: (1) individuals consume content; (2) individuals interact with content; (3) the products of the individual interactions are aggregated; (4) these products are networked for social use; and (5) individuals form and sustain social relations for collaboration and collective action. In this last stage the museum no longer has the feel of a static space, but is full of potentially interesting, challenging, and enriching encounters with other people.[32]

In 2006 the Ontario Science Center opened an entire wing devoted to user-generated materials. In one project, users designed shoes from various materials. The staff provided materials, design ideas, and consulting, and users interacted creatively with the content provided to make unique shoes. New visitors found the activity exciting, but after users generated thousands of pairs of shoes, staff and return visitors lost interest.

Simon suggests that instead of simply closing this exhibit or creating a small permanent collection of the most interesting shoes, the staff could "layer on" a social dimension to the exhibit, moving users from individual creative expression to judging, sorting, tagging, and commenting on the products, producing video documentaries, curating a traveling exhibition, and so on. This would involve moving to higher stages in her hierarchy of participation: aggregating the products, networking them for social use (for example, by making them available for tagging and comment and evaluation), and ultimately using social networks to form groups for collaborative work in curating, staging, documenting, and marketing an exhibit.[33]

Established Museums and Museum 2.0

The world's leading museums have embraced the web and have taken many creative steps to open up their institutions to their users.

The Metropolitan Museum of Art in New York has aggressively expanded its digital presence; it recently introduced a smartphone app that displays many of the museum's treasures and opens them for comment. Virtual visitors can now tour the museum, view its collections, zoom in on details of its prized possessions, comment on them, and blog about them. The physical building has been wired throughout for Wi-Fi, so that viewers can augment their viewing experience by linking to online materials on their phones. Director Thomas Campbell says that while these steps may not appear revolutionary, the next frontier isn't physical but philosophical—making the museum open and understandable by thoroughly rethinking the way it uses web technology.

The Smithsonian museum complex is also taking bold steps toward Museum 2.0. According to Director Michael Edson, "In the past we provided services to passive audiences. Now every user is a hero in his own journey." Through a collaboration with Flickr, the photo-sharing web service, as well as wikis and blogs supported on its website, the Smithsonian is encouraging users to experience, interact with, reuse, mash-up its resources, and share their products with others in the "Smithsonian Commons" area of the website. The Brooklyn Museum and the Victoria and Albert Museum in London are also among leaders in bringing established museums to the next stage.

A caution should be raised, however, about Michael Edson's notion of "every user a hero in his own journey." This "hero" language reflects a continuing bias toward the individual museum user; it potentially keeps users isolated and the user community fragmented and socially inert. The author Henry Jenkins[34] repeatedly warns that the new world of opportunities centers not on individual users at their devices but on the groups or communities linked and empowered by them. From this perspective Nina Simon's conception of Museum 2.0 as a "platform for participation" is more useful than "every user a hero" in highlighting the essential social dimension of the Museum 2.0 experience.

Conclusion

The world's knowledge is migrating to the open Internet. Web 2.0 tools make it available for learning and use. Tutorials and courses are available at all levels to ease learners' journeys into the worlds of knowledge. Young people are free to learn, create, exchange ideas, collaborate, and act collectively without the intervention of educational middlemen. Institutions of informal learning, including libraries and museums, are adapting to this new situation of learning and knowledge: at the informal level, Education 2.0 is coming of age.

Today's schools and colleges are also experimenting with the Internet. The next chapter explores new educational practices and policies in the attempt to discern whether or not these innovations are also building toward a new Education 2.0 paradigm.

Chapter Nine
The Web in the School

Can schools and colleges come to grips with the Internet and the World Wide Web? Can they embrace an informational paradigm and embrace Education 2.0, or are they destined to fall behind as learning migrates from entrenched institutions of higher learning to new organizations better adjusted to global network society? Having explored uses of Web 2.0 technologies in informal learning, we are ready to think about their uses in schools and colleges.

In this chapter we'll explore new developments in classrooms, new online cyber-schools, and new educational policies for integrating the Internet into educational practice. Do they move in the direction of Education 2.0 by suspending the factory paradigm's assumptions? Or do they remain trapped by outmoded hierarchical structures and practices?

Let's start with another question: why *haven't* schools, like museums and libraries and other vehicles for informal learning, already taken up Web 2.0? Will Richardson, one of the leaders of the Classroom 2.0 movement, has been leading the way for a decade. He notes that a consensus has formed among influencers, from the MacArthur Foundation to the National School Board Association, that social web tools now have essential roles in learning. The National Council of Teachers of English includes Web 2.0 literacies among its proposed standards, including "building relationships with others to pose and solve problems collaboratively" and "designing and sharing information for global communities." Richardson says that now kids are expected to be savvy editors, collaborators, and co-creators, who can learn anytime, anywhere, and follow their own passions in building personal learning networks. Nonetheless, he notes, schools continue to block web access and school districts refuse to consider full Web 2.0 introduction to their classrooms. Richardson asks, rhetorically, what stops teachers from including these potential learning enhancers in their own lives and introducing them, on their own, in their classrooms, to "better model and teach our students to navigate these spaces effectively."[1]

CLASSROOM 2.0

An e-learning or Classroom 2.0 movement has grown among teachers doing just as Richardson prescribes, complete with its own websites, blogs, and daily webinars. Steve Hargadon, an acknowledged leader of this movement, is thoughtful, balanced, and wide-ranging in his explorations of new possibilities for Internet use in schools. He gathers upwards of one hundred participants several times a week in the Blackboard virtual learning environment to discuss the latest web technologies and their applications.

Most of the participants are school teachers, district technology directors, and school administrators with a stake in the entrenched educational paradigm. They are bound about on all sides by the trappings of factory schooling: confining regulations, top-down standards, and standardized high-stakes tests. Q and A sessions in Classroom 2.0 seminars invariably turn to "what I can do with this information tomorrow morning in my school or classroom that is aligned with our state standards."

There are, nonetheless, already many web applications in school classrooms. Many schools, districts, and even some states have developed one-to-one laptop programs in which every student is issued a laptop computer in order to access learning software, virtual learning environments, learning management systems, and textbooks. Search engines are widely used in schools, though with restrictions; in some classrooms, a student is appointed each day as the class's Google jockey, responsible for following the lesson on Google in order to check claims and bring new content into the discussion. Teachers use Skype to connect their students with those in other schools, districts, and even foreign countries (e.g., for one-on-one language interchanges). Students use flip web cameras in classroom assignments and field trips to make documentaries about their schools and towns or about environmental conditions in their region. They use Flickr and YouTube to distribute these videos. Many teachers blog, and edublogging has attracted some superstars such as "Bud the Teacher"; teachers also involve students in blogging, for example, in units on citizen journalism in English or social studies classes. Will Richardson himself is a prominent edublogger, demonstrating the possible uses of Internet tools in classrooms.[2]

There are also many school-specific web tools. Blackboard has emerged as the major learning management platform, but faces competition from its open source rival Moodle. While Wikipedia is widely used as an information source, teachers are creating lessons, units, and entire courses—including video courses—on curriculum wikis, of which the most familiar is Curricki. Like entries on other wikis the materials on Curricki can be freely used, modified, augmented, and mashed up with other web tools to meet the local needs of any teacher, school, or district. While proprietary textbooks now are accompanied by websites open to purchasers, they are rivaled by free open source textbooks from publishing firms such as Flat World Publishing, which permit users to modify, delete, or augment the contents at will.[3] Channels for educational materials are found on YouTube; TeacherTube, a YouTube look-alike, archives thousands of teacher development and classroom demonstration videos. Many school-specific videos are also available through Curricki for unrestricted modification by any educator with video-editing software. It is hardly an exaggeration to say that if you can imagine an application of web tools in conventional schools and colleges it probably already exists.

Given the ubiquity of digital tools and hyperlinked online materials, learners, teachers, and learning groups not artificially constrained by factory school norms can be expected to move off in myriad divergent, highly personal learning directions. There may only be one right answer to an arithmetic question on a conventional test, but there is no limit to the number of worthwhile YouTube videos, blog posts, or contributions to wikis or software projects. This does not mean that "anything goes" or that reliable quality judgments cannot be made. They can, though this will require the gradual working out of criteria and training for judges. I'll have more to say about this point later.

Given its name and audience, however, Classroom 2.0 is tied to classrooms, the egg-crates that more or less *define* the old education paradigm; classrooms did not exist in either America's district or common schools; they are a modern managerial convenience unlikely to survive as the centers of learning in the global network future.

Flat Classroom and the Digiteen Project

One Classroom 2.0 approach—some would say the "real" Classroom 2.0—uses virtual learning environments to connect schools in different countries to boost educational outcomes and cultural integration. The strengths and weaknesses of this approach are well illustrated by Flat Classroom, a project cofounded in 2006 by Vicki Davis (Westwood Schools in the United States) and Australian Julie Lindsay (now working in Beijing, China). The project, to cite its website, "uses Web 2.0 tools to support communication and interaction as well as collaboration and creation between students and teachers from classrooms around the world."

The programs of Flat Classroom aim to develop "a deeper understanding of the effects of technology on our world that leads students to not only study but actually experience" the "flattening" impact of network technologies. The students are grouped with global partners in paired classrooms to explain trends, give personal viewpoints, and create videos containing outsourced video segments from their global classroom partners. They have access to an educational network, blogging, posting photos, videos, and a wiki, to plan their topic and build a web page on the topic, and are assessed on a common, criterion-based rubric. The videos they produce are finally reviewed by a global panel of judges.

Flat Classrooms is a good model to use in discussions of Classroom 2.0 for several reasons. First, while it cannot be claimed to be "typical" of Classroom 2.0 (we don't yet have enough examples or data to say that any example is typical), it is a frequently cited model. Second, its aims and defining features—collaborative learning within a flat, networked structure; the use of social networks, blogs, video platforms and the like—resonate with the Web 2.0 uses envisioned by leaders like Richardson. Third, several leading experts on web-based learning, including Vicki Davis herself, have suggested it as a useful model for discussion. Finally, it has won many high-profile awards for web-based educational innovation. Its selection is thus not arbitrary.

Flat Classroom sponsors a number of programs. I'll focus on Digiteen, a global learning project on digital citizenship for middle and high school youth. The program starts by linking classrooms in separate countries. The students get to know one another through a dedicated social network and videoconferencing. Then they collaborate in learning about digital citizenship, studying issues like personal online safety, digital security and privacy, netiquette, digital rights and responsibilities, the psychology of digital network use, laws governing intellectual property, and the basics of digital commerce. The students are presented with background information and selected videos on each of these issues. Then students research the issues further in their own classrooms and exchange research results with their global partners. Finally students in each classroom make videos demonstrating their learning results. Using video cameras and video-editing programs, they produce video clips and exchange them with the global partners through blogs, social networks, and videoconferencing. Eventually each class produces a final cut of the videos, incorporating some of its partner's clips.

There is obviously much to like in Digiteen. The program uses new educational technologies, conveys much useful information, fosters collaboration, helps in building global awareness, and provides capability building in new digital tools.

There are also some drawbacks. First, the setup does not make free use of the learningweb. The students do not cast their own nets far and wide. Unlike Linus Torvalds or Tavi Gevinson, they do not post on user groups or blogs saying "Hey, we're making a video about digital issues like child safety and intellectual property. Here are some of our first clips. Hope you can use them. Can you send along anything that might help, no matter how small?" Instead, the assignment of global partners is top-down. So from the get-go Digiteen learners are constrained by hierarchical arrangements.

Second, along similar lines, the two groups of global partners encounter each other only in classrooms shaped by the same transnational classroom paradigm. While the youngsters from the two groups live in otherwise different cultures, the culture of the classroom is the same. This profoundly limits Digiteen as a context for awareness of multicultural diversity.

Third, the curricular materials presented up front in each classroom about each digital issue are carefully selected and organized in advance to shape an approved viewpoint on digital citizenship. Students do not freely discuss personal safety issues and come to their own conclusions: they are told up front that the Internet is a dangerous place. They do not discuss intellectual copyright issues; they are told up front how ethically wrong and legally risky it is to use copyrighted files. This viewpoint is baked into the prespecified learning objectives of the program derived from curriculum standards for digital literacy.

These predetermined learning objectives compromise the research done by the students. In practice, their search is limited to materials supporting the approved viewpoint. Imagine instead that students were prodded to find materials asserting multiple viewpoints, for example, that the dangers of the Internet are overblown or that the current intellectual property regime is an unethical power grab by big multinational media conglomerates that bankroll corrupt legislators, a point of view that would undermine ethical obligations to comply with copyright laws. Given Internet norms prevailing in the youth culture, some young people in an intellectually open environment would surely accept such claims and incorporate them in their videos. Genuine research involves thinking about information materials. Thinking is selecting and organizing materials to make arguments and support conclusions. If Digiteen's objectives include learning that the Internet is dangerous and that use of copyrighted materials is unethical and risky, it closes down thinking about the issues it addresses; the conclusions are already baked in.

We can compare Digiteen with a more completely networked approach to digital citizenship where students used the web to self-organize for learning. This would not imply there would be no roles for teachers or that anything goes. Every successful learning program builds in definite constraints so that efforts don't fly off in all directions at once. So, teachers may pose initial questions but students could also network to dialogue about their own questions. Some resources may be suggested, but students could also search and exchange materials freely. Potential global partners may be arranged, but students could also self-organize to find additional partners for collaborative products. Product criteria may be suggested for consideration, but students would also be encouraged to assess video clips and their final cuts by their own explicit or tacit criteria.

These concerns about Digiteen are not merely abstract. The videos made by learners in the project have a "goody-goody" feel. They express the approved viewpoint: don't talk to strangers online, don't use copyrighted files, don't surf the Internet in school unless the teacher tells you to. This may (or may not) be good digital citizenship. But as they are the polar opposite of current global youth norms and beliefs, it is reasonable to conclude that the videos result from the program's structure, not from the creative expression of its participants. Digiteen students are learning to use the web and make videos but also to comply with hierarchical classroom dictates.

These criticisms are not meant to fault Vicki Davis, Flat Classrooms, or Digiteen. Davis is an innovative educator and her programs are as good as we are likely to get so long as educational uses of Web 2.0 remain confined within the factory school paradigm.

Web 2.0 and Virtual Schools

What about so-called virtual or cyber-schools? These have brought the entire process of schooling online, and they bear watching because, according to Clayton Christiansen, an influential thinker on organizations and innovation, such virtual schools and classrooms are likely to account for 50 percent of US secondary education by 2019.[4] Indeed this estimate may err on the conservative side; the state of Idaho has introduced a statewide digital learning academy that now pipes online courses into every school in the state. We might expect to see more fundamental change in the virtual or cyber-schools established specifically to take advantage of the new Web 2.0 possibilities. When we examine model cyber-schools, however, we find that despite their innovations in technology and space utilization, they still rely on age-grading, (virtual) egg-crating, predetermined curriculum, and standardized tests; they remain tightly bound by the factory school paradigm.[5]

Among the most radical, future-directed of these schools is the Online High School of Utah, directed by the visionary David Wiley.[6] OHSU opened its doors in 2009 to its first freshman class. The school's mantra is "focus on student learning and outsource everything else." Wiley's central idea is that schools, in addition to instructional tasks, are burdened by a number of others: financial management and accounting, government relations, grant management, public relations, facilities management, technology management, union relations, and more.[7] No individual school and few districts can afford full-time staff members dedicated to each of these specialized functions. Thus the functions are bundled together in the job descriptions of school personnel without expertise in any of them. OHSU outsources each of these tasks to specialized strategic partners in Utah,[8] for example, Agilix for its GoCourse Learning Management System, and DirectPointe Technology for laptop distribution and maintenance for each child. Wiley says,

> Partnerships with specialized organizations allow OHSU to become an organization that specializes in supporting and improving student learning—and that is the primary goal of the school. The cost savings and increased efficiencies of this model will likely become attractive to many schools in the future, whether brick and mortar or virtual, and whether traditional public, charter, or private.[9]

The school staff accordingly handles nothing but instruction. The school is committed to an "open curriculum philosophy," using open access tools exclusively:

open source software for its virtual learning environments and its learning management system, open access textbooks from such publishers as Flat World Knowledge (where Wiley is editorial director), and curriculum materials from open source providers such as Curricki and the various open courseware (OCW) projects of, for example, MIT, Carnegie Mellon, and Yale.

In the organization's charter documents, OHSU founders committed the school to using open educational resources *exclusively* throughout the entire curriculum. Open educational resources are educational materials that have been licensed in a way that follows the open content philosophy and can therefore freely (at zero cost) and legally (in full compliance with copyright law) be copied, changed, and shared.[10]

OHSU employs only a director (principal), an open curriculum development staff, and licensed teachers. In addition to producing (and retrofitting) curriculum materials and courseware for the school, the curriculum developers and teachers also make their home-grown or modified materials available through open source licenses to other schools throughout the world. The school retains a commitment, however, to sequenced curriculum and state curriculum standards. Its curriculum developers "take open educational resources as a starting point, go through a state standards curriculum alignment and gap analysis process, create missing pieces, and then assemble complete, coherent online courses."[11]

Wiley emphasizes that in disaggregating and shedding school functions, OHSU retains within its organizational boundary all *instructional* services. It is imaginable, however, that cyber-schools would also choose to outsource some or all of these services to "online instructional firms" or "educational consultants" working either as stand-alone professionals or as associates of strategic partner firms. These arrangements could provide schools with instructors possessing state-of-the-art skill sets in cyber-education, a significant advantage over certified teachers whose training was geared to physical classrooms in brick-and-mortar schools. Depending upon how such providers structured their services, advantageous roles might be found for instructors lacking teacher certificates (and union affiliation).[12] Such markets or network partners might make writers, artists and musicians, scientists, engineers, and craftsmen available to provide attractive course options in art, science, and technology education.

Even if based in the home state, network partners might still provide access to educational professionals from global markets or global strategic partners of their own. It is instructive to note that the Pennsylvania Cyber Charter School

(PA Cyber), a charter cyber-school similar to OHSU in some respects, outsources almost all instructional services to strategic partners, while the Michigan Virtual School employs one hundred part-time but only two full-time teachers.[13]

To what extent do OHSU and similar virtual or cyber-schools break from or adhere to the factory school paradigm? (1) The schools remain fundamentally age-graded, because its subject matters are structured by standards tied to annualized age-graded courses (e.g., sequenced high school courses such as algebra and physical science in grade 9, geometry and biology in grade 10, etc.); (2) while deviating from the standard delivery of instruction, the egg-crate classroom pattern remains; (3) in many cyber-schools, a single certified professional teacher directly employed by the school is assigned to each course; (4) subject matter remains organized into predetermined, presequenced curricula; (5) didactic methods—for example, lectures, discussions, and student work sheets—continue to prevail; (6) work continues to be assessed by tests of the curricular subject matters; and (7) the predominant aim remains the acquisition of basic academic skills and disciplines. In short, despite differences in the technology and space utilization, such virtual schools remain tightly controlled by the hierarchical or factory paradigm.

Emerging Policy for Internet Use in Education

To date, Classroom 2.0 and cyber-schools remain captive to the hierarchical paradigm. Are policy elites now rethinking this commitment? We can get a glimpse of their thinking by examining policy documents now emerging from Barack Obama's White House and Arne Duncan's Department of Education.

The policy report, *Transforming American Education: Learning Powered by Technology* (*TAE*), was commissioned by Congress and presented to the Obama White House in 2011. The authors, all noted experts on educational technology, based their recommendations on interviews with policy leaders in the Department of Education and the White House Office of Science and Technology Policy to assure conformity with the "priorities, goals, and insights" of policy elites. Laced with inspirational quotes from President Obama and Secretary Duncan, the report is a clear window into current policy thinking. Education visionary Will Richardson claims the report's endorsement of Web 2.0 in classrooms stands in stark opposition to its main policy initiative, Race to the Top, which features top-down standards and heavy use of high-stakes tests.[14] Is he right? Are our policy elites finally dropping the factory paradigm and embracing the Internet as an instrument for educational transformation?

Perhaps there is reason to hope. In an open letter to teachers in May 2011, Duncan writes, "Working together, we can transform teaching from the factory model designed over a century ago to one built for the information age."[15] Unfortunately, a close look at the report shows that policy makers and their expert consultants still cannot see beyond a hierarchical approach to learning and schooling, even when embracing digital technologies.[16]

The introduction to *Transforming American Education* calls boldly for "revolution not evolution"; it sets out to "rethink basic assumptions" and "redesign the system" and implement "fundamental changes" (x).[17] The language of "design and implement" runs throughout the report. The idea that a complex system like public education can be planned and controlled, designed and implemented, however, is one of those "basic assumptions" of the industrial era that needs to be re-thought, a point to which I will return shortly.

Despite this revolutionary rhetoric, the authors say they accept the *purposes* of the present system and seek only to change the *means* for achieving them. This doesn't sound like fundamental change, because paradigm change challenges entrenched purposes. Did Jefferson agree with King George about basic purposes of government? Did Galileo agree with the Church about the basic purposes of science? Did the French Impressionists agree with the Academy about the basic purposes of art? New paradigms overturn accepted ends and means.

In the event, the language of "revolution" is rapidly dropped and the report returns to tired claims about education as "key to economic growth," so that in our "competitive world" we want to retain our status as "number one." We need a "productive" system with "seamlessly integrated" components for "maximum efficiency" in meeting specified learning objectives. "Every learner" must graduate from high schools with world-class standards, and 60 percent must complete college. Is this back to the future, or forward to the past?

Transforming American Education vs. Education 2.0 and the Learningweb Revolution

Let's compare the proposed reforms of the Obama administration with Education 2.0—the informational paradigm suggested by the shifts we find in informal education (in Library and Museum 2.0), for example, the shift from central control to networked user autonomy.

The policy report offers a high-tech central control model for education, a mere technical updating of the hierarchically organized factory school. On its educational vision, national standards will generate standardized goals, objectives, and twenty-first-century competencies. Assessment will be narrowly limited to measuring the attainment of specified learning objectives, preventing the use of the new digital tools for unpredicted significant learning.

Education 2.0, on the other hand, conceives education as initiation—it rejects the scholastic and narrowly reductive aims of the entrenched system, just as Horace Mann and the common school leaders moved beyond the purposes of the district schools of seventeenth-century Puritan New England, and Benjamin Franklin rejected those of the colonial liberal arts colleges. In light of new powers distributed to individuals and groups by the new tools, the learningweb revolution, as framed by visionaries like Will Richardson and Alan Gauntlet—and by Curtis Bonk and Judy Breck, whose views we consider in the next chapter—reconceives education as preparation for effective performance in worthwhile adult activities in global network society. It thoroughly rejects the idea of education as the industrial production of prespecified individual learning objectives. The revolution aims to enhance citizens in their individual and collective fitness for living. This aim cannot be met through packages of standard learning objectives. It requires thousands of hours of learning experiences that channel learners' unique interests and passions and connect learners to situations of adult life.[18]

Learning

Transforming American Education sees the new digital technologies as tools for enhancing school learning. Acknowledging that kids with access already use them widely and in creative ways outside of school, it notes that they can't now use them in school because the curriculum has not been reshaped to incorporate them and schools constrain their use due to safety and privacy concerns. Poor kids in poor districts, moreover, don't have access to the new digital tools in school or out. Thus the report offers a new approach that "seamlessly integrates" in- and out-of-school learning. Schools need to offer broadband Internet and digital devices, as well as course choices to get kids engaged and prevent them from dropping out. At least 60 percent should earn a tertiary diploma.

The report proposes that curriculum contents be reorganized around national curriculum standards and translated into specific learning objectives including new twenty-first-century competencies, emphasizing the science, technology, engineering, and mathematics complex (STEM). The report pictures a technologically rich curriculum grounded in new sciences of learning.

Education 2.0 by contrast conceives learners as autonomous, autopoetic (self-shaping), emergent individuals already motivated to learn by goals inherent in their biological and cultural conditioning. Significant learning, on this view, is not attaining ready-made learning objectives; the significance of each learning experience is shaped by the learners' own ways of making sense of their own experience.

Educators in this new paradigm thus don't have to motivate learning. Learners are readily engaged in experiences that they personally relate to, and they learn continuously from them. Educators can be useful insofar as they establish conditions where learners' already present motivations can be leveraged to enhance subsequent learning power. In general, learner motivations are not mysterious: they include the desire, for example, to act autonomously, to feel capable, to be recognized as valuable, to learn what they think of as useful for future tasks and responsibilities, to belong to groups and share with other members, and more generally to be moving toward the good life as they see it by gaining resources and capabilities to create it.

The new technologies provide limitless means for tapping into these motivations: to learn a program like Photoshop makes one feel more capable and enables one to create products that others can use and admire. Facebook helps young people make friends and communicate with them. Developing high-tech skills in general makes young people feel better about themselves and their abilities to achieve their goals.

Because these tools are readily learned through social exchange and ubiquitous online video tutorials, kids who have access to the tools learn to use them quickly without instruction. Twenty-first-century professionals pick up these capabilities in the same ways and for the same reason: because the tools serve their purposes. Teachers and learners are no different: they use the tools out of school because they are useful; they don't use these tools in school because the tools don't link to opportunities presented in these tightly controlled environments.

Nothing assures this failure to connect tools and needs better than the steady diet of ready-made, predigested standard school content, objectives, and competencies. Learningweb revolutionaries see prespecified learning objectives in school as existing largely to fill time in a controlled environment. They appeal to the motivations of bureaucrats for preplanning and control but are deadly to most young people.

Learningweb revolutionaries argue that we won't need any new learning sciences to guide our practices. The conclusions from learning science cited in *TAE*—that different parts of the brain control different kinds of learning—sound like a twenty-first-century version of phrenology. The trend in recent brain studies has been quite the opposite: that the brain and its cell masses are very plastic and that significant learning and knowledge use involves the whole brain, not isolable parts. Only learning reduced to objectives and competencies is likely to draw on isolable areas of the brain.

Learningweb revolutionaries thus recommend that instead of thinking about school content in terms of standards and learning objectives, we think of it instead in terms of its demonstrable contributions to concrete lives in their social contexts, to initiation in worthwhile adult activities. Forget about the so-called new learning sciences; they have little to teach us once we drop the reductive, specified learning objectives approach to content. Instead, follow the exciting new developments in the neurosciences more broadly to discover the amazing potentials of young people. Make sure that digital tools are broadly and equitably distributed. Free teachers from constraints to experiment with new approaches connected to existing learner motivations. Use information management systems to track results of teacher experiments and circulate them to other teachers, not to manage a lifelong data trail for individual students.

Assessment

Transforming American Education remains wedded to the measurement of learning objectives, asserting merely that we need more up-to-date objectives, in particular "21st century competencies" and new and better ways to measure them. The report has a throwaway line about possible learning activities that lie "beyond" specified learning objectives, but it never again mentions such activities. Instead, continuous measurement-based assessment is proposed to provide actionable feedback throughout instruction to improve performance on subsequent learning objectives.

The main use of new digital technologies, for the policy authors, is to generate feedback to improve learning and motivate students. This feedback is then to be tied right back to the preexisting analytical frameworks; student learning still must be analyzed against fixed assessment standards. Those assessing student performances cannot respond to them as unique wholes, but only as they can be analyzed to conform to checklists of prespecified learning objectives.

Finally, the report insists on a national definition of learning standards so that measurements across different municipalities, states, and regions can produce data for analysis and feedback for continuous improvement. This policy would require changes in state and federal regulations to permit the collection and storage of a lifelong data trail for individuals while protecting their privacy rights.

Education 2.0, by contrast, denies that the most important results of learning are analyzable and measurable. What matters most lies beyond analysis and measurement because it is *emergent*.[19] Evaluating emergent wholes in terms of their parts gets things backwards. Poems and drawings provide simple examples, but human achievements of all kinds can be understood along the same lines. Poems are made out of words with preexisting meanings; drawings are made from color patches with independent visual properties. However, the placement and interaction of words in poems, and color patches in drawings, create new wholes. While the poems and drawings depend on their preexisting parts, they are more than the sum of these parts—and the meanings of their parts are dependent upon their unique positions in those wholes: the words take on new senses and the colors new visual impacts. The same applies to performances in the sciences and humanities: their properties are emergent in the same way. Art, science, or humanities products—the things properly conceived of as academic achievements when not blinded by such spurious pseudo-achievements as learning objectives and test scores—involve selection and placement of parts in new relationships and attending to the interactive effects. Each of these is a new creation, not predicable from or reducible to the parts. Producing these achievements is not a matter of using standard parts in standard ways to get a standard product that can be assessed against a checklist of standard criteria. Rather, these productions draw on unique personal experiences, interactions with others engaged in similar pursuits, and persistent experimentation and self-determined learning leading to unique creative insights of individuals or collaborative groups. This is precisely what the new digital tools facilitate and Education 2.0 accentuates.

With compulsory learning objectives and high-stakes measurements, learning will always be organized to achieve the measurable, not what lies beyond it. By contrast, Education 2.0 emphasizes informed and competent human judgments of particular projects and performances by those on the scene, not test scores, to generate actionable feedback geared to individual learners. Such feedback is shaped not to improve scores on tests but to improve individual capabilities and fitness. The primary mode of evaluation is thus authentic assessment; standard academic assessments play a very subordinate role.[20]

Teaching

TAE authors and learningweb revolutionaries agree that the new digital tools make many new things possible and that these tools must be made accessible to all learners. They also agree that the tools make it possible to end teacher isolation and to usher in a new era of teacher innovation, exchange, and collaboration. The differences, however, are stark.

TAE claims that a technology gap exists between teachers and professionals in other fields, creating a paucity of tech-savvy teachers. The report calls on teacher training programs to train teachers to use the new tools. The report laments teachers' lack of commitment to data collection, assessment, and utilization, to "evidence-based teaching." It calls on colleges of education to generate lifelong personal learning networks powered by the new digital technologies to inculcate "scientific attitudes" about teaching throughout the profession and to prompt teachers to embrace new high-tech digital classrooms. Teachers, the report insists, must use knowledge about students derived from formative assessment to improve achievement of standardized goals, objectives, and competencies. This is the factory model with a vengeance.

Education 2.0 sees the technology gap quite differently. Individuals readily master the new digital tools by themselves or from friends and colleagues when they see good uses for them. Other professionals—doctors, lawyers, financial advisors—do not learn to use digital technologies in professional school classrooms; they learn them on the fly, as needed. If professionals adopt the tools in their work, and students adopt them outside of school, while neither teachers nor students adopt them in school, the problem must lie in the school context rather than in the training or capabilities of teachers or students. There is no technology gap in the teaching profession, only in the schooling context. The new technologies will only be adopted by educators when the educational context changes to make their abundant and creative use necessary and beneficial. To promote Internet use for learning, we need to shift to Education 2.0 and open learning up—free it from predetermined learning objectives and free teaching to respond to the evolving needs of learners in the learningweb.

When students use the new digital tools in creative ways, teachers will need all of the resources at their disposal just to keep up. They will form their own personal learning networks based on their own affinities and are likely to eschew those imposed in a top-down fashion. They will learn or invent new and unpredicted teaching strategies, alone or in collaboration with local or online colleagues. All of this is already happening without any top-down pressure from state policy or colleges of education, as teachers experiment with the web.

Conclusion

Classroom 2.0, cyber-schools, and government policies for educational technology utilization have not yet grasped the full potential of the Internet to transform education. They remain stuck in the old factory school model. In this section we have anticipated a new network learning paradigm to replace the factory school. In Part III we develop this complexity-based network paradigm for the learningweb, outline the structure of "open networked learning centers" as successor institutions to today's schools, and provide some illustrative examples of programs in these learning centers.

Part Three
Education 2.0:
A Network Paradigm for Education

CHAPTER TEN
NEW EDUCATIONAL VISIONS

The factory school has outlawed or narrowly confined the learningweb. Some Education 2.0 visionaries, meanwhile, have already shown how education can give up failed efforts to retrofit the Internet to the factory school and engage with the web on its own terms. The Internet, as these visionaries see it, can free learners like Tavi Gevinson and Jayralin Herrera and others from teachers, normative curricula, fixed time schedules, and enclosed classroom spaces. Mobile devices such as laptops and smartphones permit people to learn anywhere, at anytime, from anyone.

Curtis Bonk and Judy Breck, two of the most penetrating of these "ubiquitous learning" visionaries, offer many suggestive ideas as starting points in thinking through new possibilities. In this chapter, after sharing some of their most suggestive and useful ideas, I argue that their visions still remain too abstract as they stand to guide educational development in the Web 2.0 era. They are views from the mountaintop of the new education, but do not yet bring us to the promised land of a new educational paradigm. Our immediate goal is to understand and critique these visions. In the following two chapters we build on them to formulate concrete goals for the learningweb revolution that can be reached by taking specific action steps.

Curtis Bonk: Mobile Visionary

Curtis Bonk has been everywhere, seen everything, and met everyone in the web-based learning space, and his book, *The World Is Open*, documents everything he has learned. Bonk summarizes these lessons in ten trends opening up education today; these "openers" are in his view creating a new educational situation where everyone will be able to learn anything from anyone at any place and time. They include e-books, open source software, open access textbooks, open courseware, web reference works and repositories, and online learning communities.

Bonk's Education 2.0 Vision

We have already discussed these trends in earlier chapters. Bonk reflects on these and makes a number of predictions about the various educational commonplaces that come together in a grand vision for Education 2.0.

Regarding *learners,* Bonk predicts that those now excluded from the Web 2.0 world will gradually all be included; that personalized learning will largely replace conventional curriculum-based learning; that learners will document learning outcomes with personal portfolios of blogs, videos, and information products, not test results; that learners will form personal networks with colearners from around the world; and that a new culture of learning will emerge, placing a high value on individuals dedicated to learning.

Regarding *teachers,* he predicts that teachers of many types, for many kinds of subject matters, will make themselves available at all hours, for both young and older people; that teacher sharing of educational resources, materials, curricula, and courseware on the open Internet will be the expected norm; and that teachers skilled in guiding e-learning—super e-mentors—will emerge as a distinct professional group.

Regarding *educational settings,* he predicts that high bandwidth access points for mobile learning will exist everywhere; that many kinds of blended learning settings will emerge, combining online, face to face, on-site, and mobile experience; that this learning will be packaged in new kinds of courses and diploma programs; that learning will become self-determined, chosen and directed by learners; and that the lines separating workplaces, learning spaces, entertainment spaces, and homes will disappear as work time *becomes* learning time and vice versa.

Regarding *assessment,* he predicts that the focus of learning will shift from instructor-based academic content to authentic problem solving and product making, requiring a shift from test-based academic assessment to authentic assessment in real-world settings.

Regarding *policy,* he predicts that governments will respond to popular demands for increased access to free education so that fee-free learning zones will proliferate.

Regarding *aims,* he predicts that a new breed of high-powered Aristotle-like individuals with mastery of the world's knowledge will emerge. Their mastery will consist in various combinations of generalist grasp of the map of knowledge; broad knowledge in specific fields; and search, retrieval, and interpretation skills. Their existence in large numbers will inaugurate "a new age of learning" and "a new age of being human."

Because Bonk's vision converges in many ways with Breck's, I'll wait until I've outlined her vision before discussing it.

Judy Breck: Handschooling Visionary

While Curtis Bonk has gone everywhere and seen everything about new web-based learning, Judy Breck has observed the same trends from one special vantage point, her homework website. Her vision is not, like Bonk's, predictive; it is philosophical and prescriptive: she tells us what we *should do,* not merely what we should *expect to see.*

Breck's main conclusions are that learning on the Internet platform is the natural way to learn; this kind of learning doesn't require either pedagogical assistance or curricular sequencing; that open access knowledge, unlike school knowledge, is organized in networks rather than hierarchies; that moving within that network, guided by the association of ideas and following ideas where they lead, is how the best thinkers and achievers learn. She urges us to stop trying to fix the schools—they are an obsolete learning platform. Instead, we should allow them gradually to fade away, while directing our efforts toward placing mobile Internet devices in the hands of all young learners for self-directed learning, an approach she labels "handschooling."

Online Learning

At homeworkcentral.com Breck created a site where students could find support materials for learning every school and college topic. She identified approximately

35,000 such topics, discovering that these do not exist under hierarchical categories (e.g., math, science, or history), as in school and college curricula, but rather are cross-linked in knowledge *networks*. A fish, for example, could be found in subnetworks of zoology, oceanography, animal behavior, culinary arts, and sports fishing. Links between these topics had already been forged by web users following associations reflecting their particular interests, and registered by search engines like Google; the web mirrors Vannevar Bush's Memex in supporting associative thought processes while leaving permanent memory traces.

In online learning, Breck notes, three networks come together: the online information network, a learner's mental network, and its underlying neural network. This meeting of networks is the basis for Brecks's big revolutionary idea: the neural and mental networks of learners are *mirrored by* the Internet—when minds interact with it, they see themselves *reflected* and thus feel "at home." Engaging with the Internet is "the natural way to learn."

High schools and colleges by contrast are organized into hierarchical departments: for example, math, biology, literature. Libraries similarly organize books by, for example, the Dewey Decimal System. These hierarchies are practical: curricula and libraries need specific places for bits and chunks of knowledge. On the web this practical problem disappears. There is no need to *place* any bit or chunk anywhere; all bits can be linked endlessly in limitless networks; knowledge is "omnidirectionally interrelated."[1]

The Natural Way to Learn

Breck contrasts static curriculum-based learning with a dynamic hyperlinked alternative that she calls "moving the center.[2] What is that? Breck notes that whenever anyone attends to *anything*, two things can happen: (1) there is a momentary flood of meanings as that awareness creates a probe of memory storage, represented in the brain as action potentials in neural networks, followed by a dropping away of attention as the observer moves on to something else, or (2) a more-than-momentary flood, as the object of attention becomes a center of consciousness. In this second case what is known and remembered about such objects is retrieved more intensively from storage (and other sources of information at hand) and connected together with the central object in a dynamic pattern of meaning and expectation.

When you add a mobile Internet to this situation, however, the entirety of human information lies ready at hand. Bits and chunks of knowledge from the

Internet combine with bits and chunks from memory and the environment in rich and expanding patterns, stimulating new questions, ideas, and patterns and leading to new inquiries and discoveries.

For Breck, the way to learn is to get interested, pay attention, follow connections, bring up lots of bits and chunks from memory, fold in knowledge and information at hand, allow new patterns to emerge of themselves, and then select and synthesize these to construct new knowledge to share. By comparison, the curricular method is tightly constrained and information poor. Teachers lead learners by the hand through predetermined knowledge pathways that (1) leave out most of the potential information at hand, (2) represent only one among the limitless ways of connecting the various bits and chunks presented, (3) have nothing whatever to do with the prior knowledge or interests or aims of any of the learners, and (4) create nothing to share.

The Natural Way to Teach

Learners do not naturally engage with knowledge as selected, shaped, and sequenced by others. An extra force of effort is required, leading to fatigue. And if on occasion the sequence contains a chunk of knowledge that *does* engage learners, what then happens? They move spontaneously to method (2) above, the moving center. They focus in and stop to think, pulling in meanings from memory storage and seeking additional knowledge or information at hand to form a pattern. They may ask a question, wish to share and exchange an idea forming in their minds, or seek additional information from sources at hand or the Internet. At that point the teacher says "now children, we must move on," pulling learners abruptly from their own thinking and learning processes. That is why school learning bores and enervates so many students, especially those most interested and engaged in learning.

Authoring an interactive, hyperlinked website, by contrast, is the natural way to teach in a network environment. Following the associations in their own minds, teachers can broaden and deepen their understanding, connecting their ideas in new ways and arriving at new meanings. Teachers can then author websites based on these associations, with many hyperlinks to related hyperlinked sites. Students can use the websites as starting points in an unpredicted journey guided by their own interests and questions; when they do so they are not moving down a preset line but creating an *aggregation*; they remain the center of learning.

Just as each dynamic pattern of ideas in our minds leaves a trace in our neural networks, each pattern of connections we make online leaves a trace. This contributes to the dual vetting process of networked knowledge. To *vet* a putative presentation of knowledge means to examine it carefully with the eyes of an expert and then to select or qualify it as worthwhile. School knowledge for Breck is secondhand; it is shaped by educational professionals to suit their preconceptions and the demands of their various constituencies. Knowledge on the web is by contrast doubly vetted by real experts.

The Grand Idea

This leads to what Breck calls "The Grand Idea" (Idea 80), which is remarkably similar to Curtis Bonk's grand idea. Aristotle, Breck says, was the last human being to absorb and synthesize in one mind all of his world's available knowledge. The library at Alexandria had all of this knowledge and more on its shelves, but it was not connected up and synthesized in one super-mind. Like the vast storehouse of knowledge generated by World War II, as viewed by Vannevar Bush, it was inert and inaccessible. Today the online knowledge sphere possesses almost all bits and chunks and organized patterns of knowledge, and every day more and more connections are forged by experts so that new patterns take shape. A contemporary equivalent of the Aristotelian mind is thus mirrored on the Internet; while this digital knowledge net is merely mechanical and cannot comprehend ideas, Breck says, our interactions with it can help us become knowledgeable and synthetic thinkers like Aristotle.

Breck's Education 2.0 Vision

For Breck, the challenge before us is adjusting today's learning situation to the virtual knowledge ecology, requiring that we break from the attitudes underlying the entrenched factory school and classroom paradigm. Schools as we know them are obsolete and cannot be fixed. It is also an error endemic to schools online: Classroom 2.0 and virtual schools with online pedagogues and conventional curricula retain the linear, sequential approach to learning that is no more natural online than off. Since the entire world of knowledge can now be placed in the hands of every learner for creative use, moreover, it is inexcusable to block most of it off and present only a small and selected remainder in a static, impersonal manner in a curriculum.

136   CHAPTER TEN

Adapting Education to the Internet Environment

If we are to stop fixing the schools, what are we to do? Breck says that in the period of mass education in the late nineteenth and early twentieth centuries educational institutions acquired many auxiliary roles beyond learning cognitive knowledge. Schools devoted themselves to nurturing and socializing children, disciplining young people, and providing space for "articulation," by which she means debating, acting, and other forms of collaboration, in addition to facilitating cognitive learning.

What role will existing schools play in the new education? Breck offers three choices. One is for schools to retain the auxiliary functions and abandon cognitive learning, morphing into community centers and leaving the young to acquire knowledge elsewhere. Breck adds that many schools appear already to have chosen this "no knowledge" option, and many young people have in turn come to rely on knowledge acquired through laptops and mobile devices for all their serious learning.

A second choice would be to transform schools into spaces for engaging with the virtual knowledge ecology. In this case, auxiliary functions of schools—socialization, discipline, articulation—would have to migrate elsewhere. But despite all the buzz about online learning, she sees no evidence that educational leaders are moving in the direction of making online knowledge the center of the school experience (concurring with our findings in Chapter Nine).

The third choice would simply be to allow schools gradually to fade away. Young people armed with mobile Internet computers would simply learn on their own or, along with their families, seek new kinds of teachers; eventually new forms of teaching-learning institutions would emerge. This third option, apparently so far off the chart, would according to Breck actually not require young people to adapt very much. Breck observes that in all her experiences as a teacher, web designer, debate coach, and education author, she has yet to meet a single child, rich or poor, who was not an active Internet user. Engagement with knowledge online, she insists, is the natural way to learn; the hyperlinked knowledge network mirrors the structure of the mind and its underlying brain. By contrast schools are artificial spaces with meager, disconnected, secondhand knowledge. Young people do not adapt naturally to them; they never have and simply cannot.

Breck prescribes this third option. As education adjusts to the Internet, it will have to "start from scratch." For her the learningweb revolution involves an institutional *rupture*. Those nations and regions with the weakest installed school base, in the Siberian steppes or the Australian outback, may develop new paradigms for learning and bypass mass higher schooling, just as nations with weak fixed telephone services have been early adopters of mobile phones. Where the schools are strong, however, educational establishments will simply stand in the path of change.[3] Curtis Bonk, in conversation, has made the same prediction.[4] To embark on our new path, Breck says, we must leave the past entirely behind.

Breck and the Educational Commonplaces

Let's look at the educational commonplaces as reinterpreted by Breck:

1. Learners. The minds and brains of learners are networks like the virtual knowledge network, so learning from direct engagement with knowledge in the Internet ecology is the natural way to learn. Online learners do not need the hand-holding or the constraints of teacher-directed, static, information-poor, curricular learning.

The elementary branches—reading, writing, and arithmetic—will in her view take care of themselves; electronic toys already have built in keyboards and calculators and there is an abundance of excellent software for learning reading, writing, and arithmetic. Kids are already teaching themselves these skills. Once learners are fourteen and older, they can learn on their own, following their own aims and mental prompts. Once they have access to Internet-based knowledge, restricting them to a few predigested and presequenced online bits and chunks—selected without regard to their interests or aims in order to protect them from adult harms—smacks of censorship, propaganda, or misplaced sentimentality.

2. Teachers. For Breck, "pedagogy" means "leading the young to learning situations and knowledge." But young people with Internet access don't need pedagogues because they don't need to be led to knowledge: it is already there in its entirety right in their hands.

The Internet has separated knowledge from pedagogical scheduling, and thus the entire notion of teaching has to be rethought (Idea 47). Most teachers today fear the wild world of the Internet and think they have to select, evaluate, and sequence bits and chunks of knowledge and then control, filter, refashion, and dish them out to learners. Search engines do this better than teachers, and they also direct learners to sites curated by the world's leading experts, who then link learners to the further knowledge they regard as the very best. Learners do not need teachers for any of these conventional tasks.

In the Internet learning environment some teachers will be learning coaches, focused on critical reasoning, thoughtful judgment, and effective presentation (Idea 61) based on the liberal arts of logic and rhetoric. Others will be website designers organizing materials as "moving centers" for learner exploration through multiple hyperlink pathways that, through reiterated linking, move outward to the entire world of knowledge. Learners and their parents may find other kinds of offline teachers useful. It is not possible to say exactly what kinds of teachers will be demanded, but learners and their parents will seek them as they need them and eventually new teaching institutions will emerge (Idea 83).

We will still need older people to nurture and socialize the young and, when necessary, to discipline them. However important they may be, Breck insists, these tasks have nothing to do with education. Once we rethink education as access to knowledge and cognitive learning, society will find many people interested in and good at these auxiliary tasks. We can, like Bonk, think of these people as "teachers," but they will be freed from responsibility for facilitating cognitive learning.

3. Subject Matters. Schools organize subject matters under hierarchical supercategories (math, science, literature, history, etc.) and sequence them in curricula. Breck agrees with Vannevar Bush that knowledge is organized not in such hierarchies but rather in a network. In general there is no inherent cognitive sequence of learning topics from the easier to the more difficult. Rather knowledge builds up in learners through aggregation; they attend, bring up mental associations, and think through connections while folding in knowledge at hand to see new patterns and construct new knowledge.

4. Settings. In Breck's handschooling paradigm the primary setting for learning is the virtual knowledge ecology itself. With mobile Internet devices the education setting is complete. Learners can engage knowledge directly and learn in the natural way.

They can learn at home, in coffeehouses or libraries, forests or seashores, or wherever they can get Internet access. Schools may reconstruct themselves as environments fully engaged with the world of knowledge online, but they have so far shown no inclination to move in this direction. Meanwhile, society will still need institutions for socializing and disciplining young people. It will also need spaces for "articulation" such as playhouses for theatrical performances and workshops for apprenticeship learning. Some schools have already abandoned serious efforts to facilitate cognitive learning and have morphed into community centers. However important they may be to society, for Breck these centers have nothing to do with education.

5. *Aims and Assessment.* For Breck, education means engaging learners in what Franklin called "philosophical" or "useful" knowledge: knowledge common to humankind, unbiased and vetted by experts. The ultimate aim of the educated person is to be, like Aristotle, the master of knowledge: someone who possesses broad general knowledge, excellent search and evaluation skills, and thought processes that can be put to creative and productive use.

When we abandon static curricula approaches to learning, standardized tests will become irrelevant. Assessment can then become authentic, that is, it can examine knowledge acquisition and use in real-world situations or close approximations.

CONVERGENCE OF EDUCATION 2.0 VISIONS

The learningweb leaders have been guided tacitly by the kinds of ideas that Judy Breck's work renders explicitly. It is not really surprising, then, that Curtis Bonk's forecasts based on recent trends in online learning overlap with Breck's prescriptions. Education 2.0, based on this convergence, will do the following:

- View teens as young adults with mature and often astounding mental and psychological capabilities, with reductive and sentimental views of teens as "adolescents" resisted.
- Place personalized, web-based learning at the center of the educational experience, with the normative curriculum playing a greatly reduced role.
- Organize learning activities around the fashioning of information products—blogs, websites, curated web exhibits, scientific reports, artistic productions—requiring fluid intelligence and cooperation, with memorization and crystallized intelligence playing a greatly reduced role.
- Make use of many kinds of teachers in differentiated roles, with personal learning mentors, web guides, and educational website designers at the center, and instructors playing a greatly reduced role.
- Make learning available 24/7 in many spaces, with classrooms and scheduled lessons playing a greatly reduced role.
- Provide a variety of formats for learning—short courses, workshops, interviews, apprenticeships and internships—and new forms for documenting achievement, with diplomas playing a reduced role.
- Aim at a combination of broad general knowledge, highly individualized expert capabilities, and mastery of the web and basic digital tools.

Some Complications and Hurdles

This new vision for education is catching on. Author Quinn Cummings has discovered, in coping with her daughter's education, that conventional schooling versus homeschooling is no longer a binary decision: no longer "either-or" but "both-and." She suspects that others will "reach the same conclusion as they adapt to new social and economic realities."

> Online classes have already become part of an extended curriculum for many students. Relevant learning experiences will originate from the large redbrick building down the street, from a recreation center downtown, from a music studio in Seattle or a lecture hall in London. As our habits evolve, it won't be homeschooling as we've known it, but it won't be brick-and-mortar schooling, either. I call it "roam schooling."

Cummings asks us to imagine high school youngsters spending a part of their days in a local brick-and-mortar school, a few afternoons a week logged into an online art history seminar taught by a grad student in Paris, and a few more in computer animation classes at the local community college, while studying web design on YouTube and meeting with a tutor at the public library for exam prep in AP chemistry. Meanwhile, they practice Spanish on Skype and take cooking lessons at a nearby restaurant on Saturday mornings. She asks, "Is this homeschooling or regular school?" Her point is that the fixed idea of the "real school" has evaporated and the idea of "homeschool" is morphing into something entirely different—into Education 2.0. To those who think it can't happen because the industrial paradigm is too deeply entrenched, Cummings points out that "the music business looked like an invincible Goliath before digital technology raised its slingshot."

According to these web learning and roam schooling visionaries, young people can be freed to move through their worlds armed with mobile devices, following their ideas where they lead and finding teachers and mentors as well as colearners as they go. They can then exchange, collaborate, and act collectively to shape their worlds. They will have in hand the entirety of the world's knowledge, as well as tutorials and expertorials to assist them in forming mature capabilities. The young can learn in a natural way rather than being force-fed a preset compulsory curriculum.

This vision offers much to build on. Knowledge is already widely available on the open Internet; the online knowledge base is already adequate for school and college learning and most research purposes, and as scholars shift from commercial to open access publication, the open knowledgeweb will move toward completion. Young web natives already possess many tools for knowledge creation, collaboration, and collective action and know how to use them. Freeing up their time from a rigid normative curriculum for self-directed solo and peer learning is in itself a big step forward. Independent web-based learning will surely play a major role in new educational arrangements.

Unanswered Questions

This enticing picture, however, leaves too many basic questions unanswered. Let's start with the picture of the revolutionary goal culture—the vision of educational commonplaces in the new paradigm—focusing on learning, teaching, subject matters, and setting.

Learning: How will learners shape their ends and choose among millions of possible valuable topics for study? While every situation offers valuable lessons, how will learners find the best among billions of possibilities? Some, like Tavi Gevinson or Mark Salzman, will discover these on their own. Others will not; as Priyasha tells us, they will need guidance and support from older students and adults. How will they avoid becoming overwhelmed? Who will guide and mentor them? If cognitive education is sharply set off from what Breck calls socialization and articulation, that is, from learning to fit into society and solve problems in contexts of knowledge use, how will learners "find themselves" and gain sponsorship for entry into society? How will they form the future adult identities that will powerfully motivate their present learning?

Teaching: Let's grant that everyone may have something valuable to teach. We still need to know how they will make it available and why they will want to—at least on a steady basis. Some knowledgeable people already freely generate periodic content, incidental to their other tasks. Others, however, will be needed for more sustained and focused contributions to the young. The Troy Exhibition website, a favorite of Judy Breck, is not just an isolated individual's hobby; it is the product of a team of paid professionals. If we want such web portals for all areas of knowledge, will we not need frameworks to encourage their creation and pay their creators—perhaps along the lines of public broadcasting?[5] Bonk and Breck agree that many new kinds of teachers will be necessary, and they will emerge to meet needs. Perhaps we can't expect them at this stage to specify exactly what kinds in detail. But some hints are necessary to guide the generation of these teachers. Curtis Bonk speaks of new super-mentors and e-learning guides. Breck identifies learning coaches to train learners in the selection and logical organization of knowledge through the liberal arts of logic and rhetoric. Neither says anything about how such teachers will be discovered or trained. Perhaps they will eventually come from teacher training colleges. Perhaps we'll find them on LinkedIn. School directors or families searching for them today will have a hard time locating them.

Educational Settings: The world and the community may be the best teachers, and young people with mobile devices can learn a lot anywhere. But most of the richest learning spaces—the shops, offices, farms, and factories—are now in private hands and closed to young people. To gain access, young people will have to gain rights of access or pass through security. Who will provide access to learning spaces? The young will need connections or new rights. How will they get them?

Such questions about the new educational visions proliferate. Bonk, Breck, and Cummings provide a few hints, at best only a rough sketch, of the learningweb goal culture—not enough to guide revolutionary action steps. To take decisive action the learningweb revolution needs a more detailed map.

TRANSITION TO THE NEW EDUCATION

Breck is right about the basic choice before us: the outmoded hierarchical path versus the open Internet learning platform. The hierarchical paradigm is no longer acceptable; we need to find our way forward to Education 2.0. Many educators, as Bonk documents, now grasp this basic fact.

Breck's strategy is to "start from scratch": equip young people with mobile devices and then allow a new infrastructure of learning to self-organize—to take shape by itself. History suggests that such *ruptural* strategies may not be realistic. Most institutional revolutions are *interstitial*, involving transition stages, not radical breaks. While new paradigm models form, new paradigm behaviors are also inserted into older institutions and undermine them, sometimes very rapidly.

Breck rejects the interstitial strategy of inserting new paradigm behaviors into the old institution, pouring new wine into old wineskins, rightly arguing that the school conventions cannot accommodate self-directed online learning and adding that schools have shown no openness to it. But shifts from the district school to the common school in the 1830s and from the liberal arts college to the research university in the 1870s followed interstitial pathways. Common school behaviors and norms infiltrated the district schools; graduate and professional programs penetrated the colleges. Leaders did not "fix" the older organizations; when anomalies could no longer be ignored, new models emerged and established leaders added new and incompatible elements into older organizations, "transforming" them into new kinds of organizations with new aims and behaviors—operating under new paradigms.

The interstitial transformation of higher education is particularly clear. New universities operating under a new paradigm—Cornell, Johns Hopkins, the land grant colleges—took shape after the Civil War when the need for professional training in scientific research, engineering, agriculture, and commerce became pressing and elites demanded and sponsored them. Harvard, the University of Pennsylvania, and other Ivy League colleges in the United States (and Oxford and Cambridge in England) accepted similar graduate and professional programs only after long resistance; but when they did so they abandoned their old liberal arts college paradigm and rapidly evolved into new organizations—research universities with professional school complexes—with new roles in the emerging industrial order. The learningweb revolution is likely to follow a similar pathway.

EDUCATION AS INSTITUTIONALIZED PRACTICE

A more fundamental problem with the sketchy models offered by many new educators is that they detach education from its institutional context. As discussed in Chapter One, institutions are adaptive tools to help people fulfill their needs, solve their problems, and attain their goals. Like all significant areas of human behavior, learning is bounded about by institutional norms: rules, laws, community conventions. You want to go out and have a conversation? You go to a coffeehouse. You want to find a book to read? You go to the library. You want wild and kinky sex? Even that is institutionalized—in red-light districts, laws regulating prostitution, and new norms of behavior in the wake of the sexual revolution.

Institutions build up around every significant area of human behavior. Whatever people want to do, institutions provide pathways and constraints—roles and positions and offices, directives and laws, sanctions and punishments. Without institutions it is almost impossible to act: too many choices, too much uncertainty, too few constraints, too little guidance or precedent. Actions have meaning only as defined by institutions. Social life without institutional norms falls into disorder and meaninglessness. This does not mean that every behavior has to be defined and regulated by law and policed by government officials. Institutions take shape in civil society, sometimes without the benefit of law, sometimes in direct opposition to it—consider ceremonies recognizing permanent bonds between gays before the question of legalizing gay marriage even arose. This example shows, institutions evolve and change.

While schools and colleges are at the heart of our educational institution today, they have not always been. Education in colonial New England was conducted largely in the family and the workshop. Puritan families were obligated to raise pious, literate, and productive children. Schooling was weakly institutionalized: school laws were undemanding and often disregarded. Colleges existed to prepare future ministers and learned professionals to read classical texts in ancient languages.

In post–Civil War society the educational institution has defined positions, generated new positions, and assigned almost everyone—doctors, lawyers, engineers, nurses, teachers, social workers, and even dropouts—to their social positions. When we speak in broad terms about "modern society," we are referring to this kind of institutional order, one shaped by the academic allocation of social positions.

Breck's definition of education as the acquisition of knowledge in the sense defined by Francis Bacon, the enlightenment, and Franklin—what has been called academic knowledge—restricts education to its cognitive dimensions. Her great breakthrough consists in showing how the web detaches cognitive knowledge from schools and colleges; knowledge in this sense is no longer "academic." By defining education in terms of cognitive knowledge, however, Breck detaches it from the related social functions of schools and colleges, what she calls socialization and articulation. In other words Breck retains something akin to the narrow sense of "education" (Chapter Two). This allows her to dismiss schools or their functional equivalents too quickly. For her, once society handles education by equipping the young with mobile web devices and dropping support for schools, it can shape new and different agencies as needed for any residual non-educational functions.

The problem is that education in the broad and primary sense—education as initiation, as bringing young people along into the worthwhile activities of a social world—*cannot* be detached from socialization and articulation. It cannot be set apart from relating with other people and gaining opportunities for adapting and adjusting cognitive knowledge to messy real-world problems. Let's consider one of Breck's examples of articulation: performing with others in theater spaces. Is this education, or is it not? Let's grant that the text of every significant play is available online, along with videos of many scenes and productions, critical commentaries, and even YouTube acting tutorials. The cognitive aspects of dramatic education are thus handled. But do we want to, or can we, divorce the cognitive tasks from learning to perform with others under direction (articulation) or socialization into the world of theater? These are intertwined dimensions of a unified dramatic education. As argued in Chapter Two, education involves close connections between "I know," "I understand," "I can do," and "I adapt and adjust." Education in dramatic literature thus requires articulation in performance spaces, and fortunately most schools have them.

Perhaps schools and colleges, in absorbing web-based learning, can morph into organizations easing these connections. Breck is right in insisting that so far they have shown no inclination to do so. But there just may be no real alternatives. We will need something *akin* to schools to bring together all of these interrelated educational functions.

Schools and colleges as we now know them may not exist in the future. If they do, they will have to adjust to the new realities, and some school and college leaders are already adjusting—think about MIT's open courseware, Flat World's open source textbooks, Harvard's shift to open access scholarly publishing, and edX. But if not, they will be replaced by other organizations ordained by new institutional norms, in a new institutional order articulating education with other institutions—cultural, political, social, and economic—to retain or restore a measure of coherence to social life. Some of these may be, like the Harvard or the University of Pennsylvania of the 1870s, older organizations that have been transformed to function under a new paradigm.

Any new educational arrangements will have to articulate with other emerging institutions in a postmodern, postindustrial institutional order. Their routines will have to correspond with the expectations of information society in the same way factory school norms, as demonstrated by Robert Dreeben, corresponded with those of industrial society. Open networked learning—roam schooling—is not in itself a helpful guide in rearing and nourishing the young, because in itself it is not a new set of norms but more like a mere rejection of older norms, and thus cannot be made into an institution or adjusted to other institutions in a social order. The Internet has done a lot of things, but it has not yet nullified Sociology 101.

Bonk and Breck, despite their suggestive and even brilliant ideas, leave us with more constructive work to do. Their predictions and prescriptions do not yet offer a usable new paradigm, for by definition a paradigm is an idea suitable for embodiment in concrete organizations that become normative models. Without a sufficiently clear ground plan there can be no concrete embodiments to serve as obligatory models, hence no new paradigm.

In the next two chapters I develop a conception of Education 2.0 as a more concrete goal culture for the learningweb revolution, focusing on the complex network organizations we need to replace hierarchical factory schools and on the open learning centers that will take their place.

CHAPTER ELEVEN
COMPLEX ORGANIZATIONS

> If the property of complexity could somehow be transformed into visible brightness so that it would stand out more clearly to our senses, the biological world would become a walking field of light compared to the physical world.... Human beings would stand out like blazing suns of complexity, flashing bursts of meanings to each other through the dull night of the physical world between. We would hurt each other's eyes!
> —John Radar Platt (1918–1992), professor
> of physics, University of Chicago

COMPLEXITY EXPLAINED

The visions of Curtis Bonk, Judy Breck, and other learningweb revolutionaries are, as they stand, too open-ended to generate a concrete "goal culture" for the learningweb revolution. We need to replace the "anyone armed with web access-learning-anything-from-anyone-anytime-anywhere" vision with a more concrete conceptual model—one suitable for embodiment in real-world educational organizations articulated with the emerging institutions of global network society.

Complexity theory can guide the development of this model.[1] Complexity suggests itself as a useful heuristic as it offers an alternative to hierarchy; it abandons the failed attempts to solve educational problems by industrial logic—the top-down control of predetermined means to predictable ends. Some wit put it this way: networked complexity replaces "Ready, Aim, Fire" with "Ready, Fire, Aim!" It explains how reasonable actors can start with little more than an intuition grounded in experience, take action even without a clear aim, and harvest the positive results continually while at the same time adjusting and modifying their aims. Complexity indicates how we can transform static organizations like today's schools into dynamic new networked organizations like RAND and ARPA—and Google and Amazon—operating in "perpetual beta."

Renouncing industrial age, means-to-an-end logic, complexity addresses the maintenance of orderly, effective process in information-rich environments where significant interactions and viral feedback loops make it impossible—either in principle or as a practical matter—to predict or control organizational behavior. By specifying necessary constraints on spontaneity to prevent such systems from flying into disorder, complexity theory helps us set limits on an "everything goes" vision when we move beyond the factory paradigm.[2]

Complexity Theory

The first step on our side excursion into complexity theory is to define some key terms and relate them to education.[3] In complexity theory a *system* is a set of interacting parts behaving as a whole and distinguishable from an *environment* by identifiable boundaries. The system's way of acting, its *function*, depends upon the nature and arrangement of the parts. Because parts *interact*, they are referred to as *actors* or *agents*. Systems may include *diverse types* of agents, who follow similar or different *rules or strategies*. The pattern of interactions among the parts determines the system's *structure*. In a *top-down* structure characteristic of twentieth-century hierarchical industrial factory organizations, the primary interactions involve *directives* from higher positions in a hierarchy to those below, and *reports* from lower positions to those above. *Restructuring* a system means changing its interaction patterns.

A school can be conceived of as a system, with agents including students, teachers, and administrators of various types, employing various strategies in their interactions to meet their explicit and tacit goals, including both system goals like learning algebra or history and personal goals like obtaining competence, belonging to a group, or preserving self-esteem. The behavior of the school itself depends on these interactions among agents. The structure of the school is determined by its patterns of interaction. Restructuring the school would involve creating new interaction patterns, for example, moving from top-down hierarchy to a network pattern with many significant interactions among peers.

A system is then said to be *complex* to the extent that there are *strong interactions* among the parts, where strong interactions are by definition those that significantly influence the probability of future events in the system or its environment. Interactions in a system are likely to be strong to the extent that they involve many and diverse agents following diverse rules or strategies. Young learners are more likely to change behaviors after interacting with new and unusual peers operating by different sets of personal rules than by interacting with peers just like themselves; consider the impact stylish urban black youngsters can have on the behaviors of students in a previously all-white suburban school. The first and most significant feature of complex systems is this: *the stronger the interactions, the more difficult it is to interpret, predict, or control the system.* In *complex adaptive systems* agents seek to adapt to changing conditions in the system or environment to achieve their goals. *Complex human systems* are all inherently adaptive.

Schools, like other hierarchies, are human systems with great inherent complexity. Many types of students and staff can potentially interact in unpredictable but powerful ways. But factory schools are organized to dampen complexity by blocking many potentially significant interactions. Teachers interact with other teachers, but their behaviors are largely scripted by top-down directives, so their exchanges in the teachers' room or around the water cooler are not likely to be in the relevant sense "significant," altering their teacher behaviors very much. Students interact strongly in halls and cafeterias, but classroom interactions are sharply curtailed to simplify classroom management.

Historically, *leadership* has attempted to reduce complexity in the system to maintain control. Charles Perrow (1977), exploring unexpected technological crises such as the Three Mile Island nuclear accident, however, speculated that high technology systems are inherently complex and hence incapable of control. In the 1990s a new idea of a "complex organization" evolved, one that embraces the impossibility of control and adapts to change by releasing instead of suppressing inherent organizational complexity, then harnesses the values resulting from the self-organizing processes to enhance organizational fitness.

Self-Organization

Many leading philosophers and economists since the eighteenth century have been fascinated by the phenomenon of "spontaneous order."[4] The idea is straightforward enough: the spontaneous, undirected actions of local agents, possessing local knowledge and acting in accordance with local rules, can often generate more orderly and effective behavior of a system than top-down control. Consider a flock of birds. The breathtaking flocking patterns are not determined by any overall "flock-mind," some super-intelligence imposed on all the individual birds. Rather, the patterns result "of themselves" as each bird adjusts its distance from those on its side and front, based, that is, on perception of the local environment, in accordance with hardwired behavioral rules. When agents interact following *local rules and strategies,* they are said to display *self (as distinct from imposed) organization.*

In schools, teachers seek to control learner behavior by preventing interactions: "stay in your seats," "don't talk to your neighbors." But they sometimes loosen control to tease out latent capabilities in the classroom. In *To Sir with Love,* the Sidney Poitier character throws the textbook in the wastebasket, agrees to treat the students as adults, and frees them to determine through their interactions what they want to learn. His hope, eventually fulfilled, is that by his shift into a "guide on the side" his students will learn valuable life lessons he can't teach in a top-down fashion. He is banking on the self-organizing capabilities of his classroom as an organization.

Control Parameters and Phase Transitions

Complexity theory studies self-organizing systems, seeking to understand how order can emerge of itself. Some features of the system, labeled the system's *control parameters,* are considered basic; these include the *number and diversity of interacting agents and strategies* and the *rate of flow of information* circulating in the system. Changes in these parameters affect the stability of systems and can prompt what complexity theorists call *phase transitions,* or transitions from one qualitative phase of behavior to another, such as a shift from order to disorder or back.

In schools, students from diverse ethnic and language groups and social classes can strain the one-size-fits-all logic of a curriculum. In changing neighborhoods, the increasing diversity of students in local schools can outstrip the pace of curriculum readjustment and behavioral management. The interactions of the groups can lead to unpredicted new behaviors and aims that strain established practices. With strong in-group identifications characterizing each of several new student groups, tensions can burst into hostile conflicts. These changes can push a school into a *phase transition*; a tense equilibrium can unpredictably fly into disorder. Similarly, a school may attempt to keep a tight lid on unpleasant and disruptive information, such as the impending dismissal of a popular teacher, but the grapevine can rapidly spread incendiary rumors and undermine order.

In large complex organizations we cannot expect order to be maintained entirely through the self-organizing activities of workers at lower levels. The leadership function remains essential, though it no longer takes the form of behavioral control. Leaders establish the working context and governing principles of the organizations, and they coordinate the numerous activities flowing spontaneously from distinct work groups. They also maintain some control over the number and diversity of actors interacting in a given task, and by introducing new rules and procedures they can tighten or loosen the actors' freedom of interaction. They can tightly restrict the flow of information in a system or, on the other hand, provide rich channels of communication among agents. When the late Robert Rodale ran Rodale Press, for example, he met frequently with authors and scholars and brought them into interaction with his editorial staff. The press also had an internal "information sieve," a publication whose editors scanned world news daily for items related to company business and distributed relevant items to staff. Everyone at the press was fielding a rich flow of information on a daily basis. As a result, the company never settled into fixed ideas or behaviors; it was always learning and trying new things.[5]

Leaders hold the levers for control parameters. This leads to an important principle of the pragmatics of complexity: *leaders can exercise some control over emergence of phase transitions in complex situations by manipulating control parameters, even though they cannot control the transitions themselves or predict or determine the posttransition system.*

The Emergence of Order at the Edge of Chaos

When normal system behavior becomes destabilized by such feedback processes, the system can fall into disorder, but it can also spontaneously enter a *phase transition* to a new order at what is called *the edge of chaos*. The processes within such phase transitions, and the details of the emergent order, cannot be controlled. New structures, exhibiting new properties not previously witnessed in the system, may emerge. Agents following diverse rules and strategies in their local interactions all contribute to an unpredictable new order that does not conform to any design conceived or imposed by leaders or determined by the environment. In the Rodale example, the flood of new ideas might have destabilized operations, but it did not; instead it stimulated intense discussions leading to specific new projects.

In the school in the changing neighborhood, considered above, increased diversity threatens to send the school into disorder. Hostile conflicts mark classroom discussions; fights break out in the halls. Tightening controls by policing the halls or suppressing classroom discussions may only make matters worse. Learning can slowly grind to a halt. Leaders cannot control the situation but can play with control parameters, for example, by introducing new elements into the situation such as community leaders who dampen conflict while opening a space where the opposing groups, following unpredicted strategies of their own, bring the situation back from the brink.

This introduces the central idea of *complex organizations*: in such organizations effective adaptation regularly results from *self-organized emergence* rather than *direct central control*. Functional stability and order can be continuously maintained not just through planning, strategy, or tight control of operations, but through successions of creative interactions at the edge of chaos. Leaders cannot control outcomes because the system is complex—causal links between means and desired ends in complex systems simply cannot be mapped; the leaders simply don't in general know what effects interventions will have. Leaders can, however, provoke and modulate phase transitions, allowing new adaptive order to emerge from self-organization.

Complexity and Global Networks

Complexity theory, as noted earlier, is particularly relevant for organizations operating in today's global network environment, because global networks ratchet up complexity. In the industrial period individuals had only a few standard mass-communication channels for receiving information and even fewer means for exchanging ideas and collaborating in groups. Organizational leaders in industrial hierarchies minimized differences among workers through standardization, and severely curtailed lateral communications among workers that affected operations, to suppress complexity and enhance control. As a result diverse individuals brought many latent capabilities to workplaces that remained undetected, untapped, and undeveloped.

In the *information era* of the early years of the twenty-first century, by contrast, information networks have linked the human community on a global scale.

There is exponentially more information flow, diversity of agent and strategy types, and strong interactions among ever-more powerful individuals and groups, with increasingly unpredictable results. Teens with Internet access, like Tavi Gevinson, Jayralin Herrera, or Priyasha from Indonesia, can, by casting nets, approximate what Robert Rodale did for Rodale Press in the 1980s: network with experts and circulate the results of their interactions. As argued earlier, new digital tools are already making it significantly easier for people to create and communicate, exchange information and ideas, form new groups, cooperate in tasks, collaborate in producing new knowledge or ideas or artifacts, and act collectively for common ends. The result of these increasingly strong interactions is that unpredicted events with significant consequences are now commonplace. Amazing things happen daily, but even routine operations are difficult to control. Complexity theory has become popular today because it promises a way to maintain or restore order in the global network environment without the need for impossible-to-provide levels of top-down control.

COMPLEX ORGANIZATIONS

Complex organization is a paradigm shift introducing *meta-strategies* to help organizations to continually reinvent themselves as changing circumstances dictate.[6] Dee Hock, an early theorist of complex organizations, spoke of the need for new forms of organization that were "infinitely malleable and yet extremely durable."[7] Various models have been proposed to capture these two virtues: for example, the flat, modular, networked, responsive, or customer-centered organization. The idea of complex organization functions at a different level, offering not just another fixed organizational design but rather guidelines for *continuous organizational redesign*.

Complex Organization Rebalances Center and Periphery

Embracing complexity involves changing the relationship between central leadership and participants: shifting power to the periphery where decisions can be based on local information (this shift is baked into the architecture of the Internet, as we saw earlier in Chapter Six). Teachers, for example, are positioned to know far more about their students than principals, can make more nuanced decisions about them, and can respond more rapidly and effectively when not compelled to seek official permission for responsive actions. When this shift of power occurs, operational units become self-organizing, solving problems through local interactions to find emergent, rather than prescribed, solutions. Leadership gives up command and control but takes on two other functions: (1) establishing a suitable context for creative self-organization within work units and (2) coordinating the emergent results to keep the organization as a whole coherent and effective.

An example will make these ideas clear. In a school a new art teacher might take an interest in fashion design. There are few channels for this interest in a hierarchical school, where the course of study is imposed from above and shaped to meet preexisting objectives. In a complex organization, however, the context permits this teacher to make her interest known and attract some students to join her improvised "design studio." In time a history teacher and a technology teacher begin to participate by adding units in the history of design and fabric-making techniques. At this stage neither teachers nor leaders know what will come of the studio, but they remain open and attentive to developments. They are "ready." They have "fired." But they have not yet formed a clear overall "aim" for the studio.

Now suppose that one of the students—a new Tavi Gevinson—wins an award, is featured in a teen fashion magazine article, and creates a lot of buzz. People from the fashion industry show interest. They offer internships for studio students. More students and staff want to join the studio and they demand more resources to support it. The leaders do not resist, and the new demands create strain throughout the organization as resources must be shifted from other programs, pushing the school into a phase transition.

At this point students, teachers, and leaders may all feel merely that something valuable will come of this new center of activity—even if they don't quite know what that is and know they can't entirely control it. At the "edge of chaos" teachers, leaders, students, parents, industry consultants, and volunteers can then be prompted to work toward a clear aim for the studio, and leaders can coordinate the fashion design studio, as one of the school's featured programs, with other school functions in a new non-equilibrium order.

Establishing a Context for Creative Self-Organization

The primary role of central authority in complex organizations is to establish and maintain a suitable, limiting context for decisions and operations throughout the organization. Three components of context are (1) mission, (2) governance, and (3) structural design.⁸

Mission: A mission statement notes organization purposes, constituencies, and built-in constraints. Stating these up front forces leaders to confront difficult choices about what the organization *is* and what it must deliver to whom to justify its existence, leaving little wiggle room for convenient exceptions.⁹ For Alfred Sloan, *General Motors exists to make money by making motor cars.* This statement identifies the primary purpose (making money), the primary constituency (shareholders), and the primary constraint (making nothing except motor cars). A science high school, for example, may have the mission of providing a challenging course of study (purpose) for learners with high test scores in math and science (clientele) who aim for admission to highly competitive colleges (constraint).

Governing Principles: Governing principles define constraints on action—what *cannot* be done, what *will not be permitted.* In complex organizations they do not specify what *will* be done: this is left to the actors in operational units. These principles define a space for work free from micromanagement, like the space within which the design studio was first established. The science high school may designate such basic operating principles as these: that minimal test scores be established for admission, that courses have labs, and that seniors present a final project.

Structural Design: Structural design maps relations among work units and outcomes needed from each for the organization to work as a whole. Work units can change over time: a computer company may close its printer division and open a phone division; a college may close an academic department and open an honors program or research center. An art department may split into art and design programs. Science High's *structural design* may specify math and science as separate departments but also require interdepartmental plans for all advanced science courses.¹⁰

Assigning, Developing, and Sourcing Capabilities

Central leadership bears ultimate responsibility for who participates in the organization. Subject to external regulations, and with input from work units, it bears responsibility for hiring and firing workers and assuring that suitable capabilities are available within operational units for assigned tasks. These capabilities can be provided through hiring and developing suitable employees, by facilitating personnel shifts within organizational programs, and by enabling work units to source additional staff capabilities externally.

Hiring and Developing Capabilities: In the industrial paradigm employees were hired to meet specific and stable task requirements, and in accord with the norms of universalism and specificity (Chapter Three) were defined in terms of their positions and roles. In the informational era, however, tasks can change rapidly and unpredictably. New work groups must be assembled based on rapid judgments about what capabilities are needed to respond to novel challenges.

Human groups are already rich in diverse capabilities. In the industrial paradigm, as noted earlier (Chapters Two and Three), capabilities not associated directly with the specific tasks workers were hired to perform remained undetected, undeveloped, and untapped. Today work groups require unpredicted capabilities; organizations are best served by hiring broadly capable employees and learning as much about their capabilities as possible. Dreeben's norms of independence, universalism, and specificity would be toxic in today's world. Google, for example, seeks highly intelligent and resourceful people and assigns—and reassigns—them as needed, making careful note of emergent capabilities. It also encourages employees to develop altogether new capabilities by granting them 20 percent release time for their own projects and then closely following the projects and the employees' growth and building upon them, a practice other complex organizations might emulate.

Sourcing Capabilities: As groups confront unpredicted tasks, there is no a priori reason to suppose the needed capabilities will exist in-house. In fact, as the tasks change, it is much more likely that the most suitable people work elsewhere, because in-house employees were selected for the old tasks. The Internet now makes people and capabilities highly visible and assessable, reducing transaction costs in hiring employees and contract workers and making outsourcing economical (see the discussion of Shirky's *Here Comes Everybody* earlier). Work units have to find the capabilities they need, whether in-house or in the market. Complex organizations need clear procedures for finding capabilities and getting them to where they are most needed.

Conventional high schools have retained the same structural design for 150 years: fixed departments teaching fixed courses with hierarchically organized fixed topics. Departments and courses have changed very slowly. A teacher could be hired to teach geometry and teach more or less the same course for life. Today, however, with most of the world's information stock on hand in every classroom and good courseware available online for every conventional subject, what is most needed is shaping new learning experiences to meet the changing needs of learners. These can be developed by existing teachers once their latent capabilities are tapped, while high-skilled teachers with cutting-edge knowledge and experience can be located online anywhere in the world, assessed, hired under contract, and brought on board to perform tasks, online or physically, at low cost.

Manipulating Control Parameters to Provoke Phase Transitions

Organizations can exhibit order, disorder, or phase transition at the edge of chaos. Over time most settle into standard operating procedures that can become stagnant and detract from adaptive fitness. Leadership in complex organizations has to maintain a healthy climate of innovation by prodding participants to try out new, more adaptive behavior patterns; in a school this may mean designing new courses or workshops. Leaders must work against a natural tendency in organizations to lock in to suboptimal behaviors, caused by groupthink and dependence upon cash cows.[11]

Groupthink stems from lack of diversity of agent types and strategies, for example, when all of the workers are drawn from the same ethnic groups, have similar training, and accept the same operational paradigms. To break groupthink, leaders have to introduce new agent types with different "takes" on situations and different strategies. In schools, this may entail, for example, recruitment of teachers, contract workers, and volunteers with diverse backgrounds.

When organizations settle into successful patterns and depend on cash cows, actors can be lulled into misjudging organizational fitness in its changing environment. When most revenues derive from a single type of operation, underlying vulnerabilities remain hidden, suppressing incentives to change. School personnel, for example, can today hardly imagine significant changes in teaching and learning because standard practices have long produced steady tax revenues. Today, however, public revenues are migrating to charter schools promising something new and different, and conventional schools, blinded by their successes, can't evolve to meet new needs.

Coordination and Restructuring

Finally, central leadership is responsible for organizational durability. The leadership task is to maintain a big-picture view of the entire organization and its various work groups as they self-organize to meet new challenges. Leaders must envision possible synergies and reassign capabilities and source new capabilities to realize them. They may in the process intentionally destabilize the organization and then bring people together at the edge of chaos to re-vision a new order. Central leaders can generate but cannot control this process; stakeholders must work together to establish a new, unpredicted order.

The School as a Complex Organization

The factory school paradigm is based on hierarchical control. Despite the vast information flows and the new capabilities generated by the Internet, recent reform policies have actually strengthened hierarchy. But top-down control works against diversity of teaching strategies, is blind to diversity of teacher and student capabilities, and nullifies the new flows of information and strong local interactions they can unleash. The result: good schools are locked into suboptimal operations, while those serving young people most in need stagnate in gross disorder.

Complexity theory, by contrast, offers guidelines for harnessing the inherent complexity of learning organizations in the network environment by *embracing* complexity and *provoking* phase transitions at the edge of chaos. This allows new, more adaptive teaching-learning strategies to emerge from self-organization. The complex learning organization is, in Dee Hock's terms *durable* yet *infinitely malleable*.

In the next chapter I apply the model of complex organization to a concrete educational organization, the Anderson-Armstrong Learning Center, an imaginary complex open learning center intended as a suggestive model for the transformed high schools of tomorrow.

CHAPTER TWELVE
OPEN LEARNING CENTERS

Join me in a brief side trip to New York City and Ridgefield, Connecticut, to learn some valuable lessons about complex unpredicted learning paths as pianist Thelonious Monk and writer Mark Salzman "follow the moving center" in their educational journeys. We attend to the adaptive, improvising spirit of these learners and their teachers. This spirit is a key feature of education as initiation in network society. Monk and Salzman can serve as role models because today's young people, in adjusting to life, will need to be more like Monk and Salzman, more flexible and adaptive and self-determining, than the compliant, rule-book-bound learners of industrial society. In network society learners who remain bound by the norms and routines of the factory school will find themselves poorly adapted, unable to grab hold of today's opportunities.

THE EDUCATION OF THELONIOUS MONK

Thelonious Monk was an iconic American composer, innovative pianist, and leader in the transition from swing to modern jazz. His mother, Barbara, came to New York from Rocky Mount, North Carolina, in 1922 hoping to find better educational opportunities for her children than existed in the segregated South. Active in church music, Barbara became her son's first piano teacher. The young Monk also took lessons from Alberta Simmons, a master of ragtime and classical jazz. Besides Barbara, however, Monk's biographer Robin Kelley states, "the most important influence on Monk's early development wasn't a person but an institution—the Columbus Hill Neighborhood Center."[1]

The Center, funded by a grant from John D. Rockefeller Jr., took over the Henrietta Industrial School at 224 West 63rd Street in 1928 and transformed it into a hub of community life. It became the "true center of social life for black youth" in Monk's San Juan Hill neighborhood, with a staff of twenty-three volunteers and twenty regular employees serving over 800 young people in its programs by 1930. Strict rules of behavior were enforced, and despite the neighborhood's reputation for violence, the Center was an oasis of peace and security. Mavis Swire, one of Monk's contemporaries at the Center, said, "It was the greatest thing in our lives ... [the staff] had a way of making you feel like you could do great things. You can do more with your life."[2]

By his teen years Monk was already carving out his own musical path. He never participated in the Center's orchestra, but he joined the music program and took second place in its annual piano competition in 1933. He was an average student in elementary school and junior high, excelling only in music. But that was enough to get him admitted to Stuyvesant High School, the most prestigious school in the city. After fewer than two years, however, Monk more or less dropped out, attending rarely and earning zeros in all of his junior year classes.

Meanwhile, he formed a trio in 1933 with two other musicians from the Columbus Hill Center (renamed the Columbus Hill Community Center that year) that played at local restaurants and dances.[3] In 1934 the famous Apollo Theater in Harlem launched its "audition nights" on Monday evenings, where contestants competed for the ten-dollar first prize. Monk's trio, his family remembers, "Won every time they went up." Even more important were his Friday evening gigs at the Columbus Hill Center, where the trio played for the fledgling dancers and singers in the neighborhood and became local heroes.[4]

When Stuyvesant "transferred" him to his local high school after his junior year, Monk simply dropped out for good and at age sixteen went on the road in the band of an evangelical preacher. When he returned home to New York at nineteen in 1937, he was a mature young man and a professional musician. Significantly, he once again frequented Columbus Hill Center, exchanging ideas with other young musicians including sixteen-year-old trumpeter Benny Harris, with whom he formed a quintet. In 1937, Harris met Dizzy Gillespie, adopted his modern harmonic ideas, and spread them in Monk's circle at the Columbus Hill Center, inspiring Monk's further adventures in modern jazz.[5]

* * *

Let's take note of some key elements of Monk's education. He came from a musical home, was immersed in church and secular black music from birth, and classical jazz from age nine. He was passionate about music. Although bright and curious, he was an indifferent school student and by age fifteen had drifted away from standard academic learning, rarely attending the high school where he was not valued despite his prodigious accomplishments, which were probably unknown to anyone there. No one at Stuyvesant was telling him he could do "great things." The community center, on the other hand, afforded him a secure, serious environment for self-directed learning, where he studied music, collaborated with other young musicians, formed his identity as a musical innovator, created a group that earned money, won prizes, contributed to the community, and established its members as local stars. The staff at the center "held a crown over his head and expected him to grow into it." Even after his high school years, he returned to the Center, tutored young musicians, and linked up with adult role models. He was a "nobody" at Stuyvesant, but a "somebody" at the Center, valued for who he was. No one at the center planned or controlled Monk's evolution, but they responded creatively to the signals he was sending them; the staff there "had a way of making you feel like you could do great things."

* * *

Some will complain that Monk's neglect of schooling makes him a poor educational model. Teddy Wilson, the iconic swing pianist and star of the Benny Goodman Trio, however, saw Monk as unusually well educated: "Monk knew my playing very well, as well as that of [Art] Tatum, [Earl] Hines, and [Fats] Waller. He was exceedingly well grounded in the piano players who preceded him, adding his own originality to a very solid foundation."[6] This complaint thus brings us back to the meaning of education. What was served up at Stuyvesant, however excellent in its own way, was largely irrelevant to Monk's educational needs. We can only think of Monk as neglecting his education if we confuse education with schooling or with education in the *narrow* sense. In the *broad* sense of education as initiation into worthwhile adult activities, Monk's education was exemplary.

The Education of Mark Salzman

Mark Salzman is a cellist, teacher of juvenile delinquents, and author of novels and memoirs including the classic memoir *Iron and Silk,* which describes his experiences in China as an English teacher and martial arts student.

Salzman grew up in suburban Ridgefield, Connecticut. His father, a social worker devoted to both oil painting and astronomy, engaged young Mark in intellectual and artistic activities from his earliest years. His mother, a piano teacher, was his first music teacher; she encouraged his passionate devotion to the cello. In *Lost in Place,* a memoir of his school days, Salzman narrates that at age thirteen he became enamored of Kung Fu and Zen.[7] Discovering that his junior high school offered courses in neither, he longed to quit school. Reflecting on Lao Tzu's dictum that "In the pursuit of learning, every day something is acquired; in the pursuit of truth, every day something is dropped," his school revulsion deepened; he came to believe that school learning was actually harming him as a person. "If I had to sit through a class five days a week called 'Plucking All Your Hairs Out and Re-Arranging Them in Stacks of Prime Numbers' it wouldn't have seemed better or worse than my actual classes" (108).

All this changed when Salzman entered tenth grade and enrolled in "Richard Rowland's" world history course.[8] When he told Rowland about his dissatisfaction with conventional schooling, Rowland didn't contradict him. Instead, he demanded to know what Salzman was *doing* about it. Salzman explained his martial arts classes and self-directed studies in Chinese philosophy. Rowland made it clear that he would get nowhere in these studies unless he put them into their Chinese cultural context and learned Chinese (109).

Rowland did not cling to the conventional curriculum. Instead he offered to teach Salzman Chinese if he agreed to work very hard. Rowland recommended a textbook and got language tapes and flashcards for him and shared lecture notes and books from a graduate course in Chinese history. Shaken and discouraged by the difficulty of these studies, Salzman was nonetheless stirred when Rowland shot back that everyone who hoped ever to understand anything in life would have to work very hard. Salzman got with the program: "The difficulty was more than compensated by the excitement I felt knowing that I was doing something any adult would have to respect, and the work became a kind of pleasure" (111).

Rowland thought that Salzman should get academic credit for his extracurricular cultural and language studies, and the two of them drew up a proposal for an independent studies course. One of the members of the committee, an art teacher, was so impressed with Salzman's proposal and his evident seriousness that she offered to supervise an additional independent study course in Chinese calligraphy. Realizing that he could not learn calligraphy on his own, Salzman located a tutor, a graduate of the art school of the Chinese University of Hong Kong. As he worked on his second independent study proposal, Salzman wondered why he couldn't design for himself an entire curriculum in Chinese studies.

His second proposal, however, resulted in a call from the vice principal, who "explained the strict state and federal regulations covering the curriculum offered in each grade of every high school." When Salzman explained how enthusiastic he was about his "unregulated" studies, how motivated he was to learn, the vice principal said that he had no choice but to enforce the regulations:

> Think of the school as a huge ocean liner. It's out there on the ocean, it's overcrowded, the engine is overworked, but it's moving slowly in the right direction. Then imagine that one kid falls overboard. We simply cannot turn the whole ocean liner around just for him. (116)

The only choice was to stay on deck, the VP explained, "sighing and looking tired" (116).

The ever-resourceful Mr. Rowland was fired midyear for an unrelated deviation from school rules, but Salzman surprisingly found another Chinese tutor in eleventh grade, the French teacher "Jacob Friedman" who had spent a sabbatical year in Taiwan learning to read and speak Mandarin (132). Nonetheless, Salzman's willingness to submit to conventional schooling abruptly ended. He plotted to drop out creatively, by applying to colleges for early admission but upon acceptance leaving high school but not showing up at college. He was accepted at Yale—the woman who interviewed him was an Asian culture scholar—and he then delayed his admission, spending an agonizing unstructured year by himself.

Yale rescued him. His freshman year was a "long, uninterrupted stretch of happiness" (225) and his sophomore year was even more enjoyable. "The more advanced the courses and the heavier the course load, the more turned on I got.... Every teacher clearly felt passionate about his or her subject and they gave the impression ... of stretching their minds to the limit, which I found highly contagious" (225, 231).

The rest of the story is well known. Salzman graduated Phi Beta Kappa and summa cum laude from Yale in 1982. Equipped with knowledge of Chinese language and culture, Salzman spent the next two years in China, studying martial arts with Kung Fu master and movie actor Pan Qing Fu. He published his award-winning memoir *Iron and Silk*, based on that experience, in 1986 and starred in the movie version, which he wrote and directed, in 1990. Salzman today lives with his wife, Chinese American (and Academy Award–winning movie director) Jennifer Yu and their two daughters in Los Angeles. He has written several novels and memoirs, including *True Notebooks* (2003), a book about his experience as teacher of delinquent boys, and he continues to play the cello.[9]

* * *

There are important lessons we can learn from the education of Mark Salzman. Like many teens, Salzman had passionate interests and devoted himself to them. He found school suffocating. Amazing teachers reached out to him, taking it upon themselves, on their own time, to creatively guide his independent studies. His history teacher had studied Chinese history in graduate school; his French teacher could read and write Mandarin; his art teacher volunteered to guide him in calligraphy. These teachers were hardly confined by limiting definitions of a school teacher. Violating the norms of universalism and specificity, they viewed Salzman holistically, as an amazing teen. Salzman also found unexpected resources in his community; demonstrating naïve resourcefulness, he found his uncertified master calligraphy tutor by inquiring in a local Chinese restaurant. Though Salzman completely rejected the standard college prep program at his high school, the ad hoc education that gradually organized itself around him there, in violation of standards and regulations, prepared him ideally for supervised study at Yale under leading scholars and for his subsequent rich creative life.

OPEN LEARNING CENTERS

In a school as a complex organization dedicated to assisting the learning of its young charges Monk's musical discoveries and Salzman's explorations of Chinese studies could have readily been accommodated, as could Jayralin Herrera's philosophical writing or Tavi Gevinson's blogging about fashion. The efforts of Salzman's teachers Rowland and Friedman would have been recognized and rewarded. Recruiting skilled community members to the school faculty would be routine. Passionate learners like Salzman would have been valued, recognized in school ritual ceremonies, and assured that they could "do great things," not viewed as abject passengers in danger of falling overboard.

By combining the best elements of Stuyvesant High, the Columbus Hill Community Center, and Ridgefield High, and then adding the open Internet, we can envision high schools as complex organizations, or what I will be calling "open learning centers." Learners there can attain an excellent high school education while following their own stars, channeling their passions, building capabilities, and linking to the larger adult world.

Organizational Context

Some educational leaders are already using the term "learning center" for new alternative school-like organizations, in recognition of the limits of schooling as the compulsory structure for learning. Indeed, some of the most obvious names for learning centers have already been grabbed up: we already have, for example, Franklin and Edison learning centers.

In what follows I lay out some broad guidelines for the kind of learning centers I will be prescribing as models for Education 2.0, illustrated by an imaginary example named for visionary young inventors Mary Anderson, inventor of the spring-driven windshield wiper in 1903 at age fifteen, and Edwin Armstrong, inventor of amplification by positive feedback—enabling the shift from the crystal set to the modern radio—when still a young college student. (Armstrong, who had been experimenting with radio since childhood, also invented today's wideband FM radio.) We'll locate the "Anderson-Armstrong Learning Center" (AALC) in "Metropolis," a large American metropolitan area. AALC has a central building (like Columbus Hill, a retrofitted central city school), and peripheral spaces: storefronts, unoccupied homes, workspaces, and gardens throughout the metro region.[10]

The fundamental conceptual shift that differentiates complex learning centers from factory schools is the move from hierarchical factory-like organization employing means-ends reasoning to complex organization. The centers turn their backs on standard means to predefined, measurable standard ends. Instead, they set teachers and learners free to interact and devise local learning projects with their own emergent ends, based on local information about teacher capabilities, learner aims, and available resources and opportunities. The centers stimulate complex learning and then harvest complex, emergent educational value. They grab hold of unpredicted opportunities and shape them into valuable learning experiences. They get ready, fire, take stock of initial results, and then take aim, operating in "perpetual beta."

Mission

The overriding purpose of AALC is to foster the education of all young people in the Metropolis region. AALC assists them in their learning endeavors and in composing and orienting their lives. AALC staff members initiate learners into worthwhile adult activities and carry them into the adult world. All activities of the center are designed to tap into the aims and passions of learners, to support and intensify their learning, and to link them to significant adult activities. College preparation—building up the academic capabilities of those whose aspirations require supervised study under academic knowledge producers—plays an important but not dominant role. The pathways to worthwhile adult activities simply do not always pass through college campuses; higher education's monopoly power over these pathways—the academic allocation of social position—is artificial and unsustainable. AALC draws on its community networks and the Internet to link learners to adult opportunities.

AALC's clientele includes all young adults in Metropolis who choose to participate, from the completion of elementary and middle school until they are settled into college and/or careers: roughly age fourteen until the early twenties. AALC offers mentoring, instruction, tutoring, and access to the Internet and digital tools to achieve their purpose. Through links to other community organizations such as workplaces, design studios, art galleries, theaters, and the like they connect young people with the community.

Governance and Structural Design

Open learning centers combine narrowly academic with community initiation functions. AALC has a director and two associate directors, one each for its academic and community initiation arms. It currently has both standing academic departments and impermanent community-oriented programs but they interact regularly. Currently its community theater and videography certificate programs are thriving, and a network design and technology program is being piloted. Following the pattern of RAND (discussed earlier), AALC is a complex organization where the physical layout encourages constant interactions of staff and students across units. Following Robert Rodale's model, the directors network with thought leaders and scholars, bring them into contact with AALC staff, and circulate their ideas to stimulate innovation and prevent the center from settling into a static, suboptimal pattern. Directors, staff members, and even student learners can propose new courses and programs, and staff can be reassigned from one work unit to another as needed.

As participants in a complex organization, when staff members or directors at AALC sense new opportunities and interests, they can seize upon them rapidly and respond with new learning experiences, courses, and programs. When several digital technology firms recently moved to Metropolis from California to save on property rents and labor costs, for example, the news stimulated local interest, especially after the children of the designers and engineers registered at AALC. Networking with the officers and employees of these firms, AALC directors first brought them to AALC to explain their products, work processes, and opportunities for apprenticeships and employment. The firms' employees and AALC teachers rapidly collaborated on short courses and in short order pressed for a pilot certificate program in network design and technology. One instructor from each of the English, science, and mathematics departments transferred to the new program to work with volunteer mentors and teachers from the new firms. Some learners in the program were soon brought into the firms as members of working groups, doing most of their tasks online using Web 2.0 tools. Their learning was assessed by firm employees and program teachers based on authentic criteria.

Like Monk at Columbus Hill, learners at AALC also use the center's facilities in creative ways for autodidactic and collaborative learning. All students have laptops or mobile Internet devices; those lacking their own can borrow one from AALC. Learners produce blogs like Tavi Gevinson, and they engage in science or humanities research like Aiden Dwyer and Samantha Garvey, alone or under staff supervision (see Chapter Four). Like Mark Salzman at Ridgefield, they are encouraged by teachers to follow their own interests, learning in a natural way by "casting nets," following links, keeping journals , and adapting to unpredicted opportunities. Staff members offer multidimensional assistance to learners on an as-needed basis, and they convey to all learners that they can "do great things." They support student learning by offering ad hoc short-form learning experiences—short courses, workshops, seminars, demonstrations, laboratories, training sessions, field trips, presentations, and consultations, and so on—in response to unpredicted events or student interests without prior approval of authorities.

The Academic Program in the Open Learning Center

In conventional high schools teachers are hired based on qualifications for a single course, for example, algebra, chemistry, or American history. The algebra teacher, however, may also be a native Arabic speaker, an amateur astronomer, a religious scholar, a competitive soccer player, and an informed cinema fan; these capabilities remain undetected and untapped because of the operation of the norms of universalism and specificity. This robs schools of available staff capabilities and renders schools as work organizations that are narrowly confining for teachers. The monopoly possessed by certified teachers also locks other adults with valuable capabilities out of the school space.

Like high schools, open learning centers also employ full-time professional educators. But they draw upon the full range of their capabilities and the educators grow in unpredicted ways. Leaders—like those at Google—follow these growth patterns, and acknowledge, reward, and make direct use of growing capabilities.

Professional Educators

The professional educators at AALC fall into four broad categories: mentors, academic instructors, media guides, and focus teachers.

Mentors are educators responsible for the overall coherence of each mentee's learning. Learners in the center are assigned mentors to provide guidance, draw out interests and passions, and monitor progress. Mentors know their mentees' life predicaments, passions and aversions, learning strengths and weaknesses. They do not control learners' educations, but they work with learners to make sense of them as they unfold; they are harnessing complexity to connect each mentee's prior learning history to current and future opportunities. Like the "Aristotles" envisioned by Curt Bonk and Judy Breck (Chapter Ten), mentors possess a sophisticated grasp of the map of knowledge and high-level search and assessment skills. Many have had college majors in the liberal arts and sciences.

Media guides are experts in computer-based learning. AALC has a large media center and peripheral learning sites with Wi-Fi. Their media guides follow online trends and opportunities. They can locate appropriate learning materials for every learning need. They dispense DVDs and URLs for use in the media center, hallways, homes, workplaces, cafes, and parks. They regularly interact with learners to discover whether the materials are effective. Media guides are similar to Curtis Bonk's "super e-learning mentors."

When learners are unable to keep pace in classroom-based courses, media guides offer online tutorials or propose that the learners be transferred to online courses where they can proceed at a slower pace. Because there is no normative "school year" at AALC, these students are not thought of as falling behind. Media guides are available from 7 AM until 10 PM in the media lab and on AALC's chat lines to help learners find resources.

Academic teachers and instructors deliver standard courses and short-form learning experiences as needs and opportunities arise; they are counterparts of today's standard school teachers. Open learning centers recruit them from the top half of their college classes. Working alone or in teams, they design courses, organize syllabi, deliver instruction, prescribe auxiliary lessons (in media lab and focus center), generate enrichment workshops and other short-form learning experiences, and conduct examinations; they are fully functioning knowledge professionals. AALC currently employs a professional instructional staff capable of delivering the entire standard high school curriculum plus many innovative courses.

Focus teachers, trained to diagnose and treat specific learning difficulties, work with learners on a one-to-one basis in the focus lab. Instructors, mentors, and media guides all can assign learners to the focus lab, but learners regularly go on their own to get extra help.

Academic Courses

Open learning centers offer a complete four-year academic diploma course. AALC offers four years each of math, science, social studies, English, and foreign languages; like PA Cyber (Chapter Nine), it provides options to fulfill diploma requirements in these fields.

But even in its traditional academic program AALC embraces complexity. Teachers know that excellent online courses and tutorials are available for every topic, so they feel little need to offer extensive didactic instruction. Instead they lay out broad conceptual frameworks, connect their students to online or video lectures in the media center, conduct discussions to deepen understanding and bring out underlying intellectual values, and demonstrate academic techniques. Much of their time is taken up with individual or group consultations, working with learners on independent study and collaborative projects related to the core course content.

Most of the academic courses are organized on a "core + option modules" pattern. Core content is reduced to no more than 50 percent of course time. The rest is devoted to modules selected by students from a menu of options or designed by learners themselves or in conjunction with teachers. Teachers lead discussions and provide training in academic skills. Students are examined on both core and option content.

Teachers also organize innovative courses and short-form experiences. Here are two examples: (1) two Indian American academic instructors joined with two community volunteers to offer a first-year course in Sanskrit, responding to requests from the Indian immigrant community; (2) a team of social studies and math instructors offered a four-hour workshop sponsored by the network design and technology program on "Network Technologies in the Arab Spring" and embedded optional questions about this topic in the final exams of their courses.

Academic Assessment

Open learning centers embrace complexity in assessment, by offering both tests of specific learning and in-depth examinations of multidimensional learning.

Marc Tucker's treatment of this distinction is worth quoting and exploring, both for its insight and its shortcomings. In a recent *Education Week* blog post, he says,

> To get persnickety, one should say "test" when we mean to assess what a student knows and can do irrespective of the particular curriculum to which the student is exposed and "examination" when our aim is to find out the degree to which the student has mastered a particular curriculum.[11]

To clarify this distinction, let's look at an analogy with medicine. When doctors perform physical *examinations,* they go through standard examination procedures. But if they discover something out of the ordinary, they press further; exams can take an unpredicted course. At the end of their exams doctors may send out for lab *tests,* for example, a white blood count to confirm a diagnosis. A test is narrow; its result can often be expressed in simple numbers. Examinations on the other hand require human judgment and their results are multidimensional.

In this sense, PISA is a *test*: it measures knowledge of, for example, math or science, without reference to a specific curriculum. This is necessary in international comparisons, because different nations use different curricula. A course *examination,* on the other hand, is an in-depth, multidimensional investigation of all course-related learning, prespecified and emergent. Good academic courses carefully interweave didactic with discursive and heuristic episodes: "I know" is articulated with "I understand" and "I can do." A course examination is a detailed, open-ended inquiry of course-based learning. As Tucker puts it in that article, "the adequacy of an examination ... is the degree to which it captures the essence of the course." If the essence of a course is mere rote memorization of knowledge content that can be assessed by any test, it is simply a very bad course. And why would we assign a live teacher, capable of responding to the individual questions and misconceptions of specific young learners based on years of experience, to teach such a course? The instruction could be more effectively provided by a computer program or video course.

Tucker is a proponent of standards-based education, and he proposes that sixteen-year-old high school students be given state board examinations based on demanding standards. Students who pass can then leave high school and move on to apprenticeships or community colleges. Students aiming for the university can move on to demanding college preparatory programs. On Tucker's approach, schools will prepare students for the board exams but state examiners will be appointed to conduct them.[12]

State boards for sixteen-year-olds is a promising idea. But I think Tucker gets his own terms mixed up. Why would local teachers not be better positioned as *examiners* of learning than off-site state-appointed judges? The locals know the guiding essence of their own courses in their specific school contexts. If learners engage in independent study, their local teachers can assess it. If learners work on a team project, their local teachers can examine them on their methods and results. Learning is an unpredictable journey; the essence of good teaching lies in guiding and assisting it. If courses lead to unpredicted learning, teachers can examine students on it—external boards couldn't even know about it.

Tests, on the other hand, are designed to be straightforward and objective; as in medicine, their role is narrow but essential. If we want to find out whether a patient suspected of cancer has a low blood count we do a lab test. If we want to find out if a learner possesses particular elements of core knowledge, we do a knowledge test. We might agree that all high school students should acquire core knowledge to avoid gross and inexcusable ignorance. We might support a state test of this knowledge at age sixteen. But we should never take core knowledge to be the sole or even primary outcome of education. Education is initiation into worthwhile adult activities and communities. No test can ever determine whether this is being accomplished.

AALC recognizes both the value and limitations of tests. While Tucker prescribes state board *exams* for all sixteen-year-olds, based on state standards, AALC merely prepares its sixteen-year-olds for *tests* on core knowledge drawn from the first two academic years. AALC courses devote limited time to basic concepts and knowledge, but it also equips its media center with powerful test prep software and provides live test coaching and tutoring. AALC regards test prep as a mere add-on to its academic program. AALC informs learners and parents that while it will take every step to assist learners in preparing for the tests, responsibility for test performance rests entirely on learners. AALC's instructors *never* teach for the test. Its academic courses are rich in both prespecified and emergent content, offering many opportunities for self-determined learning and collaborative projects. Its course *examinations* investigate all these dimensions of learning. No state bureaucrats can perform comparable examinations.

Open Staffing

In addition to regular professional staff, open learning centers also draw upon external providers of educational services on a contract or volunteer basis (including students, parents, and community members).

I have been developing throughout this book a case for both the inevitability and the desirability of open staffing. Our entrenched paradigm of education took shape in the industrial era. That era has ended; we now live in the society of global information networks, and we are now building new models of living, complete with new means of livelihood and new forms of learning. I earlier noted the shift from permanent jobs to contract work.[13] While we may slow down this transition through political movements like Occupy and unions for freelance workers, and build a new social contract to accommodate our new employment structures, a trend toward contract work is built into the spread of global networks.[14]

Teachers, like lawyers, are professional workers. Almost all teachers now work as employees for large organizations. But they already face competition from temporary, part-time contract workers, working directly for schools or indirectly as workers for education provider firms. All instruction at PA Cyber, for example, is served up by teachers working for external provider firms. Do they all have teaching certificates? Are they full-time employees with benefits? I doubt it. Online education, furthermore, is a global business. Why bring great math teachers from the Philippines or India and deal with all the hassles of immigration and employment here when they can be contracted to deliver instructional services from their home nations at a fraction of the cost? Why ignore the free time available for contract work and volunteerism already existing in the community, time that will greatly expand if advanced societies move to abbreviated work weeks to alleviate unemployment? It is this fountain of time and energy that will generate all of those unpredicted teachers and learning guides of the future that Bonk and Breck anticipate.

Full-time teachers have central roles in open learning centers as mentors, instructors, media guides, and focus teachers, but the centers also rely on contract workers and external provider firms for many academic and community initiation tasks. When there are too few students for a calculus or physics course, students enroll in online classes. When students wish to study biotechnology or need guidance with independent research like Samantha Garvey, the homeless young estuary ecologist mentioned in Chapter Four, AALC may contract with a teacher from a provider firm or local university. AALC's academic program is thus not limited by the capabilities of its regular staff. The other side of this coin is that when AALC's instructors have or develop special capabilities (e.g., in Asian languages), they are urged, like the teachers at the Utah Open High School (Chapter Nine), to create courses and websites in these areas, for AALC learners and those elsewhere.

Wikinomic Schools

What might schools look like if they embraced open staffing? Don Tapscott and Anthony Williams, in *Wikinomics,* distinguish several kinds of networked organizations;[15] three are directly relevant for education staffing, providing starting points for thinking about this issue.

1. Peer production. Organizations like Linux and Wikipedia offer innovative, large-scale products comparable to those of commercial hierarchies like Microsoft, drawing only on contributions from volunteers. Curricki, a platform for free open source multimedia learning materials, is a good example in education. Curricki materials are produced by teachers for online open source distribution using low-cost digital tools. Video lectures, text materials, and learning software of near-commercial quality can now be produced even for the "long tail" of users (e.g., instruction on languages with few remaining native speakers).

The OpenCourseWare Consortium gathers courses from leading universities and puts them online for free. Five hundred universities contribute; MIT offers all of its courses. MIT's costs are low but these courses sustain its reputation as the world's leading technical university. Sal Khan is almost single-handedly producing courseware for every school and college subject. The goal of his academy: "we hope to empower everyone, everywhere with a free, world-class education." This is an idea worth contemplating.

2. Idea and knowledge work marketplaces. Firms like Innocentive provide a market for ideas, inventions, and uniquely qualified contract workers to fill needs not met by firms' patents and employees. Firms buy or sell their cognitive surpluses, for example, unused patents, even unused employee time. If the smartest people work elsewhere, this is where you find them.

Teacher marketplaces already exist. American schools find licensed teachers in other states or overseas. If a school does not have enough students to field a physics or calculus class it can buy an online course for even one student.

An important opportunity lies in areas where demand can arise even though no courses or credentialed teachers currently exist (e.g., hip hop, complexity studies). Unexpected but valuable subject areas emerge as possible topics for education as soon as teachers and learners "cast nets." Good materials and competent providers can be found and assessed online. Not every competent provider will be a credentialed teacher.

3. Platforms for participation. Amazon, eBay, and Android market are platforms; they invite others to build business operations on their infrastructure. School districts are now migrating to "portfolio management"—coordinating diverse kinds of schools and providers. It is not a large step from portfolio to "platform management"—districts making their APIs public and inviting outsiders to provide no- or low-cost lessons, units, and courseware. Some charter cyber-schools already outsource all instruction; in the age of hip hop and re-mix, is the school as platform that far-fetched?

Volunteer Staffing

Volunteers are also central to open learning centers, as they were at Columbus Hill Center. Today's most popular websites are social: participants create, exchange, comment, and collaborate on content. They do so to satisfy basic human motivations: to create, to share, to build capabilities, to work with autonomy on projects with personal meaning, to belong, to be recognized, and to work together toward common ends.

For Clay Shirky, the forty-hour work week created a large cognitive surplus of time people had to channel these motivations. Today there is serious talk of a twenty-one-hour work week to spread work opportunities and alleviate youth unemployment,[16] so the cognitive surplus may expand greatly. The Internet provides the tools for people to do what they are already motivated to do, and a basic human motivation is to share with younger people and help bring them along. If it takes a village to raise a child, it takes a community to initiate young people into their adult life. Like Columbus Hill Center, AALC actively recruits volunteers to tutor and coach young learners, teach them life skills in ad hoc encounters and short-form courses, and link them to significant adult opportunities.

Open Participation

In a conventional high school young learners are framed as "school students." A female student in an algebra class, however, might also be a native Spanish speaker, an expert in Latino popular music or dance, and a baker of delicate pastries. Like Monk's musical triumphs or Salzman's martial arts exploits, these capabilities are neglected as irrelevant, reviled as cultural disadvantages or teen nonsense, or simply unknown by anyone. This robs the school of important student capabilities and renders it boring if not toxic. In the school as complex organization, teacher and student capabilities are detected and put to use.

AALC welcomes matriculated and nonmatriculated learners alike: it is open for dropouts like Monk and Salzman and also for young graduates—and serves them all on an equal, non-invidious basis. If our young Latina withdraws from academic studies for a time to start a pastry catering business with some friends, the staff responds with coaching, short courses, and encouragement, not disparagement.

This openness tames the dropout problem, as young people can't exactly drop out of AALC. Like college students, they may drop out of certain courses or even abandon narrowly academic studies for a period of time. But they are still welcomed as members of the AALC community; so long as they behave in accordance with the rules they are free to study and cast their nets in the media center, work on personal projects, join their friends, and enjoy many AALC short courses and workshops at various locations in the metro area. AALC provides a youth-friendly, constructive setting for young adults in Metropolis who have few other places where they are welcomed.

Open Time

Open learning centers are open more hours and days, and to more people, than conventional high schools. Like community centers—or convenience stores—AALC is open to serve teens and young adults in the community during school and after-school hours, evenings and even weekends. Its website is open 24/7. By staying open for long hours the center can serve a greater diversity of learners and draw on a greater array of contributors.

In conventional high schools, teachers and students punch in when the gates open in the morning and file out at the close of the working day. At AALC facilities you will find young people congregating on the lawn, in the computer labs, in seminar rooms, in shops, or at the library all evening and weekend long, working on their laptops and interacting with staff members. At 5 PM a teacher is on the lawn firing questions at learners working on a collaborative research project. At 7 PM a focus teacher is meeting students one-on-one by appointment for focused tutoring sessions. At 8 PM an actor from a local theater is coaching students on method acting for an upcoming street theater presentation. The AALC building is open until 10 PM for young Metropolis learners, who can then go home or hang out on the grounds and continue learning on their laptops and smartphones. AALC has a few open learning vans that travel on evenings and to shopping malls, parks, and other places where teens hang out; the vans provide Wi-Fi hot spots, learning materials, and staff to assist young people with their self-determined web-based learning projects like blogs and videos. The vans provide laptops, tablets, audio and video equipment, and other digital tools on short-term loan.

Open Subject Matters

Conventional high schools today offer standard courses—algebra, geometry, trigonometry; biology, chemistry, physics; American history, world history, civics; and so on, plus some occupational subjects. Tradition, accreditation standards, state regulations, and college admission requirements prescribe them as components of the obligatory diploma course. This fixed course of study, despite its educational value, has high costs, locking young people into experiences that neither engage them nor link them in clear ways to attractive adult roles.

Some virtual schools have broadened the curriculum. PA Cyber (discussed in Chapter Nine) offers course options for each year's students in each major subject matter area. As is stated on its website, "PA Cyber is built from choices, not bricks." Students don't take a standard "social studies" course but instead select from among a half dozen choices. Salzman might have found enough choices to fashion his own program in Chinese studies. This big menu is a great leap forward, but despite variation in subject matters, even the most unconventional courses (e.g., the history of rock and roll) are stuck within the standard one-year Carnegie unit format. They are shaped as "real courses" for "real schools."

Open learning centers, on the other hand, offer a great variety of subjects in many formats. Open learning centers go beyond the fixed Carnegie format, by promoting and building upon independent study and short-form learning experiences. Tavi Gevinson could build a course of study around the history and psychology of fashion; Samantha Garvey one around estuary ecology. AALC offers standard courses leading to the high school diploma, but does not privilege them. It values self-directed study, short-form learning, and diploma-oriented course work equally. It states that diploma programs are "among the important things that we do here."

Open Space and Open Learning Formats

AALC engages young people where they are with just-in-time experiences lasting a few hours, days, or weeks shaped to meet unique needs: for example, workshops on how to get a job, use a video camera, write a blog post, or parent an infant. These may be offered live or online, on or off the main campus building or community outreach centers, during or after regular teaching hours. AALC is true to its mission in serving all young people in the community. Who can deny that many kids—matriculated and nonmatriculated alike—need help today finding a job or using digital tools or caring for an infant?

The short-form experiences, moreover, serve as components in what are known at AALC as "course equivalents" or "CEs." Responding to requests from young single mothers, AALC developed a twelve-hour video lecture and demonstration course on parenting infants. Add thirty hours of supervised experience in AALC's child care center and you get credit for a "course" on parenting. AALC is planning a certificate program in human services; the parenting course will be included as an elective. If "Rock and Roll Sound Studio" (with an audio lab) counts for credit (in the digital technologies certificate program), why not "Parenting"—with a child care lab? Short-form workshops and life experiences can in this way be snapped together into courses for those matriculated in the diploma course.

Certificates of Learning

As all experiences at AALC are voluntary, the center assumes that its learners want to learn what they sign up for and de-emphasizes or abandons formal grades. Like *MITx* and Coursera learners, students can apply for assessment via examinations that can include tests, interviews, real-world performances, or work portfolios upon completion of any course. Those who pass earn a nongraded certificate of learning. Students failing to meet the mark are encouraged to do more work, study more, and repeat the assessment. Assessments take place throughout the year, so while failure to obtain a certificate at any given point is disappointing, it is not a high-stakes disaster.

Certificates of Mastery

One of the most important innovations in open learning centers is the program work unit. Programs are created and terminated as needed and are reviewed every three years for renewal. They draw on regular and short-term staff and volunteers. Directors create programs as demand arises and link them with each other and with academic departments to keep centers responsive to their changing environments. Like Rodale Press, open learning centers are always contending with new ideas and trying out new things.

A select group of program work units are tapped to create certificate learning programs, constructed from short-form and regular courses and course equivalents. Certificate programs at AALC require the equivalent of two school years (or the equivalent of ten one-year Carnegie units). Many component experiences do triple duty; the twelve-hour parenting video short course described earlier, for example, is a stand-alone short course, a component of the proposed human services certificate program, and also fulfills a social studies requirement. Further examples are considered below.

The precedent for high school certificate programs is well established; in 1997 Cisco Systems introduced multiyear network certificate programs in high schools in the United States and all over the world. More than 9,000 of these Cisco Network Academies now exist in high schools and two-year colleges, enrolling almost one million students each year. Participants in the academies earn industry-recognized certificates as "network associates" and "network professionals." Other firms have followed Cisco's example. If private firms can create and implement such programs in high schools, why can't professional educators?

What currency will these certificates possess in a society where social and economic positions are shaped by high school and diplomas—by academic allocation? In considering this question it is essential to remember that that academic allocation of social positions is a recent phenomenon. Before the 1870s not enough young people had high school diplomas for employers to consider them as job-relevant. Few universities offered professional training or diplomas before 1870. Diplomas could only become job prerequisites when enough people possessed them, and they became sufficiently standardized to be useful as filters to reduce employers' transaction costs. Academic allocation of social positions spread only in the industrial era that is now ending.

Today programs like Cisco's Network Academies and Harvard-MIT's edX are offering certificates of learning. Private firms like Microsoft have been granting them for decades. Certificate programs will certainly expand and become better institutionalized, and certificates will then be more widely recognized as currency for employment. Meanwhile, the dual visibility enjoyed by netizens reduces transaction costs, making it likely that forms of job qualification that bypass standardized diplomas and certificates will also expand.

Examples of Community Programs at Open Learning Centers

The Community Theater Certificate Program

In high schools around the world English courses contain units on theater: students read, discuss, and sometimes act out scenes from plays by Shakespeare and modern dramatists. Credentialed English teachers lecture on the texts and lead students in discussion and dramatic reading. Control is top-down; students have no role in selecting plays or learning activities. A potentially rich experience is dulled down.

AALC, by contrast, features an interdisciplinary community theater program where learning emerges from self-organized activity of learners and staff. The program offers limitless opportunities for what Judy Breck labels cognitive learning, socialization, and articulation: students learn about dramatic literature but also about how to create, cooperate, and adapt and adjust their literary learning to real-world problems. This orientation toward adjustment and adaptation, toward a kind of improvisation highlighted by jazz musicians like Thelonious Monk, is as appropriate for our digital age as an orientation to bureaucratic norms was in the industrial era.

The theater program is based on the new Internet-mediated capabilities of students, teachers, and community members to *learn, express* themselves, *exchange* information and ideas, *form groups, collaborate,* and *act collectively.* Staff members and program leaders establish the program context, its purposes, and constraints. But they cede considerable operational power to students, who select and even write plays, choose directors, organize stage design and production teams, select cast members and schedule rehearsals and performances, and market theater performances in the community and online. In the process diverse learner capabilities are detected, tapped, and developed. The production comes together as students, using familiar local strategies, search for texts on Google, take acting and stage design tutorials on YouTube, and draw on consultations with teachers or external resources such as professional actors and marketing professionals. The play and the learning are emergent results of self-organization.

Not all theater participants need enroll in the ten-unit (half-time) certificate program. Theater workshops and productions are popular short-form learning experiences. Learners earn learning certificates in acting, play writing, directing, stage design, and arts marketing. Those enrolled in the two-year program can earn a certificate of mastery in theater arts recognized in the regional theater industry. Those also matriculated in the diploma program can obtain credits in the certificate program for English, social studies, and computer science. The credits are recognized by school accrediting agencies and colleges.

The Videography Certificate Program

AALC also offers a ten-unit (half-time) high school video production certificate program initially generated by staff members in response to student requests. Not all video program participants need enroll in the certificate program; almost all AALC learners participate in some video program activities. For certificate students, the program includes training in marketing of services; negotiating with clients; shooting, editing, and refining finished products in consultation with clients; and publicizing the finished videos online. In this program all tasks are performed online. Those enrolled in the diploma course can apply academic credits in math, science, social studies, and literature to their graduation requirements. Program students acquire many hours of authentic real-world experience, building sophisticated video capabilities while adjusting and adapting to market demands. The total package is aggregated into an occupational certificate recognized by industry and counts toward a secondary school diploma recognized by colleges.

In the next chapter I offer a systematic comparison of the industrial paradigm of the factory school with the information network paradigm of the open learning center.

CHAPTER THIRTEEN
THE CLASH OF PARADIGMS

Now that we have a concrete image of the transformed school as learning center, we can state more precisely how hierarchical factory school and information network paradigms differ. Let's start by comparing their different approaches to the basic education commonplaces.

AGE-GRADING

Factory schools are organized around annual age-grades. The curriculum is organized around these age grades, for example, ninth-grade science and twelfth-grade English.

Open learning centers abandon age-grading. Learners are regarded not as freshmen or juniors, but (following Robert Epstein in *Teen 2.0*) as young adults ready to explore options, set personal goals, and make life decisions. Some regular courses may begin in September and run through June, but learners can enter and exit others throughout the calendar year. There are frequent short-form experiences, and regular courses are all offered online; students can begin them when they choose and proceed at their own pace. While some subject matters are best learned sequentially, the sequential organization of school learning is often arbitrary and illogical. Algebra 1 should be taken before Algebra 2, but must Social Studies 1 be taken before Social Studies 2? And though chemistry is the basis for modern biology, the latter is taught *before* chemistry. Conventional educators can't afford to overplay their "necessary sequence" card.

Egg-Crate Settings

Instruction in factory schools typically takes place in "egg-crate" classrooms, radiating out from central corridors. Didactic teaching predominates. Seats face forward. Nothing is permitted to distract students from teachers. New virtual learning environments (VLEs) such as Eluminate (now Blackboard Collaborate) are *virtual egg-crates*.

Open learning centers abandon egg-crate classrooms as the predominant sites for learning. In the main building, the media centers, seminar rooms, shops, and focus labs become equally important. Learners may rehearse with a band in a performance studio or work on a collaborative project in the student lounge (coffee served), or they may meet with mentors in their offices, with focus teachers in the focus lab, or with volunteer craft workers in the shop.

And those are just the learning spaces in the center building. The same student may attend classes at a local university, meet at a community garden or the seashore with project group members, work in adult workspaces alongside of successful adults as an intern or apprentice, as in the High Tech and Big Picture High Schools discussed in Chapter Fourteen, or be out in the community making oral history videos of elders or creating and running an enterprise.

Teachers

Teachers in factory schools teach conventional courses in egg-crate classrooms. They frequently feel isolated, and many resent the narrow definition of their role. Meanwhile they grow in many life dimensions beyond teaching, acquiring new capabilities they are unable to use because the curriculum renders them irrelevant.

In open learning centers, professional academic instructors give up their monopoly over teaching. Learners learn from many kinds of experience in many settings and from many kinds of teachers and community members. Professional teachers remain centrally important—they use many forms of expertise in flexible and adaptive ways—but do not dominate education. To compensate for their loss of monopoly power over teaching, learning centers assign professional teachers new and challenging professional roles: as course designers, workshop and seminar leaders, examiners, mentors, media guides, focus teachers, media-center coordinators, and program directors. These roles allow educators to draw on developing powers throughout their careers.

Centers also draw on two types of external teachers: distance educators offering online courses and contract workers organizing experiences on-site professionals cannot provide. In a changing world the best teachers of new knowledge and skills may work elsewhere. The Internet allows them to contribute from where they are located to where they are needed, and allows learners and educators to locate and assess them. Open learning centers constantly assess needs for external capabilities and bring them on board. Volunteers also contribute to all the centers' educational programs.

Learners

In factory schools learners are regarded as raw material to be shaped. They present themselves as scaffolds upon which prespecified learning objectives are arrayed. Little account is taken of their interests, passions, life experiences, and dilemmas. Their inherent complexity is reduced and simplified. They are "school students of a certain age."

Open learning centers by contrast know and care about their young participants. They regard them as young adults ready to take responsibility for their lives and learning needs. Like Priyasha—and Robert Epstein and the staff at Columbus Hill Center—learning center staff members regard them as "amazing"—functioning at peak brain development and capable of doing great things—though they may on occasion need instruction and adult guidance and support.

Subject Matter

Factory high schools feature a more or less fixed traditional course of study, with courses organized to promote standardized learning objectives. The curriculum follows a fixed sequence. All topics are organized in hierarchical categories (e.g., math, literature, science, art), robbing them of essential interdisciplinary and real-world context.

Open learning centers, like some of the new cyber-schools, offer a rich selection of discipline-based and interdisciplinary courses on limitless topics. The standard high school course is offered, but it is only one of many pathways to a diploma.

Open learning centers also offer a steady diet of short-form courses, workshops, and demonstrations. All courses are augmented by such enrichment experiences that provide rich contexts for what is learned, and they link learning to real-world activities. Self-directed learning is strongly encouraged and the results harvested for further learning.

METHODS

Didactic teaching predominates in the factory paradigm. "What is assessed gets taught." Test makers can more easily construct test items assaying didactic than other kinds of learning, so discursive and heuristic teaching methods are greatly underutilized. As high-stakes testing becomes ever more prevalent, education is reduced to teaching for the test.

In open learning centers, by contrast, didactic instructional methods play a modest role. Academic teachers rely on discursive methods to deepen understanding and on heuristic methods to build skills and broad capabilities. All academic courses aim to balance "I know," "I understand," and "I can do." Learners are also encouraged to shape their own learning experiences and to "learn by doing" in individual and collaborative projects. Community activities and certificate programs offer endless opportunities for informal learning, where learners "adapt and adjust" to real-world problem situations.

ASSESSMENT

Factory schools promote learning of specific objectives, units of behavior that are sampled and built into test items for standardized *tests,* the major tool of assessment. Learners, teachers, schools, and school districts are graded on test performance. Scores are publicized. Failing teachers can be fired; failing schools can be closed.

In open learning centers, by contrast, academic assessment is based on wide-ranging, multidimensional *examinations* conducted by local teachers, alone or in teams, grounded in their personal or tacit knowledge as competent judges. Exams may consist of tests, interviews, performances, and work portfolios; they investigate subject matter knowledge but also work ethic, creativity, skills in presentation, problem solving and collaboration, application of knowledge to community problems, and self-directed learning. Exams start with standard inquiries, but follow up on unpredicted topics arising in the course of the investigation. Course participation is not required for assessment; learners can stand for exams based on self-directed learning. Those who pass receive credits or certificates of learning.

The Validity of Authentic Assessments

Many are skeptical of the validity of authentic assessments conducted on-site by competent people—those skilled in adult activities. It can be argued, however, that competent judges are even more likely to make sound assessments than evaluators using tests based on predetermined objectives or standards. Let's imagine a horse race between the two modes of assessment and see who wins.

We start with an imaginary competition of student artists, or a science fair for student scientists. Let each competition have two teams of judges. Let the first team of judges be composed of observers trained reliably to analyze and score the projects in terms of a checklist of preexisting objectives or standard-based criteria. Let the second be composed of competent judges—in the art case, of established artists and faculty members of art colleges, and in the science case, of a comparable group of professional scientists and science professors. We will ask these judges merely to assign a score based on whatever explicit considerations, if any, they choose to apply. Suppose the scoring method is to assign each submission a score of 1 to 10. While the *analytical* judges would be restricted to checklists of criteria, the ratings of the *qualified* judges are accepted even if purely intuitive, so that when asked to say why they gave a particular submission a score of, for example, 8, the best they can say is, "I'm not sure why I gave this an 8, but it just seems like an 8 to me."

Now let the students with the highest scores from both the analytical and the qualified judgment groups be admitted to competitive art schools or university science programs, and then let us compare their grades at the end of their professional educations and their creative achievements in art and/or science five years after graduating.

No a priori reason exists to suppose that those selected by the analytical panel would do better than those selected by even the criteria-free judgments of qualified judges. If we simply assume the analytical criteria are more valid because they are analytical and reasoned, that would prejudge the horse race, assuming in advance what is to be proved. Once we grasp this simple point, we can confidently guess that those selected by the qualified judges would probably fare better. Why? Because the qualified judges, the college teachers and professional peers, will be judging student achievements by their own personal knowledge and tacit criteria, that is, by the same ever-evolving standards actually at work in the arts and sciences communities. People just like them, selected from the same populations, will be, by the very definition of competent judges, just like those assigning grades in college and professional schools and making judgments of creative achievement five years later. The competent judges will be conditioned by the same background experiences and tacit professional norms as peers. The values inherent in the students' works being judged, both in school and later in the process, will be the emergent values of the fields. Preexisting analytical frameworks for assessment are likely to deviate from or altogether miss these values. By contrast, the evolving tacit knowledge patterns of professionals are shaped precisely to seek and to grasp them.

The only a priori advantage to assessments based on prior analytical criteria is a technical one—that such measurements generate quantitative data that can be used as feedback to improve the assessment criteria and instructional treatments. The informal, qualitative, and tacit judgments of the competent judges cannot be used in that way. But note: this feedback from assessment data into the improvement of educational treatments is of little value—if any—if the analytical assessments are less valid than even the unanalyzed judgments of competent judges. And, as argued, there is good reason to suppose they would be.

This argues for a prominent role for authentic assessments in Education 2.0—those conducted in real-life situations by competent judges rather than in scholastic situations with specified predetermined criteria. Consider each learner as possessing unique talents and capabilities and a unique learning trajectory. Use the new digital tools to link teachers and outside judges for authentic assessment based on tacit knowledge and professional norms. Use assessments to generate feedback specific to individual learners so that subsequent learning experiences may enhance their capabilities and overall fitness. Because such assessments are particular and do not generate standard analytical data for computer models, there is no good reason permanently to store these assessments and jeopardize learners' subsequent privacy rights.

A Modest Role for Standardized Tests

Turning from examinations to tests, the centers support the standardized test process as providing an independent check on basic academic learning. Their media centers have powerful online test prep programs; their media directors offer test coaching; and focus teachers provide tutoring on typical test items. However, in accord with the governing principles of the learning center, the academic instructors *never* teach for the test. Neither students nor teachers are judged on test results. Test performance is entirely the responsibility of learners.

Academic instructors are judged by their ability to engage and guide learners in rich, multidimensional learning experiences, design and implement new courses, facilitate workshops, and conduct examinations. They have no test prep role—that function is assigned solely to media guides and focus teachers. In accord with their mission statements, learning centers themselves are judged on how successfully their young participants integrate into adult life in the community. When they say "no child left behind," they mean it.

Aims

Factory schools define their aims in scholastic terms, as the production of academic learning-objectives. This may have made sense when the high schools served a narrow group of learners whose occupations made direct use of the knowledge and skills built into the standard high school course. It makes no sense today in a world where secondary education is universal but traditional high school knowledge plays an insignificant role, at best, in the social and occupational lives of most learners.

Open learning centers aim to broadly educate learners, to channel their passions, and to link them to adult opportunities. Students are encouraged to take responsibility for their learning journeys and to use all of the resources of the centers to make their way. Mentors guide, but do not direct or control. Scholastic achievement is regarded as important, both in itself and as it assists learners to become initiated into worthwhile adult activities. Scholarship itself is regarded as a treasured activity.

How Open Learning Centers Resolve the Four Failures of the Factory School

We can finally show how Education 2.0 resolves the failures of the conventional high schools. The four primary failures are (1) academic failures—factory schools fail to promote academic achievement and the desired graduation rate; (2) efficiency failures—factory schools are wasteful of the energies and capabilities of students and teachers; (3) social and economic failures—factory schools fail to connect young people to worlds of opportunity; and (4) legitimacy failures—factory schools are losing their legitimacy as their failures lead citizens to withdraw their support. School reform efforts, far from resolving these problems, have further cemented the factory school model in place. How do the learningweb revolution and open learning centers resolve these problems?

Resolving Academic Failure

As we saw in Chapter Four, the actual academic successes and failures of the factory school are in dispute. Public school critics blame poor performance on bureaucratic government operated organizations. The critics promote school choice and privatization to cut through the red tape. But privatization efforts have failed to achieve meaningful improvement in either test scores or graduation rates, so government operation of schools cannot be the main problem.

Public school advocates, in turn, assert that the schools are actually doing reasonably well, given their mandate to educate all young people. They argue that public school critics are really interested not in school improvement but merely in wresting control of schools from public control to unlock profit opportunities for private firms. Parents, moreover, continue to give their own local schools high grades. The hue and cry about the schools is created not by the public but by corporate and political interests. Citizens who give their own schools high grades but the nation's schools low grades widely admit that they may be doing so because of all the negative press about public education.[1]

David Berliner, one of the most persuasive defenders of public education, has argued that the entire academic crisis has been manufactured by a coalition of business organizations, right-wing politicians, and media magnates colluding to grab hold of the schools as profit-making enterprises. The aggressive educational policy initiatives of right-wing coalitions like ALEC, and the torrent of bad news about schools on Fox News, support Berliner's argument. Not all liberal advocates of public education, however, have been convinced by the "manufactured crisis" thesis. Psychologist Lawrence Stedman, for example, while acknowledging the impact of antischool media campaigns, points to both weaknesses in Berlin's statistical analysis of school performance and unarguable failures of American students on many measures. He claims that even liberal advocates of public education must insist on school reform.

Who is right, the critics or defenders of the schools? It depends on the paradigm. Sometimes problems of this sort demand a fresh look. All sides in the current debate are looking at school performance through the single factory school lens of academic achievement and test performance. We can get a more balanced view by suspending the assumption that test scores and graduation rates are the keys to school assessment.

Earlier I argued that the demands of high standards and high graduation rates work against each other. I showed that the high school diploma would be a more valuable achievement, and generate a greater effort to achieve it, if the number of graduates were reduced to less than 60 percent, and that this would be quite acceptable if other attractive routes existed here, as they do in other advanced nations, for entry into the world of adult opportunity. Instead of struggling to improve graduation rates from 75 percent to 90 percent, we need to explore alternative routes to the adult world for high-school-aged students, even those that lower the graduation rate among eighteen-year-olds.

We also need to re-evaluate our conception of "high standards." The current content standards for high school disciplines are needlessly bloated. We have to fill each one-year Carnegie unit course with a year's worth of "stuff" regardless of its educational value. We may share or not share Lawrence Stedman's worry that most young people are unable, for example, to identify muckraking journalist Lincoln Steffens. Certainly it would be great if they could; a lot of information "should" be almost universal, though the cost of achieving universal knowledge might well be greater than the benefits. But consider this: a recent set of history standards required students also to be able to identify the Carolina Raiders. I had never heard of them, and neither had the professor peers whom I queried. It takes many years to present everyone with useless knowledge that no one really learns. We need to stop doing that.

Here is a larger problem: many of my university students were unsure whether the Revolutionary War took place before or after the Civil War, whether Lincoln was president in the eighteenth or nineteenth century, whether Eisenhower fought in Europe or Korea. This gross ignorance is shameful. We could eliminate it by making the mandated history test more like the written portion of the driver's test. There our concern is whether young drivers can safely operate an automobile. We do not test their knowledge of the internal combustion engine, even though it might be desirable for them to know how a car works, and even though that knowledge is a mandated part of the high school driver education course. Seven out of ten on the written test and you can take the practical driving test; if you pass it, you can drive. Kids study for the written test because they want a driver's license. They will not study hard for years to pass a high-standards history test without a clear life benefit, nor should they.

Instead of asking what everyone should know, we would be better off offering a very demanding academic program, assessed with high academic criteria (oral examinations, research papers and presentations, tests with open-ended and essay questions), for an *academic* diploma—the sort Marc Tucker thinks should be awarded to those remaining in college preparatory programs after most students pass their state boards and leave high school. We could then aim to eliminate shameful ignorance for everyone else by making minimum knowledge—not high academic accomplishment—a prerequisite for the practical postsecondary programs most young people want. Learners will study hard to acquire minimum knowledge needed to pass a test and get on with their lives. Such a test would be appropriate for a certificate qualifying them for practical programs.

Marc Tucker thinks that we can get 95 percent of youngsters to a high academic level, where they are ready for today's college-level courses without remediation by age sixteen. Given our current performance—about 25 percent by age eighteen—Tucker's claim cannot be taken seriously; it is akin to the grandiose policy objectives of the school reformers—to make America "best in the world" at science and math in a few years. We need to give up fantasy thinking and set realistic but challenging policy goals, perhaps moving from our current 25 percent to around 35 percent to 40 percent that can meet a high academic standard, with a lower but still meaningful standard for a polytechnic diploma for another 20 percent to 25 percent, and the elimination of gross ignorance for an additional 30 percent, with limitless opportunities for all to reenter school, earn an academic diploma, and move on to the university later in life.

The open learning center as proposed is ideally structured to achieve precisely this end. It offers a rich, friendly academic program. It provides mentoring, tutoring, and test preparation for all. It provides regionally recognized certificate programs in career-relevant skills. It can respond sensitively to the needs of especially talented youngsters by designing personalized programs around their talents and passions. It is designed explicitly to prevent any learner from falling through the cracks, getting lost, or dropping out.

Resolving Efficiency Failure

The factory school, with its high-stakes testing regime, is now pushing students out of school and teachers out of the profession. Teachers who remain are forced to devote their energies narrowly to didactic teaching for test preparation, preventing them from engaging in those discursive and heuristic episodes that add "I understand" and "I can do" to school knowledge or addressing the specific needs of their students. They know this is educational malpractice; their professional satisfaction is at an all-time low. Students, meanwhile, are bored to tears. They want to learn and are in many cases web-savvy. But instead of taking advantage of web-based resources for online courseware and independent learning, schools block websites and forbid mobile devices. The energies of teachers and learners are thus squandered.

Open learning centers, by contrast, are designed to make full use of the learningweb. By substituting real-world authentic assessment for high-stakes tests, open learning centers liberate the energies of all participants. Instead of wasting their time on senseless test prep, teachers can freely and creatively respond to learners, who in turn can freely express and develop their own interests and passions, drawing on web resources and free web-based courses ranging from Khan Academy to OCW and edX. Mentors can help youngsters to develop learning goals and projects and prod those who are lost to get serious about their lives. While mentors can't control learners, they can hold them accountable for the constructive use of their time. Online materials or modules in the media center provide backup and support for learners following their own stars. School leaders can, by casting nets, discover and assess potential teachers with suitable knowledge and skill, at a reasonable cost, to meet the needs of all learners.

Resolving Connection Failure

A high school diploma no longer differentiates young people from their peers, and it no longer provides a significant economic advantage for graduates over school dropouts. It serves as a prerequisite for college, but today even a college diploma, unless it is from a competitive school and in a major with daunting prerequisites, is no ticket to a decent job with benefits. Even graduate and professional degrees have in many cases become tickets to nowhere. Meanwhile the "college trap" keeps young people in school for years, often learning little and acquiring high debts that will cripple them economically for life. "Stay in school, go to college, get a good job" has become a costly and tired myth. Youth unemployment is soaring, and those delaying entrance to the job market rarely catch up.

Today, however, a second allocation system to adult positions is opening up outside of the college diploma route. Young people with unique capabilities, web savvy, or entrepreneurial drive can find career opportunities without college—and in some cases even high school—diplomas or professional credentials. The open learning centers respond to this new allocation situation directly, by featuring the development of web-related cutting-edge workplace capabilities and web and project management skills needed to find and exploit work opportunities. The centers aim to connect capable teen learners to work experiences and apprenticeships and to assess their learning using authentic workplace criteria rather than test scores. This can assist young people in forging future careers as unique contributors, rather than as applicants to the diminishing stock of conventional jobs.

Resolving Legitimacy Failure

The legitimacy of the high school rests on its claim to provide both an education and social and economic advantages through college preparation or workplace skills. Parents and students alike have accepted the high school, despite its discontents, because its diplomas promised the social and economic advantages they sought. While only a few students seek to get an education for its own sake, and even fewer an education defined as the standard high school curriculum, most have been willing to go through the motions to earn a diploma that could open the doors to college or the workplace. That has sustained the legitimacy of the educational system.

Critics of the public high school claim that citizens are rejecting it because of its poor academic performance. In fact, as recent studies show, most citizens are pleased with their own local schools. In record numbers, however, they think that the nation's schools as a whole are failing. They call for teachers to have more autonomy and to pay less attention to test scores.[2] Their personal complaints also focus on soaring college tuition costs and high youth unemployment rates. They still want their kids to go to college, in large measure because they are convinced that that's how they can get ahead and that job opportunities for high school grads are poor. Programs delivering workplace capabilities, and linked to dignified jobs, however, would soothe most of their worries and restore their faith in education.

By morphing into open learning centers, high schools can regain legitimacy by providing serious academic programs for the college bound and practically relevant programs connected to polytechnic training and career opportunities for those so inclined, by eliminating shameful ignorance and offering multidimensional assistance in a community-like setting for all young people until they are securely connected to college or workplace.

Conclusion

The concept of Education 2.0, open learning in the complex network organization, should now be reasonably clear. The learningweb revolution now has its "goal culture"—the open learning center. What is needed next is a "transition culture," a map of how to get from our entrenched factory schools to these complex network organizations. Questions arise about whether this is possible: Can we really build complex educational organizations? Can they become normative and become widely copied? Won't economic and political elites strive to retain tight control of education? What action steps are needed to get there? Of course there are no guarantees, but in the next chapter I argue this transition is possible and I even present a plausible transition culture.

Part Four
Educational Revolution

Chapter Fourteen
The Learningweb Revolution

The open learning center offers a concrete image of Education 2.0. Is it just a wild fantasy? Or can the learningweb revolution succeed—is this paradigm shift possible? Many serious thinkers believe it is not. I argue that it is. Despite the inertia of entrenched institutions and the investment of the state and powerful elites in conventional schools, paradigm change is possible and we can all contribute to it.

Of course, paradigm shifts do not take place in a vacuum. Horace Mann's "common school" revolution didn't happen "of itself"; it was a direct response by economic and political elites to the social and economic changes ushered in by automated production in New England factories after 1820. Today we are undergoing social and economic changes of comparable scale introduced by globalization and the spread of digital networks. These changes are generating contradictions in our educational and social arrangements comparable to those of the 1820s and 1830s and creating pressures for change.

The industrial-era educational model evolved for a nation leaving farms here and abroad for mostly routine work in industrial firms. In today's postindustrial economy such routine jobs are rapidly disappearing; decent employment now belongs only to workers with high levels of knowledge and workplace skill. Young people destined for such jobs, and their employers, understand that the factory school does not generate the needed capabilities.

To point to the most obvious contradictions: students remain individuated in school learning, but high skill and knowledge workers are expected to work in groups. Today's high school students learn cognitive routines sorted into distinct subject matter disciplines and are taught by teachers with discipline-specific credentials, but these workers are expected to connect and permute materials from multiple disciplines in nonroutine ways. Today's schools present subject matter in an orderly curriculum sequence unrelated to real-world applications, but workers must acquire and process information "just-in-time" for immediate use in messy problematic situations. Schools teach learners how to find the right answers, but knowledge workers first have to discover the right questions and then propose creative ways for answering them. There are no preset right questions or answers.

We need an education suitable for our own times. John Dewey noted a century ago that educators must consider how the content and mature organization of knowledge grow out of the practical demands of social life, and how that content is used, tested, and modified in its actual use. The series of learning activities, he argued, gradually must approximate mature knowledge-in-use just as the young people themselves gradually approximate maturity in their life roles and consequent knowledge needs.[1] Conventional schools and the curriculum produce a specific sort of learning in which memory, classification, and routine verbal-logical problem solving play a large role—it fosters "crystallized" knowledge, not the "fluid" knowledge needed by today's knowledge workers.[2]

Entrenched institutions nonetheless have a lot of staying power. New, more relevant practices cannot emerge so long as the old ones remain fixed by community habits and expectations, government policies and regulations, and pressures from industry. Indeed, thirty years of school reform efforts have only tightened the stranglehold of the factory school and made change more difficult. But these difficulties, we will see, are gradually fading away.

Is Fundamental Change Possible?

The leading educational thinkers of the industrial period, not surprisingly, applied the industrial mind-set when thinking about the change process. They conceived of educators as technicians organizing subject matters in a deliberate sequence as means to achieve societal goals and objectives.[3]

Educational thought since the 1980s, however, has been reshaped by an institutional approach that views educators not as technicians but as socialized agents embedded in institutional settings defining the meaning of their situations, establishing rules (explicit or tacit) of appropriate action, and thus shaping or constraining their actions. Agents learn these rules implicitly as they get initiated into institutional life; they learn to follow rules rather than use unbounded technical rationality to adjust means to ends.[4]

On this approach no one is in any position to engineer change. Indeed, one practical upshot of the institutional model has been to convince many educators that fundamental change simply is not in the cards. Institutional thinkers arrive at this conclusion by conceiving of change not in terms of leaders making technical adjustments of means to new ends, but as a result of political actors responding to pressures from economic and social elites by introducing new policies that have uncertain and often paradoxical effects.

The elites weigh in on education leaders, who cannot resist the policies directly. They are compelled rhetorically to support changes in the intended new curricula—talking up new goals and reformed practices. This talk, and the directives flowing from it, however, are only loosely coupled with day-to-day delivery of instruction in classrooms—the taught curriculum.[5] The leaders cannot push too hard; they depend on the day-to-day support of teachers, so they negotiate a compromise, giving teachers sufficient wiggle room to cope with the new demands. Teachers in turn depend on the compliance of students and must negotiate day-to-day demands with them. Teachers cannot push students beyond limits the students themselves establish in striving for their own multiple ends: to learn and grow, but also to avoid hard work, to look good to their peers, and to avoid humiliation. Educational change then happens, in a modest way, as elites apply pressures at the boundary of the school that are buffered by school leaders and resisted, transformed, or nullified by teachers negotiating their roles with students in classrooms.

This, in brief, is why institutional theorists think fundamental changes—paradigm shifts—can't happen. Small-scale incremental changes in the wake of changes in the intended curriculum don't alter the school's standard grammar of learning. Instead, they become, paradoxically, instruments for maintaining stability; the internal buffering and resistance transform fundamental changes into merely incremental ones.[6]

Historian Larry Cuban has analyzed past change processes to support this analysis. Progressive-era reformers, he found, sought to introduce active, problem-based learning in projects grounded in conditions approximating those of real life. Cold War reformers promoted new science curricula with advanced content and problem solving of the sort engaged in by real scientists. Both reforms aimed initially at fundamental change: they involved large changes in instructional content and method that required complementary changes in the use of time and space and in roles assigned to teachers and pupils—changes in basic education commonplaces. But school leaders in both cases engaged in "softening, selecting, and modifying" the proposed fundamental changes, "fashioning a fit" between the proposed changes and the existing grammar of schooling, so the proposed, fundamentally new forms of teaching and learning never took hold.

Instead, demands for both rational management in the progressive era and enriched disciplinary content in the Cold War era led to adoption of new textbooks and standardized tests that, instead of fundamentally changing education, reinforced the established factory school grammar.[7] Textbooks, achievement tests, and college admission requirements formed an institutional array—an institutional exoskeleton—trapping educational practice and preventing fundamental change. New curriculum content was introduced, enhancing the legitimacy of the system by demonstrating its capacity for change. But the "changes" remained superficial—meager modifications of the contents in the same old bottles. Cuban showed this process repeated "again and again and again" and argues that it will keep happening; new proposals for high-tech "twenty-first-century" educational change based on the Internet will meet the same fate.[8]

The Necessary Conditions for Fundamental Change

Is the institutional argument sound? Does it apply to today's educational situation of global digital networks and Web 2.0?

It would be foolish to insist that entrenched paradigms simply cannot disintegrate. Fundamental change sometimes occurs. The Roman empire and the Soviet Union both collapsed. Fundamental change has already occurred in American education; the industrial paradigm with its factory school is not the first educational pattern in American history. New England district schools existed prior to the factory-like common schools emerging in the industrial period. New England academies existed before American high schools. These patterns fit into an older institutional order. Today's entrenched educational pattern was once a shiny new paradigm. We have to ask, what are the necessary conditions favoring paradigm shifts, and are they emerging now?[9]

Fortunately, the institutional thinkers, by calling attention to the main constraints to fundamental change, have at the same time pointed to the conditions needed for fundamental change, for removing the constraints is precisely what makes change *possible*. I will now focus on the four constraints that these theorists identify, and argue that they are wearing away, making a paradigm shift possible.

Constraint 1. Powerful elites, the institutionalists claim, have generally supported and fostered entrenched practices and have been sustained by them. If the major corporate and policy leaders continue to support the factory school paradigm it will remain in place, even if weakened by internal anomalies and by individuals exiting the system to forge more adaptive means for themselves. Fundamental change cannot occur unless powerful elites begin to withdraw support from the status quo.

Constraint 2. Internal school processes, they say, are capable of buffering external pressures by economic and political elites for change, so elites cannot force it to happen in a top-down fashion. School leaders respond to external pressures for change by buffering them; they soften, select, and modify proposed changes and fashion a fit between them and existing contours of practice. Fundamental change cannot occur unless these internal buffering processes break down.

Constraint 3. The entrenched paradigm, they assert, is held in place by a tight institutional exoskeleton. Standard textbooks, achievement tests, and college admission requirements all prop up standard operating procedures and place a straightjacket upon the terms of public discourse about education. The public mind knows what "real education" and "real schools" are and will simply not accept anything else. Thus fundamental change cannot take place unless this deeply entrenched institutional exoskeleton is removed.

Constraint 4. Visions of change and innovative practices introduced by reformers are no more than alluring fragments. A lot of experimentation produces only a lot of experimental particles floating around the core of established practice. For the particles to converge in a fundamentally changed practice, comprehensive synthetic visions—that is, mental models linking new conceptions of subject matter units, administrative divisions, funding patterns, personnel credentials, and lines of authority—must be advanced by thinkers and taken up by credible leaders.

Fundamental Paradigm Change Is Possible

With these constraints indicated, we can map out an argument for the possibility of fundamental change. It works as follows: (1) Globalization, digital networks, and Web 2.0 technologies *are* weakening elite commitment to the factory model. (2) School reform efforts *are* destabilizing school participation and classroom interaction and straining the coping capabilities of teachers. (3) The introduction of diverse charter schools and the spread of homeschooling have challenged the entrenched image of the "real school" and created more room for legitimate experiments. Finally, (4) thought leaders are presenting coherent new visions of education in harmony with the changing social reality, around which the fragmentary insights and practices in the new experimental climate may converge. Therefore the conditions for fundamental educational change are falling into place.

1. Elites Have Withdrawn Commitment from the One-Size-Fits-All Factory Model

In response to constraint 1, the elites have already withdrawn from the one-size-fits-all model and replaced it with a model of diverse competitive providers, retaining standards and assessment by test scores, saying in effect, "schools are factories, so put them under the control of business managers who know how to run and, if necessary, close factories."

No public consensus has formed to support this new mini-factory model, however, and no credible evidence suggests that it resolves any of the failures of the factory school regime. A space now exists for a new, postfactory paradigm to emerge and gain traction.

We now find ourselves in an unsettled region, where the old factory paradigm is severely damaged, a proposed modification—private mini-factories—is failing, but no new vision has yet taken root in the public mind. The history of No Child Left Behind is instructive. Passed by an overwhelming bipartisan majority in 2001 to shore up the old paradigm, and signed into law by President George W. Bush in January 2002, the law rapidly ran into difficulties. Many states complained that it violated the constitutional clause reserving education as a power of the states, and it also imposed an unfunded mandate on the states in violation of the spending clause of the Constitution. Some states sued.

Republican legislators, historically opposed to federal control of education and unfunded mandates, distanced themselves from the law. Critics complained that it narrowed the curriculum and forced teachers to teach for the test. States, attempting to keep federal money flowing, lowered standards so their schools could demonstrate adequate yearly progress. Cheating on the tests was rampant. Even high-performing schools were labeled as failing because their already high scores left little room for improvement.

In 2006 Congress ignored President Bush's appeal to reauthorize the law, instead merely extending it on a year-to-year basis. President Obama proposed in 2010 to reform NCLB by patching its problems, with amendments to discourage teaching for the test, broaden the curriculum, and improve tests measuring student learning. Given the gridlock in Congress over all of Obama's initiatives, however, reauthorization efforts went nowhere. Without a new and improved NCLB, the Obama administration began granting NCLB waivers for states adopting a set of reforms promoted by Secretary of Education Duncan.

These waivers reflect a midcourse policy correction by elites. Instead of closing public schools only after several years of failure, as dictated by NCLB, elites are now pressing for widespread and immediate privatization.

Working through organizations such as ALEC and private philanthropies such as the Gates, Broad, and Walton foundations, economic leaders have pushed for "turning public schools around" immediately by converting them into charter schools adopting high standards, high-stakes tests, teacher merit pay for performance, closure for failing schools, and firing of teachers who fail to raise test scores. Gates has written up the formulas for turnarounds in its *Turnaround Handbook*.

Secretary of Education Arne Duncan calls the *Turnaround Handbook* the "bible" of school restructuring. During Duncan's reign as CEO of Chicago's schools, Gates and Broad invested $90 million in Duncan's turnaround effort, Chicago Renaissance 2010. They also invested a whopping and unprecedented $60 million in 2007 to get both political parties behind its school turnaround strategy. When Barack Obama was elected president in 2008 he brought Duncan, *Turnaround Handbook* in hand, to Washington. In its 2009/2010 report, the Broad Foundation crowed,

> [The] appointment of Arne Duncan, former CEO of Chicago Public Schools, as the U.S. Secretary of Education, marked the pinnacle of hope for our work

in education reform. In many ways, we feel the stars have finally aligned. With an agenda that echoes our decade of investments—charter schools, performance pay for teachers, accountability, expanded learning time, and national standards—the Obama administration is poised to cultivate and bring to fruition the seeds we and other reformers have planted.[10]

Political leaders do not merely succumb to pressures and cash from economic elites. Elected state and federal officials play an independent role in the policy process, as mediators between corporate leaders and voters. Parties are coalitions of various fragments of the voting population; to win office they generally have to appeal to both their bases and enough independent swing voters to achieve an electoral majority. The primary aim of political parties and candidates is to secure and maintain office. Policy positions are their marketing messages. Politicians won't embrace policies that turn voters away, no matter how much these are favored by the money people.

In light of the clear failures of the one-size-fits-all factory school, and the well-orchestrated campaign to discredit it, political elites have needed new policies to demonstrate their own posture of reform. They first welcomed NCLB and in turn have welcomed the diversified provider model touted by corporations and the Gates, Broad, and Walton foundations because it maintains the promise of education as a panacea while aligning with post-Reagan-Thatcher skepticism about government control in the social and educational sectors.

On the political-economy side of the change process, then, the stars did indeed align: the corporate elites, their wealthy philanthropic foundations, and both political parties got on the same page and Secretary Duncan then aggressively imposed the diversified provider model by administrative fiat. Duncan has used the Gates *Turnaround Handbook* as the guide for his signature Race to the Top initiative, and Gates has paid for the consultants hired to write the state grant applications. States suffering from huge budget deficits after the recession of 2008 have desperately sought Race to the Top money, even modifying state education laws in the process. To win Race to the Top money, states have had to adopt the *Turnaround Handbook* as their guide.

There is, however, no credible evidence that "turnaround" works. On the contrary, a 2009 Stanford University study showed that 83 percent of students in charter schools performed either worse or no better than counterparts in conventional public schools. A 2010 Vanderbilt University study showed that teacher merit pay did not produce higher test scores. A January 2010 article in the *Chicago Tribune*[11] reported that an analysis of 2009 test data showed that Renaissance 2010 did little to improve the city's educational performance, but its school closings and student reassignments contributed to a rise in youth violence. In a stinging article in *Dissent*, "How Billionaires Rule Our Schools," Joanne Barkan asks when corporations and their foundations will back off from privatization and high-stakes tests:

> After five or ten more years, the mess they're making in public schooling might be so undeniable that they'll say, "Oops, that didn't work" and step aside. But the damage might be irreparable: thousands of closed schools, worse conditions in those left open, an extreme degree of "teaching to the test," demoralized teachers, rampant corruption by private management companies, thousands of failed charter schools, and more low-income kids without a good education.[12]

Political elites do not have five or ten years; the campaign cycle is never-ending, and politicians have to respond to voter concerns just as soon as they bubble to the surface.

Resistance to both the standardization of education and the outrageous inflation in college tuition costs is now running high. School boards are demanding an end to the high-stakes test regime. Led by Texas State Educational Commissioner Robert Scott, more than one hundred of the state's school boards, responding to an "unprecedented mania" of citizens against high-stakes testing, have passed a resolution stating that "over reliance" on standardized high-stakes testing is "strangling our public schools and undermining any chance that educators have to transform a traditional system of schooling into a broad range of learning experiences that better prepares our students to live successfully and be competitive on a global stage."[13] The Occupy movement also has educational standardization and the broken link between education and occupational opportunities clearly in its sites.

The tide is now turning away from the testing regime, and political elites will not want to be tarred for persisting in supporting it. Campaign contributions from corporations and their foundations, however generous, simply cannot compensate them for the loss of office. Some policy makers from both parties are abandoning their commitment to the factory paradigm and are open to new educational ideas.

2. Institutional Buffers to Change Have Collapsed

In response to constraint 2, deindustrialization has already added significantly to classroom stress, and the high-stakes test regime imposed by NCLB has eliminated the institutional wiggle room that permitted schools to buffer pressures for change and teachers to negotiate the taught curriculum with their students. Policy makers can now impose their will on the schools. But both high-stakes testing and deindustrialization provoke student misbehavior and violence, and add to teacher stress. As a result of these combined forces, teachers today are less able to cope and are burning out, while more students, unable to raise their test scores, are being pushed out.

Teaching is a very high-stress profession; a recent study of 17,000 professional workers found that teachers and nurses suffer higher levels of stress than any other profession sampled.[14] Teachers' professional viability depends upon the ability to cope by negotiating a classroom contract with their students. Deindustrialization and high-stakes testing have wiped out their coping strategies.

Deindustrialization and Classroom Stress

Classroom management problems have mounted, especially in industrial cities, as a result of globalization and the deindustrialization of the American workforce. Large concentrations of contingent work in the service sector and persistent unemployment are found in many cities. The reduced wages and scarce jobs cause family problems that are carried into school. Ariel Kalil at the University of Chicago, for example, has shown that a father's loss of more than one job is significantly associated with a high risk of his son's being suspended or expelled from school, while Bellair and Roscigno showed a strong effect of concentrated low wage service sector work and unemployment on the likelihood of both fighting and drug use among school-aged teens.[15] The 2008 recession and the weak job recovery with high unemployment and underemployment in contingent work have further stressed already troubled classrooms.

High-Stakes Tests and Classroom Stress

When institutional thinkers first argued against the possibility of fundamental change in the early 1990s, school reform efforts lacked strong enforcement mechanisms. The next reform effort, Goals 2000, introduced in 1994, still lacked them and once again failed significantly to raise test scores or graduation rates. In 2000 the bipartisan NCLB act put sharp teeth into the enforcement mechanisms: schools failing to demonstrate annual progress would be closed, and teachers failing to raise their students' test scores would be fired. Principals could thus no longer buffer external pressures or protect their teachers; teachers could no longer cope by negotiating a classroom work contract acceptable to their students.

The high-stakes test regime thus undercut the coping strategies of teachers and learners and pushed classroom dynamics to the breaking point.[16] It's not hard to understand why. People approaching a task with a *mastery goal orientation* aim to learn and grow. They are thus likely to enjoy the task, persist longer at it despite setbacks, and eventually succeed at a higher level. They understand that learning and growing involve trial and error, so they are not afraid to fail; instead they perceive failures as opportunities to improve. Those approaching a task with a *performance orientation*, on the other hand, aim to show themselves and others how good they are. They think of ability as fixed rather than modified by effort. They see failures as threats to their self-worth, become self-conscious, and end up even more prone to poor performance. They withdraw from challenges and hide their weaknesses, and make it impossible for others to help, even further blocking their growth.[17]

The high-stakes testing regime undercuts teachers regardless of their goal orientations; it punishes failure and thus frustrates the mastery-oriented teachers who are open to experimentation and hope to learn from failures. It also exposes the failures of performance-oriented teachers, undermining both their self-worth and performance. Either way, it adds more stress to an already highly stressful situation.

High-stakes testing also imposes parallel stresses on both mastery- and performance-oriented learners; the former are blocked from trying things out and bored by rote learning, while the latter have their shortcomings exposed, become self-conscious, lose self-esteem, and perform even worse. High-stakes tests do not improve student performance, but do significantly increase misbehavior and decrease school attachment.[18]

A 2012 MetLife study reports that teacher satisfaction has now fallen to the lowest level since the annual survey was initiated, and a higher percentage of senior teachers plan to leave the profession. Breaking down institutional buffers to change by robbing teachers of wiggle room has not ushered in a new era of success, but has stressed teachers and learners past the breaking point.[19]

3. "Real Education" and "Real Schools" No Longer Exist

The singular "one best system" with its powerful image of what a "real high school" looks like has broken apart and vibrant fragments of a shadow institution have appeared alongside the mainstream institution. With so many legitimate alternatives, no one today can confidently say what "real education" or "real schools" are.

The first phase of excellence reforms aimed to intensify the standard academic curriculum and to raise test scores. Far from promoting fundamental change, however, it locked in the standardized tests and test prep routines that prevented serious change. The second phase has given rise to a variety of schools within the charter framework with different curricula and instructional methods. Given the recent networked learning innovations, technology and diversity have been combined and permuted into a dizzying array of new curricular and organizational forms. In the process, new schools have diverged more and more from the conventional pattern and the idea of what a real school looks like has gone up in smoke.

Charter School Diversity

Today you can choose from many alternative school formats in free, publicly supported charter schools. If you want to send your kids to a Montessori school, the Horizon Charter School offers its Montessori Academy.[20] A Waldorf school? The Circle of Seasons Charter School on the former campus of Penn State–Lehigh Valley welcomes you.[21]

Are you an adult high school dropout wishing to go to college but turned off by the idea of fitting in with teens at your local high school? A new adults-only charter high school has recently opened in Washington, DC.[22] Some charter schools serve homeschool families directly; the kids enroll, but only the parents attend classes—to learn about homeschool teaching; the kids continue to learn at home.[23] Or maybe you want your kids to learn at home but want them to get a structured high school education you cannot provide. Dozens of charter cyber-schools such as PA Cyber and Utah Open Charter High, discussed in Chapter Nine, exist to serve you.

Maybe your teens love horses and are thinking of becoming veterinarians. If so Arizona Agribusiness and Equine Center Red Mountain High School offers a program in equine studies where students ride and care for horses, take college courses, and even earn an associate's degree along with their diploma. In addition to the equine teachers the faculty includes licensed vets, and a vet school has partnered with AAECRM to offer its graduates a tuition discount. "I'm interested in horses, so this was a no-brainer, to go here," sixteen-year-old Megan Stephenson says. Equine teacher Vicki Grady adds, "I only wish there was a school like this when I was growing up.... It's great kids have so many options these days and can focus on their interest early."[24]

Many charter school networks offer innovative programs on multiple campuses. High Tech High serves the San Diego region with five high schools. While specializing in science and engineering, High Tech High, surprisingly, does not focus on computers and offers no virtual classes. Instead, it features personalization, real-world learning, and authentic assessment.[25] Moving even closer to the open learning model developed in Chapter Twelve, the Big Picture Schools cofounded in 1995 by former public school principals Dennis Littsky and Elliot Washor are based on ten "differentiators," including learning through real-world internships, one-student-at-a-time personalization, authentic assessment, advisors and mentors for all, school-college partnerships, and adult support—using parents and family members as mentors and as scouts for community-based learning opportunities, internships, and apprenticeships. While Big Picture Schools still include standardized tests in their assessment routines, their students are also evaluated on "exhibitions and demonstrations of achievement, on motivation, and on the habits of mind, hand, heart, and behavior that they display—reflecting the real world evaluations and assessments that all of us face in our everyday lives." Big Picture now operates seventy schools and is growing.[26] Such unique charter schools are no longer on the fringe; they are now among the standard options within the system. If they were freed from the high-stakes testing game, they would already *be* open learning centers.

Homeschooling and Unschooling

In the 1970s homeschooling was a fringe practice; those who homeschooled their kids had to suspend the deeply entrenched collective faith in schooling. Today that faith is rapidly eroding; homeschooling is now legal in every state. Although the statistics are disputed, the most conservative estimates available are that about 15,000 school-age children participated in homeschooling in 1972, 300,000 in 1988, 850,000 in 1999, and more than 1.5 million in 2007. That number increased by 7 percent from 2007 to 2010, while in the same period the number of children enrolled in schools increased by less than 1 percent, making homeschooling the fastest growing educational trend. "There's no reason to believe it would not keep going up," Gail Mulligan of the National Center for Educational Statistics recently told *USA Today*.[27] And as *Education Week* put it,

> Homeschooling, once dismissed as a fringe activity practiced by head-in-the-sand reactionaries and off-the-grid hippies, is now widely considered an integral part of the mainstream education system.[28]

The Internet and Web 2.0 technologies have made the homeschooling of teens more practicable than ever. Parents and learners can now download limitless learning materials from Wikipedia, the Khan Academy, and myriad web portals. And networked learning experiences, unlike standard school practices, fit very well with the knowledge and skill needs of future knowledge and high-skill workers.

As early as 2000, Stanford University began actively to recruit homeschooled learners, and it has remained among the most eager of elite universities to embrace them. The admissions office flags each homeschooler's application for special consideration and bases its decision on the students' own descriptions of their learning histories, letters of reference from adults outside of the family, and SAT scores. Among homeschooled students admitted to Stanford, "self-teaching" is a common theme as it demonstrates that the learners have already taken responsibility for their own learning. Asked why the university has demonstrated such an interest in this population, "admissions officers sum it up in 2 words, intellectual vitality."[29]

The new trend in homeschooling is so-called unschooling, leaving young people on their own, without a curriculum or formal subject matter lessons, to learn directly from their life experiences. Initially promoted by educational thought leader John Holt in 1985, unschooling, after a slow start, has boomed as it has incorporated web-based independent learning. Though on its face a radical departure from traditional homeschooling, unschooling (without the provocative label), has actually been a common homeschooling practice for teen education. Homeschool parents, after sitting down their preteens for formal lessons, frequently become "guides on the side," helping when called upon but encouraging independent learning. In fact, while the most popular reason for homeschooling remains religious and moral education, a surprising 65 percent of all homeschool parents in a 2007 survey included among their reasons a "non-traditional approach to children's education" or considered themselves "unschoolers who consider typical curriculums and standardized testing as counterproductive to quality education."[30]

Homeschooling, like charter schooling, is wearing away the collective American faith in standardized learning. Mitchell Stevens, in his comprehensive study of homeschooling families, *Kingdom of Children,* concluded that the fact that so many "sensible parents share this utter lack of faith in the public schools and their keepers signals an educational legitimacy crisis whose breadth and depth have yet to be fully measured."[31]

Today charter schools, homeschools, and even unschools are components of a shadow institution operating alongside the mainstream educational institution, providing legitimacy for alternative ways of organizing learning and preparing for occupational opportunities. If institutional theorists still believe that one model of "real education" and "real schools" dominates the public mind and prevents consideration of alternatives, they are all alone.

4. A New Educational Synthesis Is Emerging

Thought leaders are now offering synthetic visions of a new education aligned with contemporary technologies, work opportunities, and models of rational action. These visions are now ripe for convergence toward a new institutional pattern.

The conceptual innovations of Will Richardson, Henry Jenkins, Judy Breck, and Curtis Bonk, as noted earlier, convincingly outline and justify new practices, but do not yet, in themselves, set out a new educational paradigm. The innovative practices of High Tech High and the Big Picture Schools, moreover, are still today mere alternatives within a fractured mainstream system. But these new visions and practices take on board the new digital technologies and occupational structures and are tailor-made for the external and internal pressures educators now face.

What else is needed? William Reid offers a model of the education change process involving five phases: (1) external social change, forging (2) new groupings of elites and interested publics with new needs, who (3) place new pressures on the educational institution, leading to (4) experimentation with various innovations linked rhetorically to these constituencies, providing means whereby (5) viable inventions can form stable and coherent identities and transform the mainstream institution.[32]

A close study of prior paradigm shifts suggests, however, that phase 5 needs to be broken into several constituent parts. Before new inventions can transform the institution three other things are necessary: (6) a comprehensive vision—a goal culture of the new institution to articulate the various fragmentary inventions and assign them determinate places in the new order, and a transition culture marking out plausible steps in the change process; (7) responsible public leaders (think Horace Mann and Charles Eliot) to manage the transition, husbanding the new paradigm through thorny political and institutional obstacles; and (8) a social construction process where new practices are, in a give and take with various constituencies, adjusted to emerging real-world conditions and become entrenched.[33]

We have successfully completed the first four phases of the learningweb revolution, and the spread of inventions like High Tech High and the Big Picture Schools demonstrates that we are well into stage 5. The remaining tasks include consolidating conceptual visions of the sort presented in this book, building alliances with established political and institutional leaders and their constituents in the educational public to prepare the political and institutional ground for new practices, and finally putting them in place, at least on a pilot basis, and undergoing the process of adaptation and adjustment as educational leaders and their teachers, learners, communities, and families together forge a new educational institution.

What can be done to advance these necessary final steps in the learningweb revolution? We will take this up this question in the next and final chapter.

CHAPTER FIFTEEN
WHAT NEEDS TO BE DONE?

For the past thirty years American economic and political elites have, with ever-declining public support, been busy reforming the schools. School reform has involved a large shift of power from local communities and states to national elites and the federal government. School reform has tightened the grip of the factory paradigm on the educational system. The regime of high-stakes testing has dominated, elevating basic verbal and quantitative learning while diminishing or even destroying social and artistic subject matters. Education, defined as an adventurous journey into the world of knowledge and skill and life-affirming attitudes on the way to participation in the adult world, has been reduced to a test prep assembly line. This has to stop. The learning assembly line never worked, is now broken, and cannot be fixed. I'm with Judy Breck: *the first step is to stop fixing the schools.*

WHAT WE ALL CAN DO

To break the grip of the factory paradigm and ease the transformation to Education 2.0, all of us, in our roles as citizens and members of our various national, state, metropolitan, and municipal communities, can play our part.

We can all advocate for young people and for their educations. We can inform ourselves as members of the educational public. The information in this book is not esoteric; most has been gleaned from front-page news stories. The learningweb revolution is a fast-moving and newsworthy story, and the daily newspapers and the weekly news magazines are on top of it.

Property owners in particular are under a large school tax burden; they should educate themselves about where their tax dollars are going and about possible, more effective alternative approaches for their communities. Most of us are active users of the Internet and can learn about new uses of the web for learning. We can also share perspectives about the future of our schools with friends and neighbors and the rest of the nation; the future of our kids is surely as important as the sports scores or the new drapes. We all have to resist the temptation to jump to conclusions or, worse, to fall uncritically into a reactive mode, blaming one or another bogeyman—socialists, immigrants, secular humanists, teachers, the Internet, or worst of all, young people—for the failures of our educational arrangements. There is much we can do if we step up to the plate.

The problem lies in our outmoded factory paradigm. In a way this is good news. A paradigm is no more than a set of institutional norms and expectations. As soon as we pull away from these norms, stop believing, sharing, and imposing these myths, they collapse. Sure, the state officials can keep forcing us to send our kids to school and submit to a bloated curriculum and high-stakes tests even after large proportions of the population withdraw their assent, just as former communist governments forced workers to work in obsolete factories producing what no one wanted even after they could no longer pay them their meager wages. But coercive measures are weak, meet with powerful resistance, and eventually fail. Sometimes the collapse is sudden and completely unexpected, as it was with the Soviet system. The rapid collapse of compulsory schooling and recognition of homeschooling as a legitimate alternative is instructive as we envision the end of the factory school. Protests against the regime are spreading from citizen groups and the Occupy movement to school boards throughout even the most conservative states. I don't think officials are keen on forcing young people to submit to curricula and high-stakes tests at gunpoint.

Much can be done by each of us in our social roles and positions, as young learners, parents, citizens, and business people. School leaders and state and federal policy makers also have key contributions to make. In what follows I summarize some important steps each of them can take.

Young Learners

Young people have the largest stake in the learningweb revolution. Many hate school, yet are adept web-based learners and netcasters. They continue to go to high school and college only because they have no alternatives, are forcefully pressured by parents and other adults, and still believe that a pot of gold lies at the end of the rainbow for diploma holders. Daily news stories about unemployed college and professional school graduates with hundreds of thousands of dollars of debt should erode this over-the-rainbow myth, but what then?

It is criminal for adult society to put the heaviest burden for figuring out the world on the young. A healthy society lives in a vibrant world that wants and needs the young. The burden for change lies solidly upon the shoulders of adults. Still, there are many things today's young people can do for themselves. To them I offer this counsel:

First, stand up for yourselves and demand your basic rights as young adults, including the right to learn independently and the freedom from involuntary incarceration in uncaring, information-poor, coercive institutions. On the other side of this coin, stop complaining about your plight and take responsibility for your learning; grow up and renounce adolescence as a phony life stage engineered to strip you of adult status. As teacher "Richard Rowland" asked the young Mark Salzman: ask yourselves what you are *doing about* your situation.

Second, deepen your awareness of your own natural bents, talents, interests, and passions, and, like Thelonious Monk, Tavi Gevinson, Mark Salzman, and Jayralin Herrera, build significant capabilities around your gifts and youthful energies. Document your learning and achievements in blogs, images, sound files, and YouTube videos and aggregate these documents in personal learning portfolios. Publish these online to make yourselves dually visible—capable of being located and assessed. Through Facebook and LinkedIn, network with others, share and exchange ideas and skills, collaborate on projects, and act collectively to further your interests as young adults. Build personal networks and care for them. These steps will help you envision future possibilities and move forward in achieving your life goals.

Third, solicit support and assistance from your parents and extended family members. Enlist your parents and family members as advocates in your relations with teachers and school officials. The other side of this coin is this: don't make negative projections or assumptions about the motivations of parents or teachers; they are doing their jobs as best they can in less-than-ideal circumstances.

Respect your teachers for what they know and for the honorable profession they have chosen, and actively avoid unnecessary interpersonal conflicts with them. It is wiser to sidestep than to fight against authority. If you find school oppressive, consider homeschooling or cyber-schooling if these options are possible in your family settings.

Fourth, devote yourself to academic study if you love it. If not, devote yourself to something else you love. Take on difficult projects, build serious capabilities, and construct plans for your future. Going through the motions in high school, attending an uncompetitive college, and graduating in a field where majors are not in demand is a loser's game; it will not advance your goals and, if you take on student debt, can cripple you financially for life. Don't go to college unless you profoundly love academic study or have sharply focused professional goals that will require university-based credentials.

Parents

Parents are now standing at the turning point of paradigm change. Most of us who are now parents of teens and young adults came of age under the older educational paradigm. Some of us loved our education; others hated it or had decidedly mixed experiences. Regardless, the paradigm worked for many of us and commanded our allegiance. We learned that school was the ticket to a secure future, that if we stayed in school, obeyed the rules, studied hard, and went to college we would have decent, secure jobs.

The most important, and sometimes the most difficult, lesson every parent needs to learn is that the world changes and that what worked for us may not work well for our kids. The lessons young people learn from their life experiences, peers, or teen culture may resonate more powerfully than our well-intentioned guidance or coercive directives. It is always better to listen closely to young people and discuss issues openly than to rely on parental authority. Open up and you just may learn something. If your kids don't open up to you about their lives and predicaments, it may be because they don't expect an open-minded, caring, appreciative response (of course there may be other, more troubling explanations). In particular, today's young adults have grown up with the Internet and come of age surrounded by Web 2.0 technologies; they are better informed and more empowered than youth of previous generations. Here are some useful steps to assist them and bring them along.

First, don't expect schools and colleges to do the whole job of educating your kids. Schools and colleges are mere education instruments, useful but partial. Informal learning in many settings is also necessary. Get involved early; your kids need your help more than ever. Step up to the plate as a parent; it's your most important job.

Second, make your home a learning hub. Get rid of distractions. Turn off the TV and unplug the cable. If you can, get broadband Internet access and construct a home Wi-Fi network, and supply everyone in the family with a laptop computer or mobile device. Learn useful software programs and model their responsible use. Involve your teens in your projects at home and work as appropriate, and share your knowledge and skill generously with them. Stay informed about your children's online activities and projects, but don't horn in unless you are invited. Explore with them the limitless resources of the learningweb. Explore Khan Academy videos and OpenCourseWare offerings from the world's leading universities. Encourage your children to become voracious independent learners and support their efforts.

Third, become powerful learning advocates for your teens. Help them in negotiating their school lives. Build relationships with school officials and contribute as you can as a volunteer. Inquire what the schools are doing to assist the growth of your children and aid their initiation into adult society, and press them to do more. Join with other parents in demanding that the school put an end to boring, didactic teaching, the rigid, bloated curriculum, and endless test preparation for innumerable test days. Demand rich opportunities for independent, web-based, learner-directed learning. Consider homeschooling or cyber-schooling if it fits the needs of your children and teens and you can devote the time and attention it will take. You will learn a lot about many things, including your own kids. Spending even a year with your children as their teacher and colearner will deepen family bonds. It will also prepare you better to understand their talents and interests, challenges, and predicaments, so you can guide and assist them. Most important, adopt an open, experimental approach to your teens' educations. Try things out, build on what works. Don't push the myth that everyone has to go to college to get a decent job and that investment in college will be richly rewarded. If your kids are excellent students with a strong desire for academic knowledge, or if they have specific and realistic professional ambitions, encourage them to go to college and help if you can. But don't push your kids if this means saddling them with college debt that can permanently destroy their financial futures.

School Leaders

School leaders, including district school board members and superintendents, principals, and teacher union officials, all have a powerful stake in the entrenched educational arrangements. We cannot expect them to lead the learningweb revolution. On the contrary, most will at best adopt a posture of reform while actually buffering the pressures from both elites and grassroots citizen groups for fundamental change. The other side of this coin is that as educational professionals and leaders of the education public, school leaders are aware of the current problems with the factory paradigm. Many will openly admit that the high-stakes test regime is crazy. Many also possess a genuine and deep desire to foster learning. Their organizational and institutional commitments are balanced by professional values as educators. It would be a practical mistake to write them off. I am adopting an interstitial model of revolutionary change, bringing revolutionary practices into older institutions in order to transform them. Some school leaders will be our willing, others our unwitting, allies. So what can they do? Here is what I would suggest.

School Boards

To district school boards and their members I say, you are our elected educational leaders and the guardians of our community's schools. Take up this responsibility. Stop acting as time-servers filling out government forms or going along with the outmoded status quo. Be powerful community spokespersons for youth education. Make our schools into learning spaces, not holding pens and test prep academies. Join with school boards throughout the country in refusing to cooperate with the mis-educative high-stakes testing regime. Build strong alliances throughout the community with your constituents, and direct their efforts toward enhancing opportunities for youth learning.

Learn about current developments in business organization and leadership. Read and discuss books about nonhierarchical management models, networks, and complexity. Hire superintendents who are educational leaders, not mere managers. Either alone or with other districts, re-establish one high school as a complex open learning center!

SUPERINTENDENTS

Superintendents hire and manage principals and teachers and set the overall tone of school district operations. Here are some suggestions for them:

First, publicly reject the factory model of education as the production of specific learning objectives. Instead, think of your district and its schools as complex organizations set up to release complexity and harvest educational value—much of which will be unpredicted. Establish clear mission statements, governing principles, and constraints for the schools, but do not micromanage; trust the free intelligence of your principals and teachers to generate many wonderful results, some of them unexpected and amazing.

Second, in hiring, don't think narrowly about professional credentials. Hire principals on the basis of their superior educational backgrounds, broad educational visions, demonstrated leadership, innovativeness, and flexibility. Hire instructional staff members based on rich learning histories and broad talents and life experiences. If necessary, hire teachers on provisional licenses and work out arrangements for certification through part-time, on-the-job study. Make sure every new hire is web-savvy. Don't pigeonhole any staff members as, for example, a mere algebra teacher. Consider their entire learning histories and growth potentials as educators, leaders, and project managers working with professional peers, contract teachers, and volunteers. Keep a detailed inventory of the interests, activities, and accomplishments of your teachers, and stay alive to ways these can be fed back into the educational efforts of their schools and the district. Hire dedicated mentors with training and prior experience in counseling and coaching, and focus on teachers trained in learning technologies and capable of training and organizing volunteer tutors.

Third, advocate constantly for your schools, principals, teachers, and young learners. Consider granting your teachers 20 percent release time for creative projects; monitor these projects and their results, celebrate them publicly, and feed them back into the instructional program. Strongly encourage independent web-based learning, equip the schools to support it, and set out governing principles for teaching and curriculum that ensure plenty of time and space for it.

Build strong alliances throughout your community and beyond to build support for this educational mission and to obtain resources, especially volunteers and access to learning spaces through internships and apprenticeships.

Teachers

The revolution may take place gradually, as high schools adopt more complex strategies and morph into learning centers. Or a few districts may open pilot learning centers that catch on. Either way, because centers will continue to offer the high school curriculum and give graduates a diploma, some teachers are likely to remain in conventional roles, teaching assigned courses in traditional high school subjects. For those interested in joining the revolution, however, I offer these suggestions:

First, in your professional capacity, advocate against the factory school regime. Resist being reduced to a test-prep worker. Join teachers' groups and pressure for greater teacher autonomy and the elimination of high-stakes testing.

Second, stay abreast of new web-based education developments. Learn about and experiment with different online learning formats. Become an active online learner. Further your professional growth through courses from the Harvard-MIT edX project. Develop your own online courses. Learn to go beyond didactic teaching and take advantage of new online opportunities for discursive and heuristic teaching and learning. Document your work in podcasts and videos. Join the Classroom 2.0 movement and expand your use of Web 2.0 techniques in your teaching. Create model lessons as demonstrations of new teaching and assessment techniques, and publicize these on Twitter and Facebook. Form a personal online learning network with other professionals, share resources, collaborate on projects, and act collectively to further your professional interests.

Third, develop your extra-professional passions and become an expert and a specialist in at least one. These passions may include academic fields beyond your immediate teaching area, or they may lie entirely beyond education in the narrow sense. Either way, organize your special knowledge and skill to enable you to be a teacher, guide, mentor, or coach for young people with similar interests. Create opportunities to feed your expertise back into your school's educational programs.

Fourth, learn about and experiment with short-form learning experiences: presentations, workshops, seminars, and short courses. Design and offer these experiences for students, fellow professionals, and members of the community. Include them as option modules in your courses or those of other teachers. Talk with your principal about building some of these activities into your teaching load. Also develop your special gifts as a mentor or tutor, and find ways to include these activities in your work, for example, as a manager of volunteer mentors or tutors. Again, discover whether they can become part of your official load.

Fifth, learn how to encourage and guide independent learning. Work with students planning to enter regional or national arts, science, or humanities competitions. Organize your courses in the core + option modules format, and include independent learning experiences among the option modules students can select.

Finally, partner with individuals and groups in the community to secure resources for learning, including volunteer teachers and tutors, and opportunities for internships and apprenticeships. It takes a village to raise a child. Be open to working with contract teachers and volunteers and to managing their efforts.

Policy Makers

State and federal policy makers, in cooperation with economic elites, have led the school reform campaign. School reform has failed. The schools have been reduced to test prep academies, but still test scores haven't improved. The test regime has succeeded only in tightening the grip of the outmoded factory paradigm. Meanwhile outsourcing and high technology robots have killed jobs for high school graduates. College tuitions have grown exponentially while many with college and professional school diplomas remain unemployed. The factory paradigm is shot.

Policy makers will not want to be saddled with these failed policies forever. To them I offer these ideas.

For State Policy Makers

First, reclaim education as a reserved power of the state. Make your state one of the laboratories of democracy by piloting innovative programs and publicizing your results. Reject any and all unfunded educational mandates from the federal government. If necessary, take the federal government to court to get its hands off education in your state. The constitution is on your side, and the Supreme Court will be sympathetic. Invite the federal government to support your educational efforts through block grants. On the other side of this coin, diversity and intergroup learning are necessary elements of education today. Public provisions that discriminate against disadvantaged groups invite and demand federal scrutiny. Make all provisions for the Internet in education inclusive in their benefits and supportive of intergroup learning. The best way to do this is to foster cooperative efforts across district lines.

Second, end statewide imposition of the factory school model. Broaden curriculum mandates to encourage innovation. Get rid of compulsory high-stakes tests and mandatory "seat hour" requirements.

Third, take advantage of learningweb cost savings. Require all schools to use free open access textbooks, free and low-cost web-based courseware, and digital library collections. Establish statewide cyber-schools, and agencies to disseminate online courses to schools and learners throughout the state. Adjust state education regulations to facilitate cyber-schooling and homeschooling.

Fourth, think beyond school districts to metropolitan regions. Build up your intermediate educational agencies if your state has them, and establish them if it does not. Intermediate agencies are perfect vehicles for metropolitan area interdistrict efforts, and learning centers are designed to coordinate metropolitan resources and opportunities. For example, the intermediate district in the Harrisburg, Pennsylvania, region, in collaboration with twenty-nine regional districts, has established a regional high school for creative and performing arts, which the individual districts could not operate on their own. Like this school, regional learning centers could serve all learners in a metropolitan area. Multidistrict learning centers can bring diverse youngsters together for intergroup learning without relying upon unlawful race-based school assignments.

Fifth, work with large metropolitan school districts or intermediate districts to establish one or more open learning centers on a pilot basis, with funding set aside for research and assessment. Exempt these pilot centers from restrictive state education regulations. Start small and set aside sufficient funds for research, assessment, and dissemination of results. Follow up on successful efforts.

For Federal Policy Makers

Stop trying to fix NCLB. Re-examine the school reform efforts since A Nation at Risk and accept that they have failed. Stop trying to fix the schools from the top-down. Restore the data-gathering and dissemination functions of the Department of Education to primacy. Restore NAEP to its original mission.

Create research initiatives through the National Science Foundation and the Department of Education to rethink both educational research and teacher training for the Internet era. Broaden the research agenda beyond school-based learning to include home learning, informal learning, and web-based learner-directed learning.

Business Enterprises

The business community has a large stake in education, and it has influenced educational policy and school practice since the early industrial era. It wants the schools to supply it with an abundant population of capable workers and eager consumers, so that it can shift significant training and marketing costs to the public. It also is a supplier of products to the schools, for example, buildings, textbooks, and computers. In addition to taxes, it supports the schools through partnership programs and provisions for cooperative education in internships and apprenticeships.

The learningweb revolution offers the business community new opportunities to support youth learning, but also poses new challenges: publishing conglomerates, for example, will lobby fiercely against open access textbook regulations. Echoing Judy Breck, I urge them to turn their creative energies in new directions. For those businesses wishing to align themselves with the learningweb revolution, I offer these ideas:

First, team up with local schools. Encourage and support your employees as volunteer mentors, teachers, and tutors. Develop informative short courses about your industry for in-person or video delivery. Assist young people in learning about the real world of work in your industry. Offer internships and waged apprenticeships for young learners. Go beyond the legal minimum requirements to make sure these experiences serve educational purposes and are not exploitive. Team up with the schools to offer academic credit toward graduation for these experiences.

Second, drop diploma requirements in hiring. Where possible, hire on the basis of certificates of mastery and demonstrable capabilities. Encourage your employees to network actively in your industry to locate available young talent. Involve many young people in project teams as contract workers and help them acquire industry experiences and cutting-edge skills. Help even those who will not be hired as permanent employees to grow; what goes around will come around.

Third, encourage all employees and work teams to document their work processes through reports, blogs, and videos and then make these documents available online to give young people an inside view of work in your industry. Gather and aggregate the most informative of these in high-quality programs attractive to young learners.

Finally, sponsor local, regional, and national competitions and awards. The Intel Science Competition, originally established by Westinghouse, is perhaps the best-known example. Siemens and other corporate foundations also sponsor national competitions for high school students (including those who are homeschooled) in science, technology, and environmental sustainability research. Winners receive up to $100,000 in scholarships. These competitions and awards motivate tens of thousands of young learners to engage in independent research; their winners are invited to the White House, are featured in news stories, and serve as role models for independent learners.

Even the smallest local firms, however, can establish competitions in their own fields, offering a few hundred dollars in award money and motivating young learners to get involved in projects, recruit teachers and other adults as facilitators and coaches, and strive for their personal best.

* * *

Readers who want to learn more about the learningweb revolution can start by consulting the books, articles, and websites listed in the Appendix that follows. Stay informed, get active, join the revolution!

APPENDIX
BIBLIOGRAPHICAL NOTES AND USEFUL WEBSITES

Full references are provided in the endnotes for items cited in the text. This selective bibliographical note directs readers to works useful for background understanding.

CHAPTER ONE: YOUNG PEOPLE

The idea of young people "casting nets" to connect up with others is developed by Judy Breck, *Connectivity: The Answer to Ending Ignorance and Separation* (Lanham, MD: Scarecrow Education, 2004). Robert Epstein, *Teen 2.0: Saving Our Children and Families from the Torment of Adolescence,* develops the idea that teens, by age fourteen or fifteen, are adults functioning at peak mental development.

CHAPTER TWO: EDUCATION AND CHANGE

Bernard Bailyn, *Education in the Formation of American Society* (Chapel Hill: University of North Carolina Press, 1960), and Lawrence Cremin, "Public Education and the Education of the Public," *Teachers College Record* 77 (1975):

1–12, and *Traditions of American Education* (New York: Basic Books, 1977), urged education scholars to turn their attention from schools to consider broader educative forces in society. John Dewey had also conceived the school as only one of many educative forces, but Bailyn and Cremin went further, insisting that the family, church, and workplace, like the school, had their own "curricula"—institutionalized sequences of activities with social aims. In this way they extended the notion of education beyond schooling, while also setting some useful limitations to the study of education in that broadened sense. Wayne Urban, "The Word from a Walrus: Five Decades of the History of Education Society," *History of Education Quarterly* 50, no. 4 (2010): 429–459, has, however, recently questioned whether the Bailyn-Cremin conception of education has been a useful guide for historians of education.

Richard S. Peters, *Education as Initiation* (an inaugural lecture delivered at the University of London Institute of Education, London, University Institute of Education Studies in Education, 1964), had a profound impact on educational scholarship, teacher education, and curriculum in the United Kingdom and throughout the Anglophone world at a time when teacher education was becoming institutionalized as a university-based profession. Gert Biesta, "Education, Not Initiation," in *Philosophy of Education 1996*, ed. F. Margonis (Urbana, IL: Philosophy of Education Society, 1996), 90–98, is one of many critical responses to the initiation metaphor.

Henri-Irénée Marrou, *A History of Education in Antiquity* (Madison: University of Wisconsin Press, 1956), is the standard work on Greek and Roman education. Bruce A. Kimball, *Orators and Philosophers: A History of the Idea of Liberal Arts Education*, exp. ed. (New York: College Board, 1995), is a recent survey covering the evolution of the classical and liberal-modern educational ideals. C. P. Snow, *The Two Cultures* (London: Cambridge University Press, 1959), offers a popular treatment of the divide separating the humanities from the sciences and engineering in the modern university. Carl Bridenbaugh, *The Colonial Craftsman* (New York: New York University Press, 1950), provides a compelling account of the training and capabilities of craft workers prior to the spread of public education in America.

Mortimer Adler, *The Paediea Program: An Educational Syllabus* (New York: Touchstone, 1984), is the inspiration for the tripartite division of didactic, discursive, and heuristic elements in formal education. Malcolm Gladwell, *Outliers: The Story of Success* (New York: Little Brown, 2008), has popularized the idea that 10,000 hours of practice are needed to develop capabilities to the expert level.

Chalmers Johnson, *Revolutionary Change* (Boston: Little Brown, 1966), remains the best brief account of the concept of revolution, in terms of the development of revolutionary goal cultures and transition cultures. T. S. Kuhn, *The Structure of Scientific Revolutions*, 2nd ed. (Chicago: University of Chicago Press, 1970), introduced the notion of paradigm change to account for the growth of scientific knowledge. The term "paradigm" and Kuhn's general approach to the growth of knowledge have survived intense criticism and have been extended to account for change in numerous cultural spheres. The classical discussion of Kuhn and paradigms is Imre Lakatos and Alan Musgrave, eds., *Criticism and the Growth of Knowledge* (Cambridge: Cambridge University Press, 1970).

Chapter Three: High Schools

William Reese, *The Origin of the American High School* (New Haven: Yale University Press, 1999), is the best history of the early years of the American high school. Readers seeking to understand the subsequent evolution of the high school should consult Edward Krug, *The Shaping of the American High School*, vols. 1 and 2 (Madison: University of Wisconsin Press, 1972).

Raymond Callahan, *Education and the Cult of Efficiency* (Chicago: University of Chicago Press, 1964), is an influential useful history of the origins of the factory school. Samuel Haber, *Efficiency and Uplift Scientific Management in the Progressive Era 1890–1920* (Chicago: University of Chicago Press, 1964), places the cult of efficiency in its cultural context during the American progressive era.

Andy Green, *Education in State Formation: The Rise of Educational Systems in England, France and the USA* (New York: Palgrave-MacMillan, 1991), explains the uneven development of mass public education in terms of the needs of different nations to construct national subjects out of diverse populations assembled in their territorial boundaries. Green's theory of education as an instrument of state formation in the "cultural revolution of modernity" accounts for both the sequence of development of national educational systems and many characteristic features of mass education.

Robert Dreeben, *On What Is Learned in School* (Reading, MA: Addison-Wesley, 1968), a modern classic in sociology of education, explains the administrative procedures of schooling as constituting a "hidden curriculum" used to adjust citizen-subjects to the normative requirements of industrial societies.

A reader seeking to gain perspective on schooling—to step outside the entrenched paradigm and view schooling more objectively and dispassionately—might start with Andy Green and Robert Dreeben.

Larry Cuban, "Curriculum Stability and Change," in *Handbook of Research on Curriculum,* ed. P. W. Jackson (New York: Macmillan, 1992), 216–247, and David Tyack and Larry Cuban, *Tinkering toward Utopia: A Century of Public School Reform* (Cambridge: Harvard Press, 1995), provide an influential account of the "grammar" holding the standard features or commonplaces of schooling together.

Barton Bledstein, *The Culture of Professionalism: The Middle Classes and the Development of Higher Education in America* (New York: Norton, 1976), explains the origin and growth of the middle class as a result of the rise of university-based professional education.

CHAPTER FOUR: SCHOOL FAILURE I—ACADEMIC UNDERPERFORMANCE AND ADMINISTRATIVE INEFFICIENCY

School critics come in many varieties. Early romantic critics such as Jonathan Kozol, *Death at an Early Age: The Destruction of the Hearts and Minds of Negro Children in the Boston Public Schools* (Boston: Houghton Mifflin, 1967), and Herbert Kohl, *36 Children* (New York: Penguin, 1968), blamed school systems and teachers for ignorance, neglect, cynicism, and racism. For these critics school improvement depended upon a new breed of smarter, better educated, progressive, and activist school leaders and teachers—people like themselves. They provide inspiration for contemporary efforts like Teach for America to recruit Ivy League graduates (like the authors) to spend a period of time teaching in troubled schools.

Traditionalist critics like Max Rafferty, *Suffer, Little Children* (New York: American Library, 1963); E. D. Hirsch, *Cultural Literacy: What Every American Needs to Know* (New York: Random House, 1987); and Diane Ravitch, *Left Back: A Century of Failed School Reform* (New York: Simon and Schuster, 2000), all blame a weak curriculum—undermined by progressive instructional methods—for dumbing down our students. Their solutions, though different in many details, have been to impose more demanding academic content. Neoliberal critics from Milton Friedman, *Capitalism and Freedom* (Chicago: University of Chicago Press, 1962), to John Chubb and Terry Moe, *Politics, Markets, and American*

Schools (Washington, DC: Brookings Institution, 2000), have accounted for the failure of the public system on the basis of its monopoly status—the lack of competition that permits the schools to survive despite mediocre performance. Their solution has been to introduce competition through school vouchers or publicly funded charter schools.

Persistent critics of school reform have included David Berliner and Bruce Biddle, *The Manufactured Crisis: Myths, Fraud, and the Attack on America's Public Schools* (New York: Basic Books, 1994). A frequently cited review is Lawrence Stedman, review of Berliner and Biddle, "The Manufactured Crisis," *Education Policy Analysis Archives*, North America, 4 (January 1996).

CHAPTER FIVE: SCHOOL FAILURE II—SOCIAL IRRELEVANCE AND THE LOSS OF POLITICAL LEGITIMACY

John W. Meyer, "The Effects of Education as an Institution," *American Journal of Sociology* 83, no. 1 (1977): 55–77, explains the legitimacy of the educational system as an outgrowth not of its efficacy in fostering learning, but rather of its success in determining the social and economic destinies of graduates. Thomas F. Green, *Predicting the Behavior of the Educational System* (Syracuse, NY: Syracuse University Press, 1980), offers a penetrating account of today's school problems as stemming from system growth: once most of a cohort is "educated," being educated no longer confers any special social or economic advantage. Those groups reaching any given level of school or college attainment last get little or nothing for their efforts. Ivan Illich, *De-Schooling Society*, argued in 1970 that institutionalized schooling in America had expanded to the point of "radical monopoly" over learning; only schooling now counts as "education" in the popular mind, as the school has delegitimized abundant resources for nonschool learning. The result is that "education" has become a scarce resource, while each additional unit of schooling renders the population more and more stupid. Society needs to be "de-schooled" for education to improve.

From Carol Bird's *The Case Against College* (New York: David McKay, 1975), to Anya Kamenetz's masterly *DIY University: Edupunks, Edupreneurs, and the Coming Transformation of Higher Education* (White River Junction, VT: Chelsea Green Publishing, 2010), perceptive critics have questioned the educational and economic investment value of college education. Kamenetz draws on the insights of John Meyer and Ivan Illich.

CHAPTER SIX: THE INTERNET AND THE WORLD WIDE WEB

Johnny Ryan, *The History of the Internet and the Digital Future* (UK: Reaktion Books, 2010), provides a compelling account of the evolution of digital computers, information networks, the Internet, and the World Wide Web. Tim Berners-Lee, *Weaving the Web: The Original Design and Ultimate Destiny of the World Wide Web, by Its Inventor* (New York: HarperCollins, 1999), is Berners-Lee's own account of the development of the World Wide Web.

Albert-László Barabási, *Linked: How Everything Is Connected to Everything Else and What It Means,* and Duncan J. Watts, *Six Degrees: The Science of a Connected Age,* are accessible popular accounts of the mathematics and science of networks.

Yochai Benkler, *The Wealth of Networks: How Social Production Transforms Markets and Freedom* (New Haven, CT: Yale University Press, 2006), is an influential account of information network–based peer production. Steven Weber, *The Success of Open Source* (Cambridge, MA: Harvard University Press, 2004), drawing on detailed histories of Linux and other open source software programs, offers a framework for explaining how peer-construction within information networks can succeed as an alternative to commercial production.

CHAPTER SEVEN: WEB 2.0 AND THE NET CULTURE

Web 2.0 has a large and ever-expanding literature. The term appears to have been introduced by Darcy DiNucci in her 1999 article "Fragmented Future," *Print* 53, no. 4 (1999): 32, and became wildly popular after John Battelle and Tim O'Reilly reintroduced it at the first Web 2.0 conference in late 2004. From the start, the term referred not to new technical developments in, but rather new social uses of, the World Wide Web, including the blogs and social media that spread after 2003.

Bradley Jones, *Web 2.0 Heroes: Interviews with 20 Web 2.0 Influencers* (New York: Wiley, 2008), exposes the controversies surrounding early conceptualizations of Web 2.0. Sarah Lacey, *Once You're Lucky Twice You're Good: The Rebirth of Silicon Valley and the Rise of Web 2.0* (New York: Gotham Books, 2008), explores the business culture that spawned it. Scott Rosenberg, *Say Everything: How Blogging Began, What It Became, and Why It Matters* (New York: Crown, 2009), and Julia Angwin, *Stealing MySpace: The Battle to Control the Most Popular Website in America* (New York: Random House Digital, 2009), recount the early history of blogs and social media. Howard Rheingold, *Smart Mobs: The Next Social Revolution* (New York: Basic Books, 2002), pioneered reflection on social uses of mobile computing devices.

Rick Levine, Christopher Locke, and Doc Searls, *The Cluetrain Manifesto: The End of Business as Usual* (Cambridge, MA: Da Capo Press, 2001), set out an influential mantra to guide commerce on the social web: focus not on transactions but conversations.

Google is regarded as a model Web 2.0 firm. Its story is recounted in Ken Auletta, *Googled: The End of the World as We Know It* (New York: Penguin, 2009). Jeff Jarvis, *What Would Google Do?* (New York: HarperCollins, 2009), formulates the rules Google follows and shows how many kinds of organizations, from auto manufacturers to hospitals and universities, could gain from adopting such rules. Google rules have influenced my thinking about open learning centers.

Clay Shirky, *Here Comes Everybody: The Power of Organizing without Organizations* (New York: Penguin, 2009); Don Tapscott and Anthony Williams, *Wikinomics: How Mass Collaboration Changes Everything* (New York: Penguin, 2008); and Jeff Howe, *Crowdsourcing: Why the Power of the Crowd Is Driving the Future of Business* (New York: Random House Digital, 2009), offer influential, and overlapping, frameworks for understanding organization and commerce more generally in a world of individuals connected by social media. Clay Shirky, *Cognitive Surplus: How Technology Makes Consumers into Collaborators* (New York: Penguin Books, 2011), explains the personal motivations and potential social benefits of what has come to be called "user-generated content"—individuals creating, sharing, and collaborating on text documents, images, and videos for public use without compensation. Henry Jenkins, *Convergence Culture: Where Old and New Media Collide* (New York: New York University Press, 2007), is an influential account of Web 2.0 culture.

Andrew Keen, *The Cult of the Amateur: How Blogs, MySpace, YouTube, and the Rest of Today's User-Generated Media Are Destroying Our Economy, Our Culture, and Our Values* (New York: Doubleday, 2007), and Jaron Lanier, *You Are Not a Gadget: A Manifesto* (New York: Vintage, 2010), launch similar attacks against Web 2.0. Their complaints boil down to two: that user-generated content and mass collaboration are destroying individual creativity and surrounding us with junk; and that by destroying the market for significantly valuable cultural products, they are also eliminating significant culture-producing individuals. Lanier goes further, stating that Web 2.0 is destroying all forms of professional work and "screwing the middle class."

Keen and Lanier, rather than taking issue with accounts of how Web 2.0 *works* offered by Shirky, Tapscott, Howe, and other web gurus, condemn the cultural and social *outcomes* of Web 2.0. Their first complaint is hard to sustain: while Web 2.0 provides anyone—however untalented—with a platform for expression and collaboration, it hardly provides an audience. No one links to junk and it disappears into the "long tail," while higher-quality products often "go viral"; and many of the users generating them are not amateurs, but professionally trained creative individuals discovering new expressive outlets. The second complaint reflects the genuine social revolution inherent in Web 2.0; it is upending long-established expectations about work and social life. Some web gurus are simply boosters of Web 2.0; others, including Clay Shirky, take note of its revolutionary challenges. Keen and Lanier are nostalgic for a world that is not coming back. What we need now are new models for living, learning, and working—and a new social contract for global network society negotiated in the political sphere. If political efforts fail, then Web 2.0 itself will provide the available means—as demonstrated in the Arab Spring—for coordinating the inevitable rebellion, targeting plutocracy, not web technology.

Bill Wasik, *And Then There's This: How Stories Live and Die in Viral Culture* (New York: Viking Penguin, 2009), recounts a series of experiments the author conducted, including the generation of flashmobs, to study the social mechanisms of Web 2.0. Wasik's concern—quite different but no less disconcerting than those of Keen and Lanier—is that Web 2.0 will turn everyone into perpetual marketeers scurrying for attention and opportunity.

Chapter Eight: The Learningweb

Curtis Bonk, *The World Is Open: How Web Technology Is Revolutionizing Education* (San Francisco: Jossey-Bass, 2009), provides a comprehensive overview of web-based developments in education, while Clayton Christiansen, *Disrupting Class, How Disruptive Innovation Will Change the Way the World Learns* (New

York: McGraw-Hill, 2008), offers a framework for understanding these developments and their effects.

Although the literature on open knowledge and open science is expanding exponentially, there does not yet appear to be that single "unavoidable" book-length account of the movement. A good source is Rufus Pollack, *The Value of the Public Domain* (London: Institute for Public Policy Research, 2006), online at www.ippr.org/publication/55/1526/the-value-of-the-public-domain. Pollack is director of the Open Knowledge Foundation.

Andrew Lih, *The Wikipedia Revolution: How a Bunch of Nobodies Created the World's Greatest Encyclopedia* (New York: Hyperion, 2009), recounts the history of wikis, open encyclopedias, and Wikipedia.

There is not yet a book-length treatment of open textbooks. A useful guide for preparing open educational resources and textbooks is J. Hilton, D. Wiley, J. Stein, and A. Johnson, "The Four R's of Openness and ALMS Analysis: Frameworks for Open Educational Resources, *Open Learning: The Journal of Open and Distance Learning* 25, no. 1 (2010): 37–44.

On Web 2.0 in informal education, the best source for Library 2.0 is Michael E. Casey and Laura C. Savastinuk, *Library 2.0: A Guide to Participatory Library Service* (Medford, NJ: Information Today, 2007); for Museum 2.0, the definitive source is Nina Simon, *The Participatory Museum* (Museum 2.0, 2010). These books are full of useful guideposts for Education 2.0.

Chapter Nine: The Web in the School

There are numerous guides for using Web 2.0 tools in schools and classrooms. The go-to guide is Will Richardson, *Blogs, Wikis, Podcasts, and Other Powerful Web Tools for Classrooms*, 3rd ed. (New York: Corwin, 2010). Others include Rena Palloff, *Building Online Learning Communities: Effective Strategies for the Virtual Classroom* (San Francisco: Jossey-Bass, 2007); and David Warlick, *Classroom Blogging: A Teacher's Guide to the Blogosphere* (Lulu, 2005).

The definitive book on cyber-schools does not yet exist. For a good introduction to the topic, see David Wiley, "The Open High School of Utah: Openness, Disaggregation, and the Future of Schools," *TechTrends* 53, no. 4 (July/August 2009): 37–40.

The Obama administration's educational technology plan is *Transforming American Education: Learning Powered by Technology,* National Educational Technology Plan–Technical Working Group, Office of Educational Technology,

US Department of Education, 2010. A symposium in the journal *E-Learning and Digital Media* 8, no. 2 (2011) discussed and evaluated the plan. My assessment here originated as a contribution to that symposium.

Chapter Ten: New Educational Visions

Although differing in details, many of the new web-based education visionaries converge on key features of schools of the future. I have highlighted Curtis Bonk, *The World Is Open: How Web Technology Is Revolutionizing Education* (San Francisco: Jossey-Bass, 2009); and Judy Breck, *109 Ideas for Virtual Learning: How Open Content Will Help Close the Digital Divide* (Lanham, MD: Rowman & Littlefield, 2005). Another interesting account is Allan Collins and Richard Halverson, *Rethinking Education in the Age of Technology: The Digital Revolution and Schooling in America* (New York: Teachers College Press, 2009).

In emphasizing the need to situate change processes in their broad institutional contexts I am guided by classical sociological conceptions of "institutions," as summarized in W. Hamilton, "Social Institutions," in *The Encyclopedia of Social Sciences,* ed. E. Seligman, vol. 8 (New York: MacMillan, 1932), 84–89, and S. Eisenstadt, "Social Institutions: The Concept," in *The Encyclopedia of the Social Sciences,* ed. D. Sills, vol. 7 (New York: MacMillan, 1972), 409–421. The mutual adjustment of institutions within changing social life is analyzed in J. Turner, *The Institutional Order* (New York: Longman, 1997). Turner says, "The analysis of human social institutions begins with the recognition that social structures and systems of cultural symbols [are] used to sustain humans in an environment ... for maintaining, reproducing, and organizing a population so that it remains viable in an environment" (2, 4). The economy, polity, culture, education, and social structure are interdependent in this sense, and when one changes, the others must eventually readjust.

Chapter Eleven: Complex Organizations

Complexity is another topic with an exponentially expanding literature. The best introduction remains Malcolm Waldrop, *Complexity: The Emerging Science at the Edge of Order and Chaos* (New York: Simon and Schuster, 1992). More recent popular overviews include Steven H. Strogatz, *Sync: The Emerging Science of Spontaneous Order* (New York: Hyperion, 2003); and Len Fisher,

The Perfect Storm: The Science of Complexity in Everyday Life (New York: Basic Books, 2009).

The implications of complexity theory for organizations are explored in Ralph Stacey, *Complexity and Creativity in Organizations* (San Francisco: Berrett-Koehler, 1996); Stephan H. Haeckel, *Adaptive Enterprise: Creating and Leading Sense-And-Respond Organizations* (Cambridge, MA: Harvard Business School Press, 1999); and David Axelrod and Michael Cohen, *Harnessing Complexity, Organizational Implications of a Scientific Frontier* (New York: Free Press, 2000).

William Doll, "Complexity in the Classroom," *Educational Leadership* 47, no. 1 (1989): 65–70, is a pioneer effort to apply insights from complexity theory in the study of classrooms. Brent Davis and Dennis J. Sumara, eds., *Complexity and Education: Inquiries into Learning, Teaching, and Research*, extend Doll's work to the study of other education commonplaces. Many contemporary authors hint at schools as complex organizations but I am not aware of any prior effort building seriously on the work of Stacey, Haeckel, Axelrod, and Cohen or other complexity theorists to reconceive schools as complex organizations.

CHAPTER TWELVE: OPEN LEARNING CENTERS

Readers wishing to follow up on the opening narratives can consult Robin D. G. Kelley, *Thelonious Monk: The Life and Times of an American Original* (New York: Free Press, 2009); and Mark Salzman, *Lost in Place: Growing Up in Suburbia* (New York: Vintage, 1996).

CHAPTER FOURTEEN: THE LEARNINGWEB REVOLUTION

My formulations about revolutionary change have been shaped by Chalmers Johnson, *Revolutionary Change* (Boston: Little, Brown, 1966); and T. S. Kuhn, *The Structure of Scientific Revolutions*, 2nd ed. (Chicago: University of Chicago Press, 1970). Erik Olin Wright, *Envisioning Real Utopias* (New York: Verso, 2010), presents an overall vision of social change similar to mine: open learning centers are examples of "real utopias" in his sense. His book also helped guide the selection and organization of topics for this book.

On stages of the revolutionary change process, my formulations have been influenced by Neil Smelser, *Social Change in the Industrial Revolution* (London:

Routledge, 1959); on fundamental changes in educational practice, by William Reid, *Curriculum as Institution and Practice: Essays in the Deliberative Tradition* (Mahwah, NJ: Erlbaum, 1998), chapter 8, "The Problem of Curriculum Change," 116–140. My views on fundamental education change are developed further in Leonard J. Waks, "The Concept of Fundamental Educational Change," *Educational Theory* (2007): 277–295.

Useful Websites

General Websites

Curricki, a wiki of educational resources: www.curriki.org/
The Budapest Open Access Initiative: www.soros.org/openaccess/read.shtml
The Directory of Open Access journals: www.doaj.org/
The George Lucas Foundation's Edutopia initiative: www.edutopia.org/
Steve Hargadon's Classroom 2.0 initiative: www.classroom20.com/
The Gates Foundation's educational initiatives: www.gatesfoundation.org/united-states/Pages/education-strategy.aspx
Sal Khan's Academy: www.khanacademy.org/about
The OpenCourseWare Consortium: www.ocwconsortium.org/aboutus
OpenCourseWare courses: www.ocwconsortium.org/courses
MIT's list of most popular OpenCourseWare courses: http://ocw.mit.edu/courses/most-visited-courses/
edX—The Future of Online Education: For anyone, anywhere, anytime: https://www.edx.org/
Coursera—Take the world's best courses, online, for free: https://www.coursera.org

Informal Education

Library 2.0

Library 2.0—the future of libraries in the digital age: www.library20.com/
The Shifted Librarian (blog): http://theshiftedlibrarian.com/
Museum Two (blog): http://museumtwo.blogspot.com, see especially http://museumtwo.blogspot.com/2006/12/what-is-museum-20.html

Schools

PA Cyber: www.pacyber.org/
The Utah Open High School: www.openhighschool.org/faqs/
High Tech High Schools: www.hightechhigh.org/about/
Big Picture Schools: www.bigpicture.org/big-picture-history/

Notes

Introduction

1. John Dewey, *The School and Society* (Chicago: University of Chicago Press, 1899), chapter 1, "The School and Social Progress."

Chapter One

1. www.thestylerookie.com/2008/03/new-girl-in-town.html.
2. This dismissive comment is meant to suggest that as anomalies, exceptional people provide no insight into how the rest of us are to be regarded or treated. But first, the comment is empty; it follows from the simple tautology that no one can be anyone else. And second, anomalies are frequently the most useful cases to consider in re-evaluating our entrenched practices, especially when these are failing. Buried here also is the assumption that exceptional people are in some way a different breed or species, and not at all like "ordinary" young people. Down deep, no two people are at all alike, but "exceptions" have no more brain cells than we do. The great masses of young people have never before had the world's knowledge, or the power to manipulate it, at their fingertips. They have also been subject for the last hundred-plus years to restrictive social conditioning and containment in schools. As a result we have very little idea what a typical young person can achieve today; to find out we would have to equip many ordinary youths with web access, freedom from arbitrary restrictions, and adult guidance and support when and if needed. We may be amazed.
3. www.missminimalist.com/2011/05/real-life-minimalists-jayralin/.
4. http://itstartswith.us/simply-said-teenagers-are-awesome/.
5. Robert Epstein, *Teen 2.0: Saving Our Children and Families from the Torment of Adolescence* (Fresno, CA: Linden, 2010).
6. No author, "A Class Act—Young Inventors, The Great Idea Finder," www.ideafinder.com/features/classact/young.htm.

7. Bill Medic, "Why October Is Youth History Month," The Pro Youth Pages, Revised, 2010, www.proyouthpages.com/youthhistorymo.html.

8. No author, "German Teen Solves 300-Year-Old Mathematical Riddle Posed by Sir Isaac Newton," Foxnews.com, May 27, 2012, www.foxnews.com/world/2012/05/27/german-teen-solves-300-year-old-mathematical-riddle-posed-by-sir-isaac-newton/.

9. No author, "Real Life 'Doogie Howser' Gets His MD," NYDailyNews.com, June 4, 2012, http://articles.nydailynews.com/2012-06-04/news/32037196_1_medical-school-yano-graduation.

10. *Rhetoric* II.1389a31.

11. *Metaphysics* I.980a21.

12. John Rawls, *A Theory of Justice*, rev. ed. (Cambridge: Harvard University Press, 1999), 379.

13. Or the anatomy of frogs or the difference between sine and cosine curves or the battle of the Carolina Raiders (this last example is from a recent statement of national history standards—what every young citizen should know).

Chapter Two

1. Bernard Bailyn offered this broad definition as a guide for the scholarly study of the field of education in his seminal book *Education in the Formation of American Society* (Chapel Hill: University of North Carolina Press, 1960), 14. Lawrence Cremin wrote a favorable review of Bailyn's book and built upon Bailyn's definition in *Traditions of American Education* (New York: Basic Books, 1977), 134. Cremin had earlier defended the broad social definition of education, stating, "The important fact is that family life does educate, religious life does educate, and work does educate; and, what is more, the education of all three realms is as intentional as the education of the school, though in different ways and in different measures." See Cremin, "Public Education and the Education of the Public," *Teachers College Record* 77 (1975): 1–12.

2. The idea of education as initiation into worthwhile activities is developed in R. Peters, "Education as Initiation: An Inaugural Lecture Delivered at the University of London Institute of Education," University Institute of Education Studies in Education, London, 1964. The idea was restated in R. S. Peters, *Ethics and Education (EE)* (London: Allen and Unwin, 1966).

3. Mary Warnock, *Education: A Way Ahead* (Oxford: Blackwell, 1979). As Kelvin Beckett sums up her view, "Warnock objected to any analysis of the concept of education that suggests that this aim is more important than transmitting facts and skills." See Beckett, "R. S. Peters and the Concept of Education," *Educational Theory* 61, no. 3 (June 2011): 242.

4. Gert Biesta, "Education, Not Initiation," in *Philosophy of Education*, ed. F. Margonis (Urbana, IL: Philosophy of Education Society, 1996), 90–98.

5. Mircea Eliade, "Initiation, an Overview," in *Encyclopedia of Religion*, vol. 7, ed. Mircea Eliade (New York: Macmillan, 1987), 224.

6. B. Bernstein, H. L. Elvin, and R. S. Peters, "Ritual in Education," *Philosophical Transactions of the Royal Society of London*, Series B, Biological Sciences 251, no. 772 (Dec. 29, 1966): 429–436.

7. The broad definition of education is even encoded in American law. In a 1936 decision in the Weyl case, Judge Martin Thomas Manton writing for the United States Court of Appeals

for the Second Circuit, noted that every dictionary includes broad definitions of "education" in addition to narrow ones limiting it to school and college instruction. He ruled on that basis that charitable donations for informal education programs and public awareness campaigns in the media were equally qualified along with schools and colleges to the tax exemption granted to "education." *Weyl v. Commissioner of Internal Revenue* 48 F 2d. 811 (1931).

8. Elmore Leonard, *Elmore Leonard's 10 Rules of Writing* (New York: William Morrow, 2007), 75.

9. "The educational history of New England and, to a lesser extent, the Middle Atlantic States challenges ... that public schooling directly led to mass literacy. The surge in rates predated the mid-century public school movement and rather resulted from informal instruction in families, neighborhoods, and on the job. Sunday schools, local proprietary 'Dame' schools, and the often poorly funded, short-session district schools merely supplemented informal learning. Only long after state school boards in Massachusetts and Connecticut were founded in the late 1830s would free public schooling reverse these conditions: the home becoming the reinforcer of literacy and the school its primary generator." Gale Cengage, "Literacy," in *American History through Literature, 1820–1870,* vol. 2, ed. Janet Gabler-Hover and Robert Sattelmeyer (Farmington Hills, MI: Thomson Gale, 2006); available at www.enotes.com/literacy-reference.

10. The classic study is Carl Bridenbaugh, *The Colonial Craftsman* (New York: New York University Press, 1950).

11. C. P. Snow, *The Two Cultures* (London: Cambridge University Press, 1959).

12. "In Philadelphia Benjamin Franklin sought not only to create a local institution of higher learning, but also to provide an education that did not fit the models already established in New England and Virginia. In Europe and the colonies up to that time, such schools had emphasized the training of new clergymen. The goal of Franklin's nonsectarian, practical plan would be the education of a business and governing class rather than of clergymen.... Franklin's concept of higher education was new in the mid-18th-century western world, but is what a liberal education has now become." From *Franklin's Vision to Academy to University of Pennsylvania,* an exhibit researched, written, and created by Mary D. McConaghy, Michael Silberman, and Irina Kalashnikova, www.archives.upenn.edu/histy/features/1700s/penn1700s.html.

13. Not everyone can be exceptional. Many young people, however, can become *very good* at various pursuits and can greatly expand their general culture and adult connections by engaging in them. And we simply can't know what they can do if we deprive them of the conditions for doing it. Many "ordinary" people might simply amaze us.

14. "In 1869–70, there were only about two persons receiving high school diplomas per 100 17-year-olds (table 19). While this ratio increased to 9 per 100 during the ensuing 40 years, high school graduation remained an atypical occurrence, at least in most areas of the country.... During the 1910s, the 1920s, and the 1930s, the graduation ratios increased rapidly. In 1939–40, the ratio rose above 50 percent for the first time. During World War II, the graduation ratio dipped as some young men left school to join the armed forces. Immediately after the war, the graduation ratio resumed its upward trend, reaching 70 percent in 1959–60. A peak ratio of 77 percent was attained at the end of the 1960s. After falling to around 71 percent in 1979–80, the ratio has returned to about the same level as the late 1960s." T. D. Snyder, ed., *120 Years of American Education* (Washington, DC: Government Printing Office, 1993), 30. See the informative graphic representation of this trend in Snyder's figure 11, p. 31.

15. I am here extending the scope of initiation beyond Peters, who confined his attention primarily to school and college learning and thus spoke about initiation into worthwhile *academic* activities: doing history, math, science, but also engineering, the arts, and so on. Peters focused on the school-related phases of preparation, but clearly informal learning is also essential to initiation in adult activities. As a simple example, after medical students complete medical school they are still required to serve as interns before they can be recognized as professional doctors.

16. Mortimer Adler, a philosopher and polymath who designed a model high school program in the 1980s, offered an illuminating analysis of what is involved in this kind of learning, and my discussion is strongly influenced his analysis. Mortimer Adler, *The Paediea Program: An Educational Syllabus* (New York: Touchstone, 1984).

17. Mortimer Adler, *How to Speak, How to Listen* (New York: Scribner, 1983).

18. Malcolm Gladwell, *Outliers* (New York: Little, Brown, 2008).

19. The curriculum for mass secondary education is bloated because it is packed with contents bearing very little relevance for the great mass of its students. It is little changed since the first high schools; in 1821 it was intended for the very small group aiming to secure technical and managerial jobs in early industrial society. It was not then conceived of as an education suitable for the masses of workers. As shaped by Benjamin Franklin and George Emerson it was then relevant only to a percentage of teens. Even in 1821, however, most of those who attended high school regarded it as bloated and cherry-picked only the courses needed for their intended jobs.

20. T. S. Kuhn, *The Structure of Scientific Revolutions,* 2nd. ed. (Chicago: University of Chicago Press, 1970), 150.

Chapter Three

1. Chaim M. Rosenberg, *The Life and Times of Francis Cabot Lowell, 1775–1817* (Lanham, MD: Lexington Books, 2010).

2. R. Dreeben, *On What Is Learned in School* (Reading, MA: Addison-Wesley, 1968), esp. chapter 5.

3. See Samuel Haber, *Efficiency and Uplift Scientific Management in the Progressive Era 1890–1920* (Chicago: University of Chicago Press, 1964) for an account of the spread of scientific management thinking throughout American culture.

4. Raymond Callahan, in *Education and the Cult of Efficiency* (Chicago: University of Chicago Press, 1964), a classic study of scientific management in the schools, explains the adoption of industrial management techniques in education by reference to the vulnerable position of school leaders who were subordinate to school boards dominated by business leaders. It is more plausible to think of university-trained school administrators as inhabiting the same cultural matrix as business leaders, and hence also sharing the values and norms of the industrial culture.

5. Ibid., 6.

6. Ibid., 54.

7. William Reese, in *The Origin of the American High School* (New Haven, CT: Yale University Press, 1999), 137, tells us that the domination of teaching by textbooks was so severe that courses were frequently identified simply by the names of the textbook author rather than by the subject, a pattern carried over from the pre–Civil War college.

8. Ibid., 132.
9. Ibid., 141.
10. See D. B. Tyack and L. Cuban, *Tinkering toward Utopia: A Century of Public School Reform* (Cambridge, MA: Harvard University Press, 1995); L. Cuban, "Curriculum Stability and Change," in *Handbook of Research on Curriculum*, ed. P. W. Jackson (New York: Macmillan, 1992), 216–247; C. E. Bidwell and R. Dreeben, "School Organization and Curriculum," in *Handbook of Research on Curriculum*, 345–362.
11. Ted Sizer, "School on a Hill," *Harpers*, September 1, 2001, www.highbeam.com/doc/1G1-77702891.html.
12. K. Anderson-Levitt, "The Schoolyard Gate: Schooling and Childhood in Global Perspective," *Journal of Social History* 38, no. 4 (2005): 987–1006.
13. Dreeben, *On What Is Learned in School*.

Chapter Four

1. Larry Cuban in many places notes that placing these burdens on the schools is a way of neglecting intractable problems. Policy elites can respond directly to declining wages, for example, by raising the minimum wage. By demanding that the schools attack low wages by improving occupational education, policy elites successfully evade responsibility for direct responses to the problem of low wages.
2. This result is known to statisticians as Simpson's paradox. ANAR used scare tactics to force the states to adopt its recommended reforms. When the Sandia results were presented to David Kearns, deputy secretary of education, he allegedly told the researchers, "You bury this, or I'll bury you!" See Gerald Bracey, "Righting Wrongs," *Huffington Post*, December 3, 2007, www.huffingtonpost.com/gerald-bracey/righting-wrongs_b_75189.html. The Sandia report received almost no media attention.
3. The first TIMSS data were collected in 1995, a dozen years after ANAR; they were collected again in 1999, 2003, and 2007. In 1995 the United States ranked twenty-fourth in composite math-science scores for thirteen-year-olds (eighth grade) and was one of the few countries whose twelfth-graders did worse on both math and science than its eighth-graders. The 1999 results were similar.
4. David Berliner and Bruce Biddle, in a book published shortly after the 1995 legislation, *The Manufactured Crisis: Myths, Fraud, and the Attack on America's Public Schools* (New York: Basic Books, 1994), argued trenchantly that the alleged academic failure of the schools was a "manufactured crisis" pushed by right-wing critics aiming to dismantle public education. They argued that, contrary to the laments of school critics, test scores had not been declining. Furthermore, they said, the single-minded pursuit of high test scores was not appropriate for our American democracy. The book drew a sharp reply from many, including the liberal educational scholar Lawrence Stedman, who challenged the authors' analysis of test score results and restated the case for high academic expectations from a liberal perspective. See L. Stedman, review of Berliner and Biddle "The Manufactured Crisis," *Education Policy Analysis Archives* 4 (January 1996), http://epaa.asu.edu/ojs/article/view/624.
5. Hank Hayes, "Gov. Bredesen Warns Schools to Expect Drop in Test Scores," *TimesNews.Net*, July 31, 2010, www.timesnews.net/article.php?id=9025190.
6. Sharon Otterman, "Most New York Students Are Not College-Ready," *New

York Times, February 7, 2011, www.nytimes.com/2011/02/08/nyregion/08regents .html?pagewanted=all.

7. While US fourth-graders showed no improvement on TIMSS in science and math from 1995 to 2003, eighth-graders showed modest improvement in 2003, arriving at twentieth place in math and fifteenth place in science. And in 2007, after NCLB reforms were in place, US eighth-graders moved up to eleventh of thirty-six nations in math and ninth of forty-eight nations in science, placing eleventh overall.

8. In 2000, US fifteen-year-olds scored fifteenth in reading; in 2003, twenty-fourth in math; and in 2006, twenty-first in science. In 2009 (two years after the 2007 TIMSS), US fifteen-year-olds scored thirtieth in math, twenty-third in science, and seventeenth in reading.

9. It is difficult to imagine that, after thirty years of panicked "wake up calls," anyone still expects American students to excel in international comparisons. Why should we be shocked by our PISA performances? This boy has already cried "wolf" too often.

10. The term "Sputnik moment" is particularly inept, as the curricular reforms initiated in the panic following the Soviet launch of Sputnik were memorable, monumental failures.

11. Yong Zhao, "High Test Scores, Low Ability," *New York Times*, December 4, 2010, www.nytimes.com/roomfordebate/2010/12/02/what-is-a-college-degree-worth-in-china/ high-test-scores-low-ability.

12. Jiang Xueqin, "The Test Chinese Schools Still Fail: High Scores for Shanghai's 15-year-olds Are Actually a Sign of Weakness," *Wall Street Journal*, December 8, 2010, http://online .wsj.com/article/SB10001424052748703766704576008692493038646.html.

13. The phrase "globally competitive workforce" should give rise to serious reflection. If young workers in developing nations are more docile than their US counterparts and are willing to work for dramatically lower wages, then corporations will, whenever possible, outsource tasks to these nations. For young American workers to be competitive in this sense, they will have to become equally docile and willing to accept third-world wages. Is that a goal we should strive for as a nation?

14. Chris Hedges has recently proposed a compelling explanation of the postglobalization US test mania. "We spurn real teachers—those with the capacity to inspire children to think, those who help the young discover their gifts and potential—and replace them with instructors who teach to narrow, standardized tests. These instructors obey. They teach children to obey. And that is the point." "Why the United States Is Destroying Its Education System," *Truthout.com*, April 11, 2011, http://truth-out.org/index.php?option=com_ k2&view=item&id=396:why-the-united-states-is-destroying-its-education-system.

15. Sarah Lacy and Peter Thiel, "We're in a Bubble and It's Not the Internet; It's Higher Education," *Tech Crunch*, April 10, 2011, http://techcrunch.com/2011/04/10/ peter-thiel-were-in-a-bubble-and-its-not-the-internet-its-higher-education/.

16. See "Peter Thiel giving $100,000 to dropouts," *San Francisco Business Times*, May 26, 2011, www.bizjournals.com/sanfrancisco/morning_call/2011/05/peter-thiel-giving -100000-to-dropouts.html.

17. Audrey Watters, "Top Ed-Tech Trends of 2011: The Higher Education Bubble," *Hack Education*, December 13, 2011, www.hackeducation.com/2011/12/13/ top-ed-tech-trends-of-2011-the-higher-education-bubble/.

18. Only 20 percent of fourth-graders, 17 percent of eighth-graders, and 12 percent of seniors scored at the "proficient" level. Christine Armario and Dorie Turner, "U.S. Students' Knowledge of History Weak, Test Shows," *Durango Herald*, June 14, 2011, http:// durangoherald.com/article/20110615/NEWS05/706159961/-1/s.

19. www.dailymail.co.uk/news/article-2064149/Aidan-Dwyer-The-13-year-old-boy-genius-created-revolutionary-solar-panels-looking-tree-branches.html#ixzz1jenUcDuh; http://articles.cnn.com/2012-01-12/us/us_new-york-homeless-teen_1_macarthur-foundation-fellowships-college-scholarship-homeless-shelter?_s=PM:US. The videos of these teens discussing their sophisticated projects are simply jaw-dropping.

20. Donald Knies, a teacher in my high school, was a world traveler and author of the book *Walk the Wide World*. He taught world geography in high schools to earn money to support his travels. His presence had a profound impact on me. The full text of his book is available at www.archive.org/details/walkthewideworld013412mbp.

21. In their classic study of teacher values, Philip Jackson and Elizabeth Belford showed that on a list of eleven teaching activities, preparing students to attain specific learning objectives came in dead last. See their "Behavioral Objectives and the Joys of Teaching," *School Review* 75, no. 3 (1965).

22. Liana Heitin, "Survey: Teacher Job Satisfaction Hits a Low Point," *Ed Week Teacher*, March 7, 2012, reported that teacher job satisfaction is at the lowest it's been in more than two decades.

CHAPTER FIVE

1. John Gardner, *Excellence: Can We Be Equal and Excellent Too?* (New York: Harper, 1961).

2. See Thomas Friedman, "Average Is Over," *New York Times*, January 25, 2012, www.nytimes.com/2012/01/25/opinion/friedman-average-is-over.html.

3. Anthony Carnevale, who served as chair of President Clinton's National Commission on Employment Policy and has also advised George Bush and Barack Obama on the transition from school to work, told Anya Kamentz that "In the American system employers use post-secondary education as the sorting device for hiring ... so in the end you have the whole population headed for college and most of them don't get through." This is not an overstatement: according to Nancy Hoffman of Jobs for the Future, 94 percent of American teens now think they are headed for college.

During the Clinton years Carnevale developed a strong school to work policy, with apprenticeship programs based on government-industry partnerships. This was opposed by minority groups and progressives, and the key provisions of the bill were watered down. These left-oriented groups feared enshrining a two-track educational system in the law. They acknowledged that the present system already has two tracks—the well-off go to college, the poor don't, and the latter track—the one for the poor—doesn't work. They nonetheless saw vocational tracking as a no-no, even if the outcomes for the poor would be better. They said, "the worst thing that could happen is that we have two systems that *both* work." See Anya Kamenetz, *DIY University: Edupunks, Edupreneurs, and the Coming Transformation of Higher Education* (White River Junction, VT: Chelsea Green Publishing, 2010), 37–38.

Today neither track works. The worst thing that could happen would be if we trapped everyone into the no longer workable college track. An exciting vocational alternative would today attract the middle class and the poor and would serve both well.

4. Books making the case against the continuing economic value of a college education have included Carolyn Bird's prescient *The Case against College* (1975) and Anya Kamenetz's masterly *DIY University* mentioned in note 3. And a 2012 analysis of government data by

economists at Northeastern and Drexel Universities and the Economic Policy Institute shows the debt challenges of the young are now drastically worse.

5. "Live and Learn: Why We Have College," *The New Yorker,* June 6, 2011, www newyorker.com/arts/critics/atlarge/2011/06/06/110606crat_atlarge_menand?currentPage=all.

6. The *Atlantic* article, "In the Basement of the Ivory Tower," appeared in June 2008. See www.theatlantic.com/magazine/archive/2008/06/in-the-basement-of-the-ivory-tower/6810/. The article was expanded into a book with the same title (New York: Viking, 2011).

7. Richard Arum and Josipa Roksa, "Your So-Called Education," *New York Times,* May 14, 2011, www.nytimes.com/2011/05/15/opinion/15arum.html.

8. Hope Yen, "1 in 2 New Graduates Are Unemployed or Under-employed," Associated Press, April 23, 2012, http://news.yahoo.com/1-2-graduates-jobless-underemployed-140300522.html.

9. "The Cruel Fist of Supply and Demand Spaketh Thusly," Lawyers Against the Law School Scam (blog), July 25, 2010, www.nalp.org/uploads/NatlSummaryChartClassof09.pdf. The author asks whether anyone has "advice on how anyone on here deals with the stress of shitlaw. I know we call it shitlaw, because it is. The pay is atrocious, the benefits non-existent ... I'm drowning in debt and live paycheck to paycheck ... I've had only one day off in a year, and think I am medically exhausted. This is what happens when you have hordes of talented, intelligent, ambitious people who have spent years chasing a dream, but where that dream involves a supply and demand situation where the supply substantially exceeds the demand."

10. David Segal, "Is Law School a Losing Game?" *New York Times,* January 8, 2011, www.nytimes.com/2011/01/09/business/09law.html?pagewanted=all.

11. The phrase "the culture of professionalism" was popularized in Barton Bledstein's classic study *The Culture of Professionalism: The Middle Classes and the Development of Higher Education in America* (New York: Norton, 1976). According to Sheila Slaughter and Gary Rhoads, that "culture" of university-based professional roles backed up by educational job credentials and state licenses is now being replaced by an "academic capitalist" knowledge/learning regime. See their *Academic Capitalism and the New Economy: Markets, State and Higher Education* (Baltimore: Johns Hopkins University Press, 2009).

12. The growing significance of the "amateur" workforce is explained clearly in Jeff Howe, *Crowdsourcing: Why the Power of the Crowd Is Driving the Future of Business* (New York: Random House Digital, 2009), especially chapter 1, "The Rise of the Amateur," 23–46.

13. Peter Coy, Michelle Conlin, and Moira Herbst, "The Disposable Worker," *Bloomberg Business Week,* January 7, 2010, www.businessweek.com/magazine/content/10_03/b4163032935448.htm.

14. Hannah Seligson, "No Jobs? Young Grads Make Their Own," *New York Times,* December 11, 2010, www.nytimes.com/2010/12/12/business/12yec.html?_r=1&pagewanted=all.

15. Aziz Senni, with Jean-Marc Pitte, *L'Ascenseur social est en Panne ... J'ai pris l'escalier* (The social escalator is broken ... I took the stairs), *L'Archipel,* 2005.

16. There are persistent worries about the exploitation of contract workers and freelancers in digital sweatshops. See http://fiverr.com/, where freelancers compete for opportunities to do challenging tasks for just five dollars. On the other hand, freelance workers are also banding together for union protections; see www.freelancersunion.org/.

17. John W. Meyer, "The Effects of Education as an Institution," *American Journal of Sociology* 83, no. 1 (1977): 55–77.

Chapter Six

1. Burton H. Klein, "A Radical Proposal for R. and D.," *Fortune* 57, no. 5 (May 1958): 112.
2. Johnny Ryan, *The History of the Internet and the Digital Future* (London: Reaktion Books, 2010), 44.
3. See the Wikipedia article on Baran, http://en.wikipedia.org/wiki/Paul_Baran.
4. Philip Elmer-Dewitt, "First Nation in Cyberspace," *Time International*, December 6, 1993, no. 49, www.chemie.fu-berlin.de/outerspace/internet-article.html.
5. Hypertext was further developed by Ted Nelson at Harvard in 1960.
6. Ryan, *History of the Internet*, 25.
7. Ibid., 24.
8. In 1971 Ray Tomlinson, a BBN engineer working on ARPANET, created the code for email, which rapidly became the most widely used feature of computer networks. Because email was not in his job description he had to hide his work from his supervisors for fear that they would fire him.
9. Ryan, *History of the Internet*, 105.
10. Ibid., 107.
11. Ibid., 109.

Chapter Seven

1. Rupert Murdoch, speech to the American Society of Newspaper Editors, Washington, DC, April 13, 2005, www.guardian.co.uk/media/2005/apr/14/citynews.newmedia.
2. Julia Angwin, *Stealing MySpace: The Battle to Control the Most Popular Website in America* (New York: Random House Digital, 2009), 210.
3. The term bears an explanation. Networks consist of nodes and links. In a social network the members are the nodes, and the connections between them the links. Graph theory is that branch of mathematics that studies such objects. The term "social graph" thus indicates networks of people as seen through the lens of graph theory, as objects that can be understood in abstract terms.
4. Bradley Jones, *Web 2.0 Heroes: Interviews with 20 Web 2.0 Influencers* (New York: Wiley, 2008), 82.
5. Ibid., 93.
6. Ibid., 47.
7. DeveloperWorks Interviews: Tim Berners-Lee, podcast recorded July 28, 2006. Transcript at www.ibm.com/developerworks/podcast/dwi/cm-int082206.txt.
8. A brief survey shows how these technologies support the social and cultural features of the new web. *AJAX*, shorthand for Asynchronous JavaScript and XML, is the toolkit developers use to create the rich, interactive user experience of Web 2.0. The term *Ajax* was coined in 2005 by Jesse James Garrett in *Ajax: A New Approach to Web Applications*, February 18, 2005, www.adaptivepath.com/ideas/essays/archives/000385.php.
   AJAX made websites fast and efficient. Before AJAX each user action on the web required the entire HTML page to be reloaded from a server, causing an interruption in use experience and a high load placed on servers. With AJAX pages can be refreshed without a pause; the web can provide users with the same immediacy and usability as the software programs resident on

their desktops. Software and data files in "the cloud" became just as good as those "at home." The time lags and clunky feeling caused by server calls and page reloads have been eliminated.

Flash is a container file format for web video. Before Flash, viewing online videos required a media player such as RealPlayer to be downloaded and installed on their desktops. These players worked differently, and often poorly, with different video formats. With Flash, users did not have to take the effort to download a player; Flash downloaded automatically and became resident on more than 90 percent of networked computers. As a container, it was equally compatible with competing video formats. Flash provided an almost universal, effortless, and smooth video experience on the web.

Google Gears and Adobe AIR have further enabled the rich, responsive user experience on the web by enabling the applications on the web to work smoothly with, and take advantage of, the power and storage capabilities of users' computing devices.

Finally, LAMP stands for a group of open source software programs: Linux (operating system), Apache (server), MySQL (database), and PHP Perl or Python (scripting languages). These programs have been created and improved on the Internet by voluntary labor; they are now available at no or low cost to web developers. LAMP is an enabling technology for Web 2.0 because it has dramatically lowered the technical difficulty and cost of web development.

9. Some commentators see the history of the Internet divided into the periods before and after the dot-com bubble burst in 1999–2000. The bubble resulted from mega-million-dollar deals for companies without revenues or even business plans but with enough hype to inflate their perceived market value. In this narrative Web 2.0 is *not* marketing hype but its antagonist: the use of open source software to lubricate web development *without* mega-million-dollar venture capital deals and the requisite marketing hype.

10. See Steven Levy, "Geek Power: Steven Levy Revisits Tech Titans, Hackers, Idealists," *Wired*, April 19, 2010, www.wired.com/magazine/2010/04/ff_hackers/all/1.

11. See Fatima Yasmine, "Greplin Founder Daniel Gross on his Amazing Story behind Building the Company," Entrepreneur, The Next Web Blog, March 5, 2011, http://thenextweb.com/entrepreneur/2011/03/05/greplin-founder-daniel-gross-on-his-amazing-story-behind-building-the-company-interview/.

12. No author, "Digg Clone: Start Your Own Digg in Five Minutes Flat with PHP," *Developer Tutorials*, April 6, 2008, www.developertutorials.com/tutorials/php/digg-clone-php-mysql-digg-quickly-108/.

13. Todd Haselton, "Obama Wants 98 percent of Americans to have 4G-speed Wireless in 5 Years," Mobileburn, February 11, 2011, www.mobileburn.com/news.jsp?Id=12910.

14. Chris Gayomali, "Obama Wants 4G for 98 percent of Americans by 2016, but How Would That Work?" *Time, Techland*, February 11, 2011, http://techland.time.com/2011/02/11/obama-promises-4g-for-98-of-americans-by-2016/.

15. As measured by the Keynote Business 40 Internet Performance Index (KB40), page download time has decreased from 2.8 to 2.33 seconds from February 2006 to February 2008. No author, "Average Web Page Size Septuples Since 2003," WebSiteOptimization.com, no date, www.websiteoptimization.com/speed/tweak/average-web-page/.

16. Excellent tutorial sites include How Stuff Works, You Tube, eHow, About.com, wikihow, Instructables, videojug, and W3Schools (specializing in web development tutorials).

17. No author, "The Story: Hole in the Wall," Frontline World, October 2002, www.pbs.org/frontlineworld/stories/india/thestory.html.

18. See the website Dialupforfree, www.dialupforfree.com/.

19. Once broadband began to spread, many US cities from New York and Philadelphia

to San Francisco initiated universal access plans. In November 2010 Uruguay announced its provision of minimal 256k DSL service on its phone lines for free. No author, "Internet for All—Uruguay Offers Universal Free Broadband," *Anarchogeek*, November 26, 2010, http://anarchogeek.com/2010/11/26/internet-for-all-uruguay-offers-universal-free-broadband/.

20. Marcus A. Banks, "Universal Internet Access—Not Just a Campaign Theme," *Gotham Gazette*, October 2005, www.gothamgazette.com/article/tech/20051019/19/1617; No author, "Universal Internet Access in SC: South Carolina's Opportunity to Lead the Nation.... The Rationale and Strategy for Free e-sc," www.scpronet.com/policy-work/universal-internet-access-in-sc.

21. David Gauntlett's website is www.makingisconnecting.org/.

22. "Creativity, Participation and Connectedness: An Interview with David Gauntlett," in *Mashup Cultures*, ed. Stefan Sonvilla-Weiss (New York: Springer, 2010).

23. www.web2teachingtools.com/piclits.html.

24. This trend was given a jump start by Vice President Al Gore's "reinventing government initiative," which by 2000 had already "expanded the use of Internet gateway sites allowing one-stop transactions and more than 1,000 online forms, such as IRS electronic filing in 2000 by more than 32 million Americans." History of the National Partnership for Reinventing Government: Accomplishments, 1993–2000—A Summary, http://govinfo.library.unt.edu/npr/whoweare/appendixf.html.

25. Zunia can be found online at http://zunia.org/.

26. See, for example, Rey Currie, "What Happens When HIEs Meet Web 2.0—How Cloud Computing and Service-Oriented Architecture (SOA) Work with Healthcare Information Exchanges (HIEs)," *Health Management Technology*, no date, www.healthmgttech.com/index.php/solutions/network-infrastructure/what-happens-when-hie-meet-web-20.html.

27. Steve Lee and Lane F. Cooper, "Web 2.0 Strives to Be Collaboration Software of Choice for Enterprises," BizTechReports.Com, www-01.ibm.com/software/info/itsolutions/collaboration/web20.html.

28. Howard Rheingold, *Smart Mobs: The Next Social Revolution* (New York: Basic Books, 2002).

29. Zack Exley, "Organizing Online," *Mother Jones*, December 9, 2000, http://motherjones.com/politics/2000/12/organizing-online.

30. "Riots outside of Paris," *Global Guerrillas*, November 2, 2005, http://globalguerrillas.typepad.com/globalguerrillas/2005/11/journal_riots_o.html; Molly Moore, "French Rioting Spreads as Government Seeks an Answer," *Washington Post*, November 3, 2005, www.washingtonpost.com/wp-dyn/content/article/2005/11/02/AR2005110200492.html.

31. Jon Leyne, "No Sign Egypt Will Take the Tunisian Road," BBC News-Middle East, January 16, 2011, www.bbc.co.uk/news/world-middle-east-12202937.

32. www.miller-mccune.com/politics/the-cascading-effects-of-the-arab-spring-28575/.

33. Clay Shirky, *Cognitive Surplus: How Technology Makes Consumers into Collaborators* (New York: Penguin Books, 2011), 10.

CHAPTER EIGHT

1. The Answers website is online at http://wiki.answers.com/about/.
2. Curricki is online at www.curriki.org/.
3. In April 2012 Harvard University, noting the skyrocketing prices of commercially

published scholarly journals that are putting a damper on the spread of knowledge, officially urged its faculty members to seek publication in open access journals, to resign from the boards of all publications that keep articles behind paywalls, and to encourage their scholarly associations to take control over publication in their fields. Ian Sample, "Harvard University Says It Can't Afford Journal Publishers' Prices," guardian.co.uk, April 24, 2012, www.guardian.co.uk/science/2012/apr/24/harvard-university-journal-publishers-prices.

4. Ken Auletta, *Googled: The End of the World as We Know It* (New York: Penguin, 2009), 322.

5. Richard Stallman, "The Free Universal Encyclopedia and Learning Resource—Announcement of the Project," www.gnu.org/encyclopedia/free-encyclopedia.html.

6. Randall Stross, "Encyclopedic Knowledge, Then vs. Now," *New York Times*, May 2, 2009, www.nytimes.com/2009/05/03/business/03digi.html?_r=3&th&emc=th.

7. Curtis Bonk, *The World Is Open: How Web Technology Is Revolutionizing Education* (San Francisco: Jossey-Bass, 2009), 66.

8. Clifford Stoll, *Silicon Snake Oil: Second Thoughts on the Information Highway* (New York: Doubleday, 1995).

9. Michael Pastore provides a list of thirty important benefits of e-books at http://epublishersweekly.blogspot.com/2008/02/30-benefits-of-ebooks.html.

10. "Microsoft Closing Encarta Online Encyclopedia," AFP, March 30, 2009, www.google.com/hostednews/afp/article/ALeqM5hQSILtukjBTCfJASmw25gjPo70yA.

11. Jim Giles, "Internet Encyclopaedias Go Head to Head," *Nature*, December 15, 2005, 900–901.

12. Encyclopædia Britannica, Inc., "Fatally Flawed: Refuting the Recent Study on Encyclopedic Accuracy by the Journal *Nature*," March 2006, http://corporate.britannica.com/britannica_nature_response.pdf.

13. Stallman, "Free Universal Encyclopedia."

14. Peter Suber offers an excellent brief explanation of open knowledge, "Open Access Overview: Focusing on Open Access to Peer-Reviewed Research Articles and Their Preprints," http://legacy.earlham.edu/~peters/fos/overview.htm.

15. Sheila Slaughter and Larry Rhoads, *Academic Capitalism in the New Economy: Markets, States, and Higher Education* (Baltimore: Johns Hopkins University Press, 2004).

16. Budapest Open Access Initiative, www.soros.org/openaccess/read.shtml.

17. Directory of Open Access Journals, www.doaj.org/.

18. B.-C. Björk, P. Welling, M. Laakso, P. Majlender, T. Hedlund, et al., "Open Access to the Scientific Journal Literature: Situation 2009," *PLOS ONE* 5, no. 6 (2010): e11273. doi:10.1371/journal.pone.0011273.

19. Khan's Academy is online at www.khanacademy.org/about.

20. The Open Courseware Consortium website is at www.ocwconsortium.org/aboutus.

21. Open courses are available at www.ocwconsortium.org/courses.

22. MIT's list of most popular courses is at http://ocw.mit.edu/courses/most-visited-courses/.

23. "What Is *MITx*? Answering Common Questions about the Institute's New Approach to Online Education," MIT News, December 19, 2011, http://web.mit.edu/newsoffice/2011/mitx-faq-1219.html.

24. Steve Kolowich, "A Call for Open Textbooks," *Inside Higher Education*, October 1, 2010, www.insidehighered.com/news/2010/10/01/textbooks.

25. Wiley has recently coauthored an important statement of principles for open educational

textbooks and learning resources. J. Hilton, D. Wiley, J. Stein, and A. Johnson, "The Four R's of Openness and ALMS Analysis: Frameworks for Open Educational Resources," *Open Learning: The Journal of Open and Distance Learning* 25, no. 1 (2010): 37–44.

26. Michael E. Casey and Laura C. Savastinuk, *Library 2.0: A Guide to Participatory Library Service* (Medford, NJ: Information Today, 2007).

27. Michael E. Casey and Laura C. Savastinuk, "Library 2.0: Service for the Next-Generation Library," *Library Journal*, September 1, 2006, www.libraryjournal.com/article/CA6365200.html.

28. John Blyberg, "11 Reasons Why Library 2.0 Exists and Matters," Blyberg.net, January 9, 2006, www.blyberg.net/2006/01/09/11-reasons-why-library-20-exists-and-matters/.

29. R. David Lankes, Joanne Silverstein, Scott Nicholson, and Todd Marshall, "Participatory Networks: The Library as Conversation," Proceedings of the Sixth International Conference on Conceptions of Library and Information Science—"Featuring the Future," http://informationr.net/ir/12-4/colis/colis05.html.

30. Jessamyn West and friends, "What We Want: An OPAC Manifesto," librarian.net (blog), no date, www.librarian.net/opac/.

31. Nina Simon, "What Is Museum 2.0?" Museum Two (blog), December 1, 2006, http://museumtwo.blogspot.com/2006/12/what-is-museum-20.html; Simon, *The Participatory Museum* (Author: Museum 2.0, 2010).

32. Simon, "A Revised Theory of Social Participation via 'Me-to-We' Design," Museum Two (blog), January 25, 2010, http://museumtwo.blogspot.com/2010/01/revised-theory-of-social-participation.html.

33. Simon, "Layer On for the Long Haul: Sustaining Visitor Co-Created Experiences," Museum Two (blog), October 21, 2007, http://museumtwo.blogspot.com/2007/10/layer-on-for-long-haul-sustaining.html.

34. Henry Jenkins, *Convergence Culture: Where Old and New Media Collide* (New York: New York University Press, 2007).

CHAPTER NINE

1. Will Richardson, "Why Schools Should Break the Web 2.0 Barrier," *Threshold*, 2009, http://67techcamp.weebly.com/uploads/1/4/4/6/1446140/will_rich_web2.0_barrier.pdf.

2. Will Richardson, *Blogs, Wikis, Podcasts, and Other Powerful Web Tools for Classrooms*, 3rd ed. (New York: Corwin, 2010).

3. Flat World has adopted a "freemium" business model, making open source texts available for free online and charging competitive prices for hard copy texts and teachers' manuals.

4. Clayton Christiansen, *Disrupting Class, How Disruptive Innovation Will Change the Way the World Learns* (New York: McGraw-Hill, 2008).

5. The students remain individuated, working alone at similar workstation computers within virtual learning environments shaped for formal instruction—environments I call "virtual egg crates."

6. David Wiley, "The Open High School of Utah: Openness, Disaggregation, and the Future of Schools," *TechTrends* 53, no. 4 (July/August 2009): 37–40.

7. By placing instruction online, the facilities management task is either eliminated or placed in other hands (e.g., homes and libraries).

8. By working with strategic partners in the state, OHSU relies upon a network form

of organization as opposed to market exchange. While external to the OHSU organization, these are working partners working cooperatively with the school on all of its functions; they evolve in synch with the school, providing recurring services without the need for competitive bidding. As a team, they can also exert coordinated political leverage on state government. On the network form of organization, see W. W. Powell, "Neither Market nor Hierarchy: Network Forms of Organization," *Research in Organizational Behavior* 12: 295–336.

9. Technical Working Group, National Educational Technology Plan, US Department of Education, *Transforming American Education: Learning Powered by Technology*, 38, www2.ed.gov/about/offices/list/os/technology/netp.pdf.

10. Ibid., 38.

11. Ibid.

12. State laws may prohibit the use of uncertified, unlicensed teachers or prohibit arrangements that circumvent collective bargaining. Many school districts, however, already outsource some instructional services to partner firms, at the same time effectively outsourcing responsibility for certification and collective bargaining and opening questions about whether online teachers are certified or unionized.

13. On Michigan Virtual School, see Curtis J. Bonk, *The World Is Open: How Web Technology Is Revolutionizing Education* (San Francisco: Jossey-Bass, 2009), 105. Bonk doesn't describe the contractual relations of the part-time teachers, but it is hard to imagine that they are all certified and unionized.

14. Will Richardson, "No More One-Size-Fits-All Learning," *District Administration*, July 2010, www.districtadministration.com/article/no-more-one-size-fits-all-learning.

15. Arne Duncan, "An Open Letter from Arne Duncan to America's Teachers: In Honor of Teacher Appreciation Week," *Education Week*, May 2, 2011, www.edweek.org/ew/articles/2011/05/02/30duncan.h30.html.

16. Richardson's assessment in "No More One-Size-Fits-All Learning" that *TAE* "really is transformation through technology, not just tinkering on the edges" is thus not just overly optimistic but simply wrong.

17. Technical Working Group, *Transforming American Education*, x.

18. One key source of ideas for this revolution is Judy Breck, *109 Ideas for Virtual Learning: How Open Content Will Help Close the Digital Divide* (Lanham, MD: Rowman and Littlefield, 2005). Ironically a *TAE* author, John Seely Brown, prepared a flattering foreword for this book. (Perhaps Brown was one of the [unmentioned] dissenting authors.) Another key source for the revolution is Curtis Bonk, *The World Is Open*. These important authors are discussed in the next chapter.

19. This distinction between the prespecified versus emergent results of learning is central to contrast between the report and the learningweb revolution and is developed in detail in Chapter Eleven, on complexity.

20. Chapter Thirteen discusses reasons why authentic assessment is likely to be sounder than assessment based on analytical criteria.

Chapter Ten

1. Judy Breck, *109 Ideas for Virtual Learning: How Open Content Will Help Close the Digital Divide* (Lanham, MD: Rowman and Littlefield Education, 2005), 144.

2. Breck, *109 Ideas*, 254.

3. While Breck's tripartite division of possible futures is suggestive, I will propose in Chapter Twelve a fourth alternative, the complex open learning center combining web-based cognitive learning with the elements of what Breck calls socialization and articulation that are required for education as initiation.

4. Curtis Bonk, personal communication, Denver, Colorado, April 12, 2010.

5. This is the sort of problem Andy Keen forcefully brought to our attention in his critique of Web 2.0 culture; Andrew Keen, *The Cult of the Amateur: How Blogs, MySpace, YouTube, and the Rest of Today's User-Generated Media Are Destroying Our Economy, Our Culture, and Our Values* (New York: Doubleday, 2007). Keen is clearly wrong in claiming that user-generated content is all junk. But he is correct to insist that sustained production of excellence requires a framework that supports it economically.

CHAPTER ELEVEN

1. Many dimensions of schooling have already been reviewed through the lens of complexity. See William Doll, "Complexity in the Classroom," *Educational Leadership* 47, no. 1 (1989): 65–70; Brent Davis and Dennis J. Sumara, *Complexity and Education: Inquiries into Learning, Teaching, and Research* (Hillsdale, NJ: Lawrence Erlbaum, 2006); William Doll, Joyce Fleener, Donna Truet, and John St. Julien, eds., *Chaos, Complexity and Curriculum: A Conversation* (New York: Peter Lang, 2005); Linda Farr Darling, Anthony Clarke, and Gaalan Erickson, eds., *Collective Improvisation in a Teacher Education Community* (Dordrecht: Springer, 2007), 207–225.

2. The discussion of complexity in this section is frankly theoretical. Readers may wish to skip over it and turn immediately to Chapter Twelve, where I build on the theoretical points to construct a concrete model of a school as complex organization, and then return to this chapter to expand their understanding of the theory if they wish.

3. Complexity studies originated in a number of research institutes in the 1980s, in particular the University of Michigan and the Santa Fe Institute. See Malcolm Waldrop, *Complexity, The Emerging Science at the Edge of Order and Chaos* (New York: Simon and Schuster, 1992). At both institutions the main players included the American pragmatist philosopher Arthur Burks and two of his former graduate students, Robert Axelrod and Michael D. Cohen. The influence of Peirce and Dewey in the work of Axelrod and Cohen is evident. See, for example, Axelrod and Cohen's study of the pragmatics of complexity, *Harnessing Complexity, Organizational Implications of a Scientific Frontier* (New York: Free Press, 2000). Some scholars have noted the interplay between complexity theory and poststructuralism. See Deborah Osberg, Gert Biesta, and Paul Cilliers, "From Representation to Emergence: Complexity's Challenge to the Epistemology of Schooling," *Educational Philosophy and Theory* 40, no. 1 (2008): 213–227.

4. This notion plays a large role in Hume's theory of society and Adam Smith's conception of the market.

5. Rodale was my colleague in the Science, Technology and Society program at Penn State from the early 1980s until his untimely death in 1990. He regularly participated in our program conferences and seminars and frequently brought his colleagues, including me, to the press office at Emmaus for staff discussions.

6. Ralph Stacey, *Complexity and Creativity in Organizations* (San Francisco: Berrett-Koehler, 1996), 2.

7. See Dee Hock, "The Chaordic Organization: Out of Control and Into Order," *World Business Academy Perspectives*, 2003, www.fastforwardblog.com/wp-content/uploads/2008/11/dee-hock-the-chaordic-organization.pdf.

8. Stephan H. Haeckel, *Adaptive Enterprise: Creating and Leading Sense-and-Respond Organizations* (Cambridge, MA: Harvard Business School Press, 1999). I rely extensively on Haeckel's model of adaptive organization in this section.

9. Ibid., 115.

10. The school would thus have a structural design similar to the one adopted by RAND (Chapter Six), with free exchange between well-networked members of the structural divisions.

11. These and related obstacles to organizational responsiveness are discussed in Len Fisher, *The Perfect Storm: The Science of Complexity in Everyday Life* (New York: Basic Books, 2009).

CHAPTER TWELVE

1. Robin D. G. Kelley, *Thelonious Monk: The Life and Times of an American Original* (New York: Free Press, 2009).

2. Ibid., 14, 28–29.

3. Ibid., 34–35.

4. Ibid., 36–37.

5. Ibid., 55–56.

6. Ibid., 55.

7. Mark Salzman, *Lost in Place: Growing Up Absurd in Suburbia* (New York: Vintage, 1996).

8. I employ quotes here because Salzman has changed the names of his teachers.

9. Lawrence Weschler draws a portrait of Salzman, at age forty, pulling together the various strands of his creative life in "The Novelist and the Nun," *The New Yorker*, October 2, 2000.

10. We may imagine AALC as a cooperative project of the central district and those of the surrounding suburban and close-in rural districts. Precedents for this sort of arrangement are abundant; for example, this is the standard way of organizing vocational-technical schools.

11. Marc Tucker, "On Curriculum, Assessment and (Especially) Writing in the Modern Age," *Education Week*, January 19, 2012, http://blogs.edweek.org/edweek/top_performers/2012/01/on_curriculum_assessment_and_especially_writing_inthe_modern_age.html.

12. National Center on Education and the Economy, Marc Tucker, Chair, *Tough Choices or Tough Times: The Report of the New Commission on the Skills of the American Workforce*, rev. ed. (San Francisco: Jossey-Bass, 2008). Tucker repeats the narrative about a shortage of skilled workers, and like many others he sees the solution as directing young adults into occupations where the skill shortages are most acute. Wharton management professor Peter Capelli, *Why Good People Can't Find Good Jobs: The Skills Gap and What Companies Can Do about It* (Philadelphia: Wharton Digital Press, 2012), debunks the skills gap as mostly a myth promoted by self-serving employers and business spokespeople.

13. The shift to contract work is examined in Peter Coy, Michelle Conlin, and Moira Herbst, "The Disposable Worker," *Bloomberg Business Week*, January 7, 2010, www.businessweek.com/magazine/content/10_03/b4163032935448.htm.

14. Critics of Web 2.0 such as Andrew Keen (*The Cult of the Amateur: How Blogs, MySpace, YouTube, and the Rest of Today's User-Generated Media Are Destroying Our Economy, Our Culture, and Our Values* [New York: Doubleday, 2007]) and Jaron Lanier (*You Are Not a Gadget: A Manifesto* [New York: Vintage, 2010]), make this shift from full-time jobs with benefits to contract work the centerpiece of their attack. Both worry about the impact on creative workers who are driven out by amateurs. But Lanier extends his concern to educated workers more generally. In a recent interview Lanier put it bluntly: the trouble with Web 2.0 is that it "screws the middle class.... Web 2.0 is a formula to kill the middle class and undo centuries of social progress"; Jaron Lanier, interviewed by Erin Hartman of Random House, www.jaronlanier.com/poleconGadgetqa.html.

Without question the new capabilities of capitalist enterprise to take advantage of vanishing transactions costs to shift tasks from middle-class employees to low-cost contract workers at home or abroad pose a major challenge. This challenge, however, can hardly be met by putting a lid on Web 2.0. And this for two reasons: First, in liberal societies we have no legal apparatus for doing so, and creating such a lid would be resisted by those across the entire political spectrum. Second, many technologies with broad negative consequences—think nuclear weapons—are broadly detested. But Web 2.0 users—including Keen and Lanier—love their high-tech gadgets and could hardly live without them. The solution lies not in closing down Web 2.0 but in learning to live with it and its benefits—forging new ways of living and learning while pressing in the political sphere for a new social contract. A guiding insight is that there is nothing natural or inevitable about so-called middle-class life; it is an artifact of academic allocation. Barton Bledstein, in *The Culture of Professionalism: The Middle Classes and the Development of Higher Education in America* (New York: Norton, 1976), establishes that the very concept of middle class didn't exist before the spread of technical and professional college diplomas in the 1870s.

15. Don Tapscott and Anthony Williams, *Wikinomics: How Mass Collaboration Changes Everything* (New York: Penguin, 2008).

16. See Michael Coren, "The Case for the 21-Hour Work Week," *Fast Company*, January 11, 2012, online at http://finance.yahoo.com/news/the-case-for-a-21-hour-work-week.html.

The twenty-one-hour work week proposal responds to the worldwide crisis in overproduction and unemployment. It can be sustained only by revolutionary new institutions of distributive justice or by a radical reduction of material lifestyle expectations, or a combination of both. The Occupy movement can be read as a pressure for the former, while the contemporary wave of interest in frugality and minimalist lifestyles provides guidance toward the latter. These two trends are already merging in new social philosophies and social movements. See, for example, Van Jones, *Rebuild the Dream* (New York: Nation Books, 2012).

Chapter Thirteen

1. William J. Bushaw and Shane J. Lopez, "Betting on Teachers: The 43rd Annual Phi Delta Kappa/Gallup Poll of the Public's Attitudes toward the Public Schools," *Phi Delta Kappan* 93, no. 1 (September 2011): 8–26.

2. Bushaw and Lopez, "Betting on Teachers," table 9, p. 11.

Chapter Fourteen

1. Dewey is worth quoting at length on this point. He says, "there is all the difference in the world whether the acquisition of information is treated as an end in itself, or is made an integral portion of the training of thought. The assumption that information that has been accumulated apart from use in the recognition and solution of a problem may later on be, at will, freely employed by thought is quite false. The skill at the ready command of intelligence is the skill acquired with the aid of intelligence." John Dewey, *How We Think*, 1st ed. (New York: D.C. Heath, 1910), 52.

2. The psychologist Raymond Cattell contrasted crystallized intelligence (the use of acquired knowledge and ability to reason using learned procedures) and fluid intelligence (the ability to reason broadly, form concepts, and solve problems using novel or unfamiliar procedures). Schooling is associated with the development of crystallized intelligence. In the knowledge work environment, however, where problems are novel and unstructured, crystallized intelligence is of negligible value and may at times even interfere with fluid intelligence.

3. This "technical" conception is embedded in the curriculum models advanced by such leaders as Franklin Bobbitt and Ralph Tyler.

4. For a thorough discussion of the new institutionalism in education, see Brian Rowan and Cecil G. Miskel, *Institutional Theory and the Study of Educational Organizations: Handbook of Research on Educational Administration*, ed. J. Murphy and K. Seashore-Lewis (San Francisco: Jossey-Bass, 1999). Karl Weick, Larry Cuban, John Meyer, Ian Westbury, and William Reid have been among the figures shaping this new consensus.

5. See Karl Weick, "Educational Organizations as Loosely Coupled Systems," *Administrative Science Quarterly* 21 (1976). This classic study has been cited thousands of times and is a foundation stone for institutional analysis of educational organizations.

6. Larry Cuban, "Curriculum Stability and Change," chapter 8, *Handbook of Research on Curriculum, A Project of the American Educational Research Association*, ed. Philip W. Jackson (New York: Macmillan, 1992), 218.

7. Ibid., 232.

8. Cuban, in his DeGarmo lecture at the 2010 meeting of the American Educational Research Association, restated this argument in critiquing Allan Collins and Richard Halverson, *Rethinking Education in the Age of Technology: The Digital Revolution and Schooling in America* (New York: Teachers College Press, 2009).

9. For further discussion see Rowan and Miskel, 380.

10. See Broad Foundation, annual report, 2009–10, www.broadfoundation.org/asset/101-2009.10%20annual%20report.pdf.

11. Stephanie Banchero, "Daley School Plan Fails to Make Grade," January 17, 2010, http://articles.chicagotribune.com/2010-01-17/news/1001160276_1_charter-schools-chicago-reform-urban-education.

12. Joanne Barkin, "Got Dough? How Billionaires Rule Our Schools," *Dissent*, Winter 2011, http://www.dissentmagazine.org/article/got-dough-how-billionaires-rule-our-schools.

13. Valerie Strauss, "In Texas, a Revolt against Standardized Testing," www.washingtonpost.com/blogs/answer-sheet/post/in-texas-a-revolt-brews-against-standardized-testing/2012/03/15/gIQAI5N0VS_blog.html.

14. Andrew Smith, Carolyn Brice, Alison Collins, Victoria Matthews, and Rachel McNamara, "The Scale of Occupational Stress: A Further Analysis of the Impact of Demographic Factors and Type of Job," report for the Centre for Occupational and Health

Psychology, Department of Psychology, Cardiff University, 2000, www.hse.gov.uk/research/crr_pdf/2000/crr00311.pdf.

15. Paul E. Bellair and Vincent J. Roscigno, "Local Labor-Market Opportunity and Adolescent Delinquency," *Social Forces* 78, no. 4 (2000): 1509–1538; Ariel Kalil and Kathleen M. Ziol-Guest, "Parental Job Loss and Children's Academic Progress in Two-Parent Families," www.ipr.northwestern.edu/jcpr/workingpapers/wpfiles/KalilFINAL.pdf. See also A. Kalil and K. M. Ziol-Guest, "Parental Employment Circumstances and Children's Academic Progress," *Social Science Research* 37, no. 2 (2008): 500–515.

16. This literature is reviewed in Philip D. Parker, Andrew J. Martin, Susan Colmar, and Gregory A. Liem, "Teacher's Workplace Well-Being: Exploring a Process Model of Goal Orientation, Coping Behavior, Engagement, and Burnout," *Teaching and Teacher Education* 28, no. 4 (2012): 503–513.

17. The distinction between mastery and performance goal orientations was introduced by Carol S. Dweck, "Motivational Processes Affecting Learning," *American Psychologist* 41, no. 10 (October 1986): 1040–1048, and is currently one of the dominant concepts in educational psychology. Dweck, *Mindset: The New Psychology of Success* (New York: Random House, 2006), has renamed these orientations the growth vs. fixed mind-sets. Parker et al., "Teacher's Workplace Well-Being," use Dweck's formulations in their studies of teacher well-being.

18. Teachers are often compelled by school officials, community norms, and public policy to implement achievement orientations and competition in their classrooms, often resulting in a lack of student effort and misbehavior—all of which adds greatly to teacher stress. See M. V. Covington, "Goal Theory, Motivation, and School Achievement: An Integrative Review," *Annual Review of Psychology* 51 (2000): 171–200.

19. MetLife Survey of the American Teacher 2011: Teachers, Parents and the Economy, www.metlife.com/assets/cao/contributions/foundation/american-teacher/MetLife-Teacher-Survey-2011.pdf.

20. www.horizoncharterschools.org/about-horizon.html.

21. http://circleofseasons.org/A_Unique_Education.html.

22. Lisa Gartner, "D.C. Approves Four New Charter Schools," *Washington Examiner*, April 24, 2012, http://washingtonexaminer.com/article/530541.

23. I discuss this and other unusual charter schools in "Essay Review: Beyond the One Best System: Case-Studies of Charter Schools," *Teachers College Record* (2003).

24. www.azcentral.com/community/mesa/articles/2009/10/01/20091001mr-equineskl1002.html.

25. www.hightechhigh.org/about/.

26. www.bigpicture.org/big-picture-history/.

27. Janice Lloyd, "Homeschooling Grows," *USA Today*, January 5, 2009, www.usatoday.com/news/education/2009-01-04-homeschooling_N.htm.

28. No author, "Homeschooling," *Education Week*, July 13, 2011, www.edweek.org/ew/issues/home-schooling/.

29. Christine Foster, "In a Class by Themselves," *Stanford Magazine*, 2000, www.stanfordalumni.org/news/magazine/2000/novdec/articles/homeschooling.html.

30. Cited in C. Schelling, "Homeschooling Goes Boom in America," *WND*, January 5, 2009, www.wnd.com/2009/01/85408/.

31. Mitchell L. Stevens, *Kingdom of Children: Culture and Controversy in the Homeschooling Movement* (Princeton, NJ: Princeton University Press, 2001), 71.

32. William Reid provides an example fitting this model in his case study of England's

"sixth form" in the nineteenth century. Industrialization shifted the attention of elites from localities to the national stage, as they focused on arenas and organizations that could assist in securing a national consensus. By the 1830s the elite needed to recruit beyond the landed aristocracy for public administrators, creating a need for consensus building between aristocracy and an emerging middle class. The sixth form was changed to connect its new topics with the new national statuses; new organizational forms emerged in parallel with new institutional categories shared by the new mixed-class constituency. Such schools as Arnold's Rugby tried out new inventions linking sixth-form experiences and "leadership": the sixth became a "rite of passage"; there was a new emphasis on mimetic forms of teaching with the headmaster as sixth-form teacher providing an appropriate example of leadership. William Reid, *Curriculum as Institution and Practice: Essays in the Deliberative Tradition* (Mahwah, NJ: Erlbaum, 1998).

33. I have argued for this extended model in Leonard J. Waks, "The Concept of Fundamental Educational Change," *Educational Theory* 57, no. 3 (2007): 277–295, on both conceptual grounds and based on a case study of the paradigm shift experienced in the transition from the district to the common school.

INDEX

Abeles, Vicki, 47
Abelson, Hal, 103
Academic achievement/underachievement: achievement norm, 40–41; contradiction of high achievement and high graduation rate, 55–56; as manufactured crisis, 241(n4); open learning centers resolving academic failure, 189–192; school failure and, ix; *Turnaround Handbook,* 203–204
Academic allocation of socioeconomic positions: alternative methods for, 59–60; expansion of, 54; Internet and, 68; Internet and network allocation, 60–62; legitimacy and, 64–65; open learning centers, 193
Academic knowledge, 144
Academic underperformance, 42–43
Academically Adrift (Arum and Roksa), 57–58
The Act of Creation (Koestler), 86
Adler, Mortimer, 25–26, 240(n16)
Administration: institutional rules and patterns, 29
Adobe AIR, 246(n8)
Adult life: academic initiations as passage to, 16; crisis in legitimacy, 65; higher education, 18higher education18–19; schools' failure to prepare students, 53–54. *See also* Initiation
Adults: support for teens, 8–9; teen bloggers connecting with, 6; teen competence and performance compared with, 9
Aftab, Parry, 3, 9–10

Age-graded schooling, 38, 182–183; Online High School of Utah, 120
Aims, educational: Bonk's Education 2.0 vision, 132; factory school and open learning centers, 188; factory school paradigm, 38
AJAX (Asynchronous JavaScript), 245(n8)
Aldridge, Jane, 3
ALEC, 189–190, 202
Allen, Paul, 27
AltaVista, 95–96
Amazon, 82, 97–98, 174
American Library Association, 106
Ancient civilizations: elementary and higher education, 18–19
"Anderson-Armstrong Learning Center" (AALC), 165–173, 175–181, 252(n10)
Andreessen, Mark, 76, 81
Android, 174
Answers.com, 95
Antihierarchical philosophy, 69
AP courses, 21
Apache, 246(n8)
Appleton, Nathan, 33, 97–98
Apprenticeships, 56, 138, 243(n3)
Arab Spring, 90–91
Aristotle, 8, 29–30, 135
Arizona Agribusiness and Equine Center Red Mountain High School, 207–208
ARPA, 73–77, 148
ARPANET, 73–75, 245(n8)
Art education, 14, 83
Articulation, 136, 138, 141, 144–145

257

Arum, Richard, 57–58
Assessment: Bonk's Education 2.0 vision, 131–132; Breck's handschooling, 139; Education 2.0 policy objectives, 124–125; factory school, 38, 185–186; formal learning, 25–26; institutional rules and patterns, 29; links to national economic achievement, 47–48; No Child Left Behind and NAEP, 45; open learning centers, 170–172, 185–186, 188; PISA, 46–47; standardized tests in open learning centers, 188; validity of authentic assessments, 186–188
Associated Press, 58
Athens, ancient, 18
Atlantic Monthly, 57, 71
ATT, 71
Augmenting Human Intellect: A Conceptual Framework (Engelbart), 75
Autodidactic learning, 167
Auxiliary roles of schools, 136
Axelrod, Robert, 251(n3)

Babauta, Leo, 4
Bacon, Francis, 144
Bagley, William, 36
Bailyn, Bernard, 12, 238(n1)
Baran, Paul, 70
Barnes and Noble, 97
Battelle, John, 80
Behavioral norms, 40–41, 51
Belford, Elizabeth, 243(n21)
Bell, Terrence H., 43–44
Ben Ali, Zine El Abidine, 90–91
Berliner, David, 189–190, 241(n4)
Berners-Lee, Tim, 75–76, 81, 87–88
Bernstein, Basil, 15
Bianchini, Gina, 81
Biddle, Bruce, 241(n4)
Biesta, Gert, 14
Big Picture Schools, 208
"Bisociation" of ideas, 86–87
BitTorrent protocol, 88
Björnshauge, Lars, 101
Blackboard web tool, 114
Blogger, 78
Blogging: accomplishments of teens, 6–7; adult view of, 9–10; classroom use of, 114; creative self-expressions, 86–87; education and initiation, 13; fashion, 2–3; heuristic teaching, 25; informal learning, 27; minimalism, 3–5; net culture, 78–79; netcasting, 83; open learning centers, 167–168; Web 2.0, 81
Blyberg, John, 108
Boinodiris, Phaedra, 88

Bolt, Beranek and Newman (BEN), 72–73, 245(n8)
Bonk, Curtis, 130–132, 137, 141–142, 146, 168
Borges, Jorge Luis, 6–7
Boston Manufacturing Company, 33–34
Boston Society of Natural History, 20
Brain development, 18
Breck, Judy, 132–139, 141–142, 144, 146, 168, 251(n3)
Britain, 15, 19, 255–256(n32)
Broad Foundation, 202–203
Broadband access, 85
Brooklyn Museum, 111
Browsers, 76
BryanBoy (blogger), 3
Bryn Mawr, 15–16
Bunny Bisous blog, 3
Burks, Arthur, 251(n3)
Bush, George W., 45, 201, 243(n3)
Bush, Vannevar, 71, 135, 138
Business Angels des Cités, 63
Business community: role in paradigm change, 222–223
Business model of education, 43–44

California Open Source Textbook Project (COSTP), 105
Capabilities: hiring, sourcing and developing, 156–157
Career satisfaction, 206
Carnevale, Anthony, 243(n3)
Carter, Jimmy, 43
Casey, Michael, 107–108
Castells, Manuel, 108
Casting nets, 167–168
Cattell, Raymond, 254(n2)
Central authority, 154–158
Central control model for education, 121–122
Central High School (Philadelphia), 21
CERN, 75–76
Certificates of learning and mastery, 178–179
Certification: factory school paradigm, 38
Change, engineering, 197–199; conditions for, 199–200
Charter schools, 207–208
Chicago Renaissance 2010, 202
Chicago Tribune, 204
China, 47, 164
Chinese language and culture, 162–164
Chopin, Friederich, 7
Christiansen, Clayton, 118
Circle of Seasons Charter School, 207
Cisco Systems, 178–179
Civil unrest, 90

Clark, Jim, 76
Clark, Wesley, 72–73
Classroom 2.0, 113–117, 120–127, 135
Cloud computing, 81, 84–85, 88, 97
Cognitive surplus, 92, 175
Cohen, Michael D., 251(n3)
Collaboration: Flat Classroom, 115; global networks, 153; Internet and computers encouraging, ix–x; network paradigms in postindustrial industries, 41; online encyclopedias, 99; open learning centers, 167–168; Web 2.0, 88–89
Collective action, 89–91
College trap, 193
Colleges and universities: early exclusiveness of, 21–22; edX and Coursera, 104; employment objectives and, 243(n3); homeschooled learners, 209; open source courses, 119; OpenCourseWare, 102–103; Salman Khan, 101–102; social networking, 79–80
Collegiate Learning Association (CLA) measure of skills, 57
Colonial New England, 18, 199–200, 239(n9)
Columbus Hill Neighborhood Center, New York, 160–161, 184
Committee on Tests and Standards of Efficiency, 36
Common school revolution, 196
Commonplaces, xi, 29–32, 199
Communities of practice, 17
Community theater certificate program, 179–180
Complex human systems, 149
Complex open networked learning centers, x. *See also* Open learning centers
Complexity and complex organizations, x–xi; complexity theory, 148–152; control parameters and phase transitions, 150–151, 157; creative self-organization, 154–155; global networks, 152–153; order and chaos, 151–152; organizing capabilities, 155–157; rebalancing center and periphery, 153–154; school as complex organization, 158; self-organization, 149–150. *See also* Open learning centers
Complexity studies, 251(n3)
Complexity theory, 147–148
Congress, US: Goals 2000, 44–45; No Child Left Behind, 202; TAE report, 120
Constraints to paradigm shifts, 200
Continuous organization redesign, 153
Contract workers, 61–62, 244(n16), 253(n14)

Control parameters, 150–151
Cooper, Lane, 89
Copernicus, 29–30
Core + option modules, 170
Core-periphery relationship, 153–154
Corporate interests, 189–190
Council on Educational Technology (MIT), 103. *See also* MIT
Coursera, 104
Cramming, 37
Creativity: "bisociation" of ideas, 86–87; central authority in complex organizations, 154–155; Engelbart's dream of computers used to stimulate, 74–75; failure of didactic teaching, 50; teen brain development, 6; test-centric education stifling, 47
Cremin, Lawrence, 12, 238(n1)
Crystallized intelligence, 197, 254(n2)
Cuban, Larry, 198–199, 241(n1)
Cultural factors: PISA scores, 46–47
Cultural literacy, 190–191
Culture of professionalism, 244(n11)
Cunningham, Ward, 99
Curricki, 114, 119, 173–174
Curriculum: Breck's educational commonplace, 138; Breck's "moving the center," 133–134; complexity theory, 150–151; Digiteen, 116; and educational inefficiency, 50–51; excellence reforms, 207; factory school, 37, 184–185; hidden, 38; high school and colleges, 21; institutional rules and patterns, 29; for mass secondary education, 240(n19); Online High School of Utah, 118–119; open learning centers, 176–177, 182–185; preset, xi; Salzman's deviation from standard curriculum, 162–163; wikis, 114
Cyber-schools, 118–120

DARPA, 74
Davis, Vicki, 115, 117
Debt, student, 59, 244(n9)
Deindustrialization, 205–206
Departments, educational, 36–38
Dewey, John, viii, 14, 18, 197, 251(n3), 254(n1)
Didactic teaching-learning: factory schools, 37–39, 192; formal learning, 23, 25–26; informal learning, 26–27; open learning centers, 171, 185, 192; reform movement strengthening the factory school paradigm, 48–50
Digital Equipment Corporation (DEC), 72–73
Digital media, 79

Digiteen, 115–117
DiNucci, Darcy, 80
Diplomas: allocating social positions, 59–60; diploma inflation, 56–58; educational legitimacy, 64; entrepreneurs and, 62–63; failure to differentiate learners, 192–193; pre-industrial education, 22; trends in graduation rates, 239(n14); value in differentiating graduates' educational achievement, 54–55. *See also* Graduation rates
Directory of Open Access Journals, 101
DirectPointe Technology, 118
Discursive teaching: factory schools, 38–39, 192; formal learning, 24–26; informal learning, 26; open learning centers, 171, 185, 192; school reform movement ignoring, 49
Dissent magazine, 204
Diversity: categorization of learners, 51; charter schools, 207–208; excellence reforms, 207; group think, 157; lack of diversity in public schools, 16–17; in teachers' interests and capabilities, 53
Dreeben, Robert, 40, 51
Dropouts and dropout rates: adults-only charter schools, 207; Bill Gates, 27; didactic teaching contributing to, 49; education through life experience, 21–22; entrepreneurs, 48; hierarchical paradigm contributing to, ix; Mark Salzman, 163–164; open learning centers, 175–176; Thelonious Monk, 160
Dual visibility, 61
Duncan, Arne, 46, 120–121, 202–203
Durability, organizational, 157–158
Dwyer, Aiden, 51

eBay, 174
e-books and e-readers, 96–98
Economic achievement: digital media, 79; standardized test scores and, 47–48
Economic institutions, 28
Edge of chaos, 151–152, 154
Edson, Michael, 111
Educate America Act (Goals 2000), 44–45
Education: acquisition of information, 254(n1); broad and narrow senses of, 12; defining, 238–239(n7), 238(n1); diverse processes, 17; expectations and goals of, vii; as initiation into worthwhile activities, 12–16; as institutionalized practice, 143–146; schooling and, 17–18, 22
Education 2.0 informational paradigm, xi; Bonk's vision, 131–132; Breck's vision, 135–137; defining, 11; emerging policy for online education, 120–127; "real school" and "home school," 140–141. *See also* Open learning centers
Education Week blog, 170, 209
Educational paradigms, 29–32
Edwards, Kelman, Jr., 58, 64
edX, 104, 179, 192, 219
Efficiency, educational: academic underperformance and inefficiency, 42–43; didactic method, 49–50; factory school paradigm, 36; hierarchical organization of education, 50–52; open learning centers resolving failure of, 192
Egg-crate classrooms, 38, 114, 183
Egypt, 90–91
e-learning, 113–117
Elections, 89–90
Elementary education: ancient civilizations and, 18; heuristic teaching, 25; test scores, 242(n7)
Eliade, Mircea, 14–15
Elites, 199–204, 212
email code, 245(n8)
Emerson, George B., 20
Employment: allocating social positions, 59–60; business community role in paradigm change, 222–223; classroom behavior and parental unemployment, 205; college education and, 243(n3); decline of professionalism, 60–62; diplomas' value in obtaining, 54–55; expectations and goals of education, vii; graduating students' failure to obtain, 17; law school graduates, 59; redefining stable jobs, 62–63; value of a diploma in obtaining, 57–58. *See also* Industrial age
Encarta, 96, 98–99
Encyclopaedia Britannica, 98
Encyclopedias, online, 98–99
Encyclopedie (Diderot and D'Alembert), 98
Engelbart, Doug, 74–75
Entrenched paradigms, 200
Entrepreneurs, 48, 62–63, 82
Epstein, Robert, 6, 182
Eton, 15–16
Europe: OpenCourseWare, 103
Excellence, 43, 55–56
Exceptional people, 237(n2), 239(n13)
Exley, Zack, 89–90
Expressive objects, 86–87
Extracurriculum: informal learning, 27

Facebook, 78–80, 91
Factory school paradigm: academic failure,

189–192; age-grading, 182–183; aims of, 188; assessment, 185–186; citizens' roles in changing, 212–213; complex learning centers versus, 165–166; development of, 36–37; Digiteen, 116; efficiency failure, 192; egg-crate settings, 183; elites withdrawing commitment to, 201–204; establishment of, 31–32; the "grammar" of, 39; hierarchical organization and educational inefficiency, 50–52; inadequacy of, 196–197; industrial society and, 39–41; management techniques, 240(n4); origins of, 36; reform movement strengthening, 48–49; seven key features of, 37–38; shortcomings of, ix; subject matter, 184–185; TAE report, 121; teachers, 183–184
Farnsworth, Philo, 6
Fashion design and fashion industry, 2, 12–13, 154
Fast Company Magazine, 106
File sharing, 87–88
Finn, Chester, 46
First International Mathematics Study (1964), 44
Flash, 246(n8)
Flat Classroom, 115–117
Flat World Knowledge, 105–106, 114, 119
Flickr, 111, 113–114
Fluid intelligence, 197, 254(n2)
Focus teachers, 168–169
Ford, Brian J., 96
Formal learning, 23–27
For-profit school, 189–190
Forte, Sanford, 105
Fortune magazine, 70
"Fragmented Future," 80
Frakes, Julia, 3, 51
Franklin, Benjamin, 20, 144, 239(n12)
Free education: Khan Academy, 101–102, 192, 209
Freelance workers, 244(n16)
Freidman, Thomas, 55
Friendster, 78–79, 86–87
Frontline, 84
Frugality, 3–5
Functions of systems, 148
Funk and Wagnalls Encyclopedia, 98

Galileo, 29–30
Gardner, John, 55
Garvey, Samantha, 51, 173
Gates, Bill, 27–28, 202–203
Gates foundation, 202
Gauntlett, David, 84–87
Gellos, Lou, 62

General initiation, 15
Geographical location: blogging, 5
Georgia High School Writing Test, 45
Germany: apprenticeships, 56
Gevinson, Steve, 3
Gevinson, Tavi, 2–3, 12–13, 28, 51
Ghonim, Wael, 91–92
Gillespie, Dizzy, 160–161
Gilmore, John, 71
Gladwell, Malcolm, 26, 51
Global programs: Flat Classroom and Digiteen, 115–117
Globally competitive workforce, 47–48, 242(n13)
Glogster, 87
GNUpedia, 99–100
Goals 2000, 44–45, 205–206
Google, 78, 80–81, 95–96
Google Books, 96–97
Google Docs, 85
Google jockeys, 11, 113
GoogleGears, 246(n8)
Gore, Al, 247(n24)
Governance in complex organizations, 155, 166–168
Graduate schools: law schools, 58–59
Graduation rates: contradiction of high achievement and high graduation rate, 55–56; diploma inflation, 56–58; diplomas' failure to initiate graduates into adult life, 54–55; early high schools, 22; Goals 2000, 44–45; No Child Left Behind and state-level assessments, 45–46; trends in, 239(n14). *See also* Diplomas
Grady, Vicki, 208
"Grammar" of factory school paradigm, 39
Green, Thomas F., 55
Grella, Rebecca, 51
Greplin, 82
Gresham College, 19–20
Gross, Daniel, 82
Group think, 157
Gymnasium, 19

Handschooling, 132–139
Hargadon, Steve, 113
Hart, Michael, 96
Harvard, 20, 26–27, 33, 95, 104, 143, 179, 219, 247–248(n3)
Hedges, Chris, 242(n14)
Hegemonic paradigm, 31
Henderson, William, 59, 64
Here Comes Everyone (Shirky), 61, 156
Herrera, Jayralin, 3–5, 8, 48, 51, 65
Heuristic teaching: factory schools, 38–39,

Heuristic teaching (continued): 192; formal learning, 24–25; informal learning, 26; open learning centers, 171, 185, 192; school reform movement ignoring, 49

Hidden curriculum, 38

Hierarchical paradigm: Breck's handschooling vision, 132–133; complex learning centers, 165–166; complex organizations and global networking, 154; complexity theory as alternative to, 147–148; Digiteen, 116; educational inefficiency, 50–52; emerging policy for online education, 120–127; history and development of, 31, 34–35; Memex machine, 71–72; network paradigms and, 41; subject matter, 184–185; transition to networked learning, xi; web culture as antithesis, 69. *See also* Complexity; Factory school paradigm

High schools, 20–22; adults-only charter schools, 207; curriculum for mass education, 240(n19); test scores, 242(n7); withdrawal of economic, social, and political support, xi. *See also* Factory school paradigm

High Tech High, San Diego, 208

Higher education: ancient civilizations, 18–19; assessment in open learning centers, 171–172; bubble in, 48; curriculum for mass education, 240(n19); emergence of professionalism, 61; entrepreneurs sidestepping, 63; failure to differentiate learners, 192–193; Franklin's goal of, 239(n12); high schools and colleges, 21–22; interstitial transformation, 143; 19th-century schools, 20; teen achievements, 7; value in differentiating achievement, 57. *See also* Colleges and universities

High-stakes testing, 205–206, 221

Hock, Dee, 153, 158

Holt, John, 209

Home as learning hub, 216

Homeschooling, 140, 207–210, 213

Homework, 27, 132–139

Housework, 36

"How-to" teaching-learning. *See* Heuristic teaching

HTML (hypertext markup language), 76, 86–87, 245(n8)

Humanism, 19;

Humanities, 19–21, 30, 31

Hyperlinks, 72, 75, 96, 134

"I know" teaching-learning. *See* Didactic teaching-learning

IBM, 87–88

Identity, social networking and, 78–79

Immigrant workers: entrepreneurship among, 63; farming and manufacturing, 60. *See also* Industrial age

Independence norm, 40–41

Independent studies courses, 163

Indian Institute of Technology (IIT), 103

Industrial age: academic allocation system, 60–61; aims of educational model, 196; allocating social position, 60; British education, 255–256(n32); complexity theory as response to, 148; educational thought, 197–198; emergence of high schools, 33; factory school and industrial society, 39–41; hierarchical organization, 34–35; job training roles of schools, 54; low graduation rate, 22; mindset of, 34. *See also* Factory school paradigm

Industrial paradigm, 35–39

Industrial revolution, vii

Informal learning, 26–28, 106–111, 240(n15)

Information era, 152–153

Information Processing Techniques Office (IPTO), 73

Information sieve, 151

Initiation into adult life: creating policy for online education, 122; education as, 12–16; formal learning, 23–26; informal learning, 26–28, 240(n15); Monk and Salzman's educational experiences, 159, 162; open learning centers resolving connection failure, 192–193; particular academic initiations in general social initiation, 16–22; schools' failure to achieve, 53–54; socialization and articulation, 144–145

Innocentive, 174

Innovation: constraints on reform, 200; new educational paradigm, 210–211

Insider understanding, 13

Institutional paradigm: conditions for fundamental change, 199–200; education as institutionalized practice, 143–146; revolutionary change, 28–32

Institutional rules, 28–29

Intel science talent search, 51, 223

Intellectual property, 87–88

Intelligence, 6, 9, 254(n1)

Intergalactic Computer Network, 73. *See also* Internet

International comparisons of educational achievement, 44, 46–47, 242(n8)

Internet: academic allocation of socioeconomic positions, 68; advantages

of, ix; aims and action steps, x–xi; barriers to use in contemporary schools, x; Breck's vision of learning, 132–139; citizens' use for paradigm examination and change, 213; complexity and global networks, 153; e-books and e-readers, 96–98; Education 2.0 informational paradigm, 11; education as initiation, 12; elements of a larger vision for education, 5–6; Engelbart's mission, 74–75; as global communication hub, 22; home as learning hub, 216; homeschooling and unschooling, 209; job shortages and, vii; Khan Academy, 101–102; KnowledgeWeb, 94–101; mechanics of, 69; online encyclopedias, 98–99; open learning centers, 184; origins of, 69–70, 246(n9); potential concerns about use of, xii; schools censoring use of, 51–52; undercutting professionalism, 61–62; user expansion, 83–84; user-generated content, 91–93; Web 2.0, 78; workstations, 71–73; World Wide Web, 75–76. *See also* Blogging
Internet protocol (IP), 69
Internet service provider (ISP), 75
Interstitial revolutions, 142–143
iPad, 97–98
Iron and Silk (Salzman), 162, 164
Itstartswith.us, 6

Jackson, Patrick Tracy, 33
Jackson, Philip, 243(n21)
Jacobs, Marc, 3
Jasmine revolution, 90–91
Jay, Francine, 4
Jefferson, Thomas, 17–18
Jiang Xuchien, 47
Jobs. *See* Employment
Jobs, Steve, 80
Jones, Bradley, 81
Just society, 9

Kalil, Ariel, 205
Karp, David, 48
Kearns, David, 241(n2)
Keen, Andy, 251(n5)
Kelley, Robin, 160
Keywords, 95–96
Khan, Salman, 101–102
Khan Academy, 101–102, 192, 209
Kindle, 97–98
Kingdom of Children (Stevens), 210
Klein, Burton H., 70
Knies, Donald, 243(n20)
Knowledge, Plato on, 94
KnowledgeWeb, 94–101

Koestler, Arthur, 86
Koller, Daphne, 104
Kuhn, Thomas, 29–30

Labor force: industrial paradigm, 35–39
LAMP software, 246(n8)
Landes, Dave, 108
Languages, 21, 26
Lanier, Jaron, 253(n14)
Lao Tzu, 162
Law of last entry, 55
Law practice, 18
Law schools, 59, 64, 244(n9)
Leaders, school, 217
Leadership: control parameters, 151; education as initiation, 15; reducing complexity, 149; role in paradigm shift, 217–218
Learners: Breck's educational commonplaces, 137; categorization of, 51; factory schools and open learning centers, 184; hurdles to Education 2.0, 141; role in paradigm shift, 214–215
Learning difficulties, 169
LearningWeb, x; Digiteen, 116; informal learning, 106–111; Khan Academy, 101–102; KnowledgeWeb, 94–101; Library 2.0, 107–109; Museum 2.0, 109–111; open courses and textbooks, 101–106; open learning centers, 192; open source textbooks, 104–106; OpenCourseWare, 102–104
Lee, Steve, 89
Legitimacy, academic, 63–65, 193–194
Lib Guides, 109
Liberal arts, 19–21, 57–58
Liberal-modern education, 21
Libraries, 133
Library 2.0, x, 107–109
Licklider, J.C.R., 72–73
Limits-to-growth paradox of education, 54–55
Lincoln Lab, 72
Lindsay, Julie, 115
Linux, 173–174, 246(n8)
Literacy: colonial New England, 18, 239(n9); computer, 27; diplomas' value in signifying educational attainment, 55; PISA assessments, 46; Web 2.0 literacies, 112–113
Literacy, cultural, 190–191
Literature, 6–7, 18, 21
Littsky, Dennis, 208
Live Ops, 62
Lost in Place (Salzman), 162

Lowell, Francis Cabot, 33–34
Lowell, Massachusetts, 33

MacArthur Foundation, 112
Mahfouz, Asmaa, 91
Management, 33–34, 36, 240(n4)
Mann, Horace, 196
Mansfield Amendment, 74
Manton, Martin Thomas, 238–239(n7)
The Manufactured Crisis: Myths, Fraud, and the Attack on America's Public Schools (Berliner and Biddle), 241(n4)
Manufactured crisis thesis, 189–190
Manufacturing, 34, 60
Marketing ideas, inventions, and employees, 174
Martial arts, 162
Mass secondary education, 21
Mastery goal orientation, 206
Mathematics: age-grading, 182–183; early high school and college education, 21; Goals 2000, 44–45; international comparisons of educational achievement, 44; Online High School of Utah, 120; teen achievements, 7
McClellan, James, 12
McElroy, Neil, 73
McManus, Richard, 81
Media: digital, 79; as educative force, 17–18; home as learning hub, 216; manufactured crisis thesis, 189–190; media audiences, 85–86; open learning centers, 168–169; removable, 87–88; *Style Rookie* blog, 2; television use, 92–93; user-generated content, 91–93
Medical care, 36
Medicine, 7, 170–171
Memex machine, 71–72
Memory, brain development and, 6
Menand, Louis, 57
Mendelssohn, Felix, 7
Mental networks, 133
Mentors, 17, 168–169
Meta-strategies, 153
MetLife, 206–207
Metropolitan Museum of Art in New York, 110–111
Meyer, John, 64
Microsoft, 26–27, 62, 96, 98–99
Military, 72–74
Miller, Paul, 108
Minimalism, 3–5
Minorities, academic underachievement among, 43
Miss Minimalist blog, 4, 65

Mission, 155, 166
MIT (Massachusetts Institute of Technology), 72, 102–103, 174, 179, 219
Mitra, Sugata, 84
MITS-Altair computer, 27
MITx, 104
Monk, Barbara, 159–160
Monk, Thelonious, 159–162
Montessori Academy, 207
Moodle, 114
Moore, Sally Anne, 26, 107
Morehouse College, 15–16
Mosaic browser, 76
Motivation of students, 57–58
Moving the center, 133–134
Mozart, Wolfgang Amadeus, 7
MP3 standard, 87–88
Mubarak, Hosni, 90–91
Mulleavy, Kate and Laura, 2
Mulligan, Gail, 209
Multimedia sites, 83, 87
Murdoch, Rupert, 79
Museum 2.0, x, 109–111
Music: Monk's education, 159–162; net culture, 78–79, 83; Salzman's education, 162–164; sharing and exchanging, 87–88; teen achievements, 7
Muslim youth, 63
Mutually assured destruction, 70
MySpace, 79, 86–87
MySQL, 246(n8)

Napster, 78–79, 88
"A Nation at Risk" (ANAR), 43–44, 241(n2)
National Assessment of Education Progress (NAEP), 45, 49, 221–222
National Association of Legal Career Professionals (NALP), 59
National Association of Young Entrepreneurs, 63
National Council of Teachers of English, 112–113
National Education Association, 36
National Science Foundation (NSF), 75, 222
Nature magazine, 99
Net culture, 78–93
Netcasting, 82–83
Netscape, 76, 80–81, 88
Networking skills, 17
Networks, 60–62, 133, 152–153, 245(n3)
Networks, knowledge, 133
Neural networks, 133
New York Times, 2–3, 45
NewsCorp, 79
Newton, Sir Isaac, 7, 20, 29–30

Ng, Andrew, 104
No Child Left Behind (NCLB), 45, 201–203, 205–206, 221–222, 242(n7)
Nook, 97–98
Norms of behavior, 40–41, 51
NORSAR seismic detection agency, 74
NSFNET, 75
Nuclear threat, 69–71
Nupedia, 99

Obama, Barack, 46, 80, 84, 120–122, 202–203, 243(n3)
Obsolescence of schools, 136–137
Occupational order, 28
Occupy movement, 204, 213, 253(n16)
Olsen, Ken, 72–73
On What Is Learned in Schools (Dreeben), 40
One-size-fits-all education model, 201–204
Online High School of Utah, 106, 118–120, 207, 249–250(n8)
Online information network, 133
Online learning, x, 68, 113–117. *See also* Internet
Online teaching, x
Ontario Science Center, 110
Open access, 99–101, 118–119, 247–248(n3)
Open Knowledge, 99–101
Open learning centers: AALC, 252(n10); academic courses, 169–170; academic program, 168–179; age-graded learning, 182–183; aims of, 188; assessment, 170–172, 185–186; certificates of learning and mastery, 178–179; charter schools, 208; community theater certificate program, 179–180; curriculum, 176–177, 184–185; educators, 168–169; governance and structural design, 166–168; mission, 166; open participation, 175–176; open space and learning formats, 177–178; open staffing, 172–173; open time, 176; organizational context, 165–168; policy changes, 221; resolving academic failure, 189–192; resolving efficiency failure, 192; resolving legitimacy failure, 193–194; setting, 183; transcending traditional education, viii, x; validity of authentic assessments, 186–188; videography certificate program, 180–181; volunteer staffing, 174–175, 184; Wikinomic schools, 173–174
Open Office, 85
Open source platforms, 104–106, 114
OpenCourseWare (OCW), 102–104, 119, 174, 192
OpenCourseWare Consortium, 103

Ordinary people, 239(n13)
O'Reilly, Tim, 80
Outliers (Gladwell), 26
Outsourcing jobs: industrial and professional jobs, 60; Internet role in, xii; legal work, 59; Online High School of Utah, 118; online instruction, 119, 250(n12)
Overseas trade, 33

PA Cyber, 173, 177, 207
Packet switching networks, 70–71, 73
Page, Larry, 95–96
PageRank, 96
Paige, Rod, 56
Pan Qing Fu, 164
PaperMag blog, 3
Paradigm change: business community role in, 222–223; charter schools, 207–208; citizens' and learners' role in, 212–217; class size, 205–206; classroom management, 205; educational paradigms and commonplaces, 29–30; educational synthesis, 210–211; educators' role in, 217–220; high-stakes testing, 205–206; homeschooling and unschooling, 208–209; necessary conditions for, 199–200; policymakers' role in, 220–222; replacing one-size-fits-all education model, 201–204
Paradigms, educational, 29–32
PARC (Palo Alto Research Corporation), 74–75
Parenting, 177–178
Parents: role in paradigm shift, 215–217
The Participative Museum (Simon), 109
"Participatory Networks: The Library as Conversation," 108
Particular initiation, 15
Pascal, Blaise, 6
Patriotism, 15
PDP-1, 72–73
Pennsylvania Cyber Charter School, 119–120
Performance orientation, 206
Performing arts, 21–22
Perl, 246(n8)
Personal interests: teen bloggers, 5
Peters, Richard, 12–16
Pew Center study, 79, 83–84
Phase transitions, 150–151, 157
Philosophical insights, 4–5
Philosophy: multiparadigmatic situations, 31
PicLits, 87
Pirate Bay, 88
Platforms for participation, 174
Plato, 19, 94
Platt, John Radar, 147(quote)

Policymakers: Bonk's Education 2.0 vision, 132; Education 2.0 emerging policy for online education, 120–127; engineering change, 198–199; role in paradigm change, 220–222; school-to-work policy, 243(n3)
Political institutions, 28
Political leaders, 203
Portfolio management, 174
Postindustrial industries, 41
Practical knowledge, 95
Preparadigm situations, 31
Pressure on students: cultural factors in international comparisons, 46–47
Principles of Scientific Management (Taylor), 34
Private academies, 20
Priyasha, 5–8, 11, 28, 77, 141, 153, 184
Prodigy, 75
Professional schools, 58–59
Professionalism: culture of, 244(n11); Internet and network allocation of social position, 60–62
Program for International Student Assessment (PISA), 46–47, 171
Project Gutenberg (PG), 96
Protest, social, 89–91
PRS e-readers, 97
Public schooling, 17–18
Puritans, 20
Python, 246(n8)

Question-and-answer technology, 95

Race to Nowhere, 47
Race to the Top, 120–121, 203
RAND Corporation, 70, 76–77, 148, 167
Rawls, John, 8–9
Ray, Shouryya, 7
Reading, 26
Read/WriteWeb blog, 81
Reagan, Ronald, 43
Real-world problem solving, 49–50
Regents exams (New York), 45–46
Regional high schools, 221
Reid, William, 255–256(n32)
Reif, L. Rafael, 104
Reinventing government initiative, 247(n24)
Religious institutions, 28, 30
Remedial courses, 21
Renaissance, 19
Report links, hierarchical, 34–35
Restructuring a system, 148–149
Retrofitting new tools to old school processes, vii–viii

Revolutionary change, x, 28–32, 141
Rheingold, Harold, 89
Richardson, Will, 112–114, 120–121
Ridgefield, Connecticut, 162
"Ritual and Education," 15–16
Rituals, 15, 58
Roberts, Lawrence, 72
Robinson, Ken, 50
Rodale, Robert, 151, 251(n5)
Rodale Press, 151
Roksa, Joseph, 57–58
Role models, 17
Royal Society, 19–20
RSS (really simple syndication), 83
Rules and strategies, 149–150
Rupture, institutional, 136–137, 142

Saeed, Khalid Mohamed, 90–91
Safety concerns, 2–3, 116–117
Salaries and wages: differentiation by educational attainment, 55; globally competitive workforce, 47–48, 242(n13); response to low wages for teachers, 241(n1)
Salzman, Mark, 159, 162–164
Sandia National Laboratory, 44, 241(n2)
Sanger, Larry, 99
Santa Fe Institute, 251(n3)
SAT scores, 44, 209, 241(n2)
Satellite network, 74
School boards, 217–218
School failure, external: allocating social positions, 59–60; decline of the professional worker, 60–62; diploma inflation, 56–58; educational legitimacy, 63–65; entrepreneurship, 62–63; high achievement and high graduation rate, 55–56; limits-to-growth paradox of education, 54–55; lowering graduation rate, 56; overenrollment in law schools, 58–59; preparation for adult life, 53–54
School failure, internal: academic underperformance and inefficiency, 42–43; educational inefficiency, 50–52; high-stakes testing and, 43–48; NCLB, 45; school reform and, 48–50
School reform movement: strengthening the factory paradigm, 48–49
School year, 39
Schooling: education versus, 17–18, 22, 161–162; educational paradigms and commonplaces, 30–31. *See also* Factory school paradigm
Schools: as complex organizations, 158; complexity theory, 148–149

School-to-work policy, 243(n3)
Science, technology, engineering, and mathematics complex (STEM), 122–123
Sciences and technology: age-grading, 182–183; charter schools, 208; early high school and college education, 21; Goals 2000, 44–45; higher learning and the two cultures, 19–20; international comparisons of educational achievement, 44; Online High School of Utah, 120
Scientific management, 34
Scientific revolutions, 29–30
Scott, Robert, 204
Sea of Shoes blog, 3
Search engines, 95–96
Secondary education. *See* High schools
Security: Internet blogging, 9–10
Segal, David, 59
Self-expression, 86–87
Self-organization, 149–150, 154–155
Self-organized emergence, 152
Self-teaching, 209
Seligson, Hannah, 62
Semi-Automatic Ground Environment (SAGE), 72
Senni, Aziz, 63
Sequoia Capital, 82
Service sector jobs, 56, 252(n12)
Settings of schools, 138, 142
Shared resources, Internet, 87–88
Shirky, Clay, 61, 91-92 156, 175
Short-form learning experiences, 167–169, 177–178, 180, 182, 185, 219–220
Siemens foundation, 223
Silicon Snake Oil (Stoll), 97
Simmons, Alberta, 159–160
Simon, Nina, 109, 111
Simpson's paradox, 241(n2)
Singapore, 46–47
Sixth-form, Britain's, 255–256(n32)
Sizer, Ted, 39
Skilled workers, 252(n12)
Skills: adoption and adaptation, 26; Breck's educational commonplace, 137; CLA measure, 57; didactic teaching-learning, 23; factory school paradigm blocking mastery of, 51–52; networking skills, 17; Online High School of Utah, 120; teen bloggers, 5; 10,000 hours of practice, 26–27, 51–52
Smart mobs, 89–90
Smart Mobs: The Next Social Revolution (Rheingold), 89
Smartphones, 23, 51, 84, 110
Smith, William, 20

Smithsonian museum complex, 111
Snow, C.P., 20
Social class, 16–17
Social graph, 80
Social initiation, 16–22
Social institutions, 28
Social networking: collective action, 89; expanding the cognitive surplus, 174–175; explosive growth of, 80; Flat Classroom, 115–116; media audiences, 85–86; net culture, 78–79; social graph, 245(n3); use in the classroom, 113–114; Web 2.0 netcasting, 82–83
Socialization, 144–145
Society, the school and, viii, 12
Socioeconomic positions. *See* Academic allocation of socioeconomic positions
Specificity norm, 40–41, 51
Spontaneous order, 149–150
"Sputnik moment," 46, 242(n10)
Stallman, Richard, 95–96, 99–100
Standardized tests, 188, 190–191, 204–206, 221. *See also* Assessment
Standards, 190; Education 2.0 policy objectives, 125
Standards-based education, 171
Stanford University, 104, 203–204, 209
State, standardizing role of, 31
States' power over education, 201–202, 220–221
Stedman, Lawrence, 190
Steiner, David, 45–46
Stephenson, Megan, 208
Stevens, Mitchell, 210
Stoll, Clifford, 97
Stress, 205, 255(n18)
Strong interactions, 149
Stross, Randall, 96
Structural design of complex organizations, 155, 166–168
Structure of a system, 148
Stuyvesant High School, New York, 160–161
Style Rookie blog, 2–3
Subject matter. *See* Curriculum
Super e-learning mentors, 169
Superintendents: role in paradigm shift, 218–219
Supreme Court, US, 220–221
Swire, Mavis, 160
Symbolic behaviors, 15
Systems analysis, 70, 148

Taiwan, 47
Tapscott, Don, 173–174

Taylor, Frederick, 34
Taylor, Robert, 72–73
TCP/IP protocol, 74–75
Teachers: achievement orientations, 255(n18); Bonk's Education 2.0 vision, 131; Breck's educational commonplaces, 137; career dissatisfaction, 206; factory school paradigm and open learning centers, 183–184; Online High School of Utah, 119, 250(n12); open learning centers, 168–169, 172–173; role in paradigm shift, 219–220; stress and coping strategies, 205–206; superintendents advocating for, 218–219
TeacherTube, 114
Teaching: Breck's handschooling vision, 134–135; Education 2.0 policy objectives, 126–127; hurdles to Education 2.0, 141–142; institutional rules and patterns, 29
Teaching methods. *See* Didactic teaching-learning; Discursive teaching; Heuristic teaching
Technology: complex systems, 149; embeddedness of, viii; undercutting professionalism, 62; workstations, 71–72. *See also* Internet; Sciences and technology; Web 2.0; World Wide Web
Teen2.0: Saving Our Children and Families from the Torment of Adolescence (Epstein), 6, 182
Teens: amazing achievements, 6–8; blogging, 6–7; consumerism and minimalism in blogging, 2–6; education as initiation, 12–16; educational paradigm, 30; higher education, 18; institutional rules and patterns, 29; learning prospects and achievements of ordinary teens, 8–9; reconceiving "education" and "change," ix; voluntary aspects of education, 12–13
Television, 92
10,000 hours of practice, 26–27, 51
Test scores: academic failure and, 241(n4); Breck's handschooling, 139; decline in, 242(n8); reasons for US preoccupation with, 242(n14); teacher merit pay, 203–204; TIMSS data, 241(n3)
Textbook-based curricula, 37, 104–106
Textbooks, 240(n7)
Theater, 145, 179–180
Thiel, Peter, 48
Thiel Fellows, 48
Thomas, Dave, 21–22
Thomas, Martha Carey, 15
Three Mile Island, 149
Three R's, 18, 137

Time magazine, 76, 79, 91
Titles, professional, 62
To Sir With Love (film), 150
Tomlinson, Ray, 245(n8)
Top-down structure, 148, 221–222
Traditional education, 11. *See also* Factory school paradigm
Transaction costs, 61–62, 253(n14)
Transforming American Education: Learning Powered by Technology (TAE), 120
Trends in Mathematics and Science Study (TIMSS), 44–46, 241(n3), 242(n7)
True Notebooks (Salzman), 164
Tucker, Marc, 170–172, 191, 252(n12)
Tuition: charter schools, 208; law school, 59; resistance to inflation of, 204
Tumblr blog platform, 48
Turnaround Handbook (Gates), 202–203
Twenty-one-hour work week, 175, 253(n16)
Two cultures, 19–20
Two-track system, 243(n3)

Unemployment/underemployment: college graduates, 58; law school graduates, 59
Universal access plans, 246–247(n19)
Universalism norm, 40–41, 51
University of Chicago medical school, 7
University of Michigan, 251(n3)
Unschooling, 208–210
Unteachable students, 57–58
User-generated content, 91–93, 110
Utah. *See* Online High School of Utah

Values: Rawls's Aristotelian principle, 8–9; service sector jobs, 56
van Leeuwenhoek, Anton van, 6
Vanderbilt University study, 203–204
Vanity Fair, 80
Vegesna, Raju, 81
Venture capitalists, 48
Veterinary programs, 207–208
Vetting process of networked knowledge, 135
Victoria and Albert Museum, 111
Video lessons, 101–102
Videography certificate program, 180–181
Virtual knowledge economy, 136
Virtual schools, 118–120
Vocational tracking, 243(n3)
Voluntariness, 13
Volunteers, 174–175, 184

Wages. *See* Salaries and wages
Waivers, 202
Waldorf schools, 207
Wales, Jimmy, 99

Walk the Wide World (Knies), 243(n20)
Walton Foundation, 202
Warnock, Mary, 13
Washor, Elliot, 208
Waste and inefficiency, ix
Web 2.0: accessibility and mobility, 83–84; advantages of, x; collaboration, 88–89; collective action, 89–91; creative self-expression, 86–87; as development phase, 81–82; explosive growth of, 80–81; informal learning, 107; interactive technologies, 245(n8); netcasting, 82–83; online encyclopedias, 98–99; Open Knowledge, 99–101; power, ease, and affordability, 84–85; sharing and exchange, 87–88; shifting end users from central control, 68; social and commercial factors, 82; transaction costs, 253(n14); web culture, 85–86
Web cams, 113–114
Web site creation, 82
Weinberg, Sidney, 21–22
Wells, Maynard, 62
Wharton, Edith, 6
"Why" learning. *See* Discursive teaching
Wi-Fi, 84–85, 110–111
Wikileaks, 88
Wikinomic schools, 173–174
Wikinomics (Tapscott and William), 173–174
Wikipedia, 92, 95, 99, 114, 209
Wiley, David A., 106, 118–119
William, Anthony, 173–174
Wilson, Teddy, 161
Wohlstetter, Alfred, 70
Work week, 175, 253(n16)
Workstations, 71–75
World Book Encyclopedia, 98
The World Is Open (Book), 131
World Wide Web: advantages of, ix; origins of, 75–76; schools blocking access to, 112–113; sharing and exchanging, 87–88
Wren, Christopher, 19

Xerox, 74–75
XML, 245(n8)

Yale College, 163–164
Yano, Sho, 7
Yong Zhao, 47
Youth culture, 15–16
YouTube, 91, 95, 113–114

Zen Habits blog, 4
Zen philosophy, 162
Zuckerberg, Mark, 79–80, 82
Zunia Knowledge Exchange, 88

ABOUT THE AUTHOR

Leonard J. Waks is Professor Emeritus of Educational Leadership and Policy Studies at Temple University, Philadelphia. Waks has earned doctorates in philosophy and organizational studies, and he taught at Purdue, Stanford, and Penn State before joining the Temple faculty. He is co-founder of the National Technological Literacy Conferences, and author of the book *Technology's School* as well as more than 100 scholarly articles and book chapters.

Made in the USA
Monee, IL
18 January 2023

25503913R00157